A PRIDE OF PRYDES

An account of the lives and times of
some of the many descendants of

James Pride and Helen Selkirk

by

Eve Pryde-Roberts

Published in 2015 by Eve Pryde-Roberts, Wales, UK

Copyright © Eve Pryde-Roberts 2015

E-book published 2017 also subject to Copyright

as is the paperback edition made available on Amazon

in January 2018

For my Dad

Joseph Anthony Pryde

1909 - 1985

CHAPTER CONTENTS

Photographs The quality of photographs in this book is variable (especially in the e-edition and the Amazon paperback version, as in an effort to make the book affordable original colour photographs are presented in monochrome) but they serve their purpose as best they can. All individual photographs of living persons are included with their permission. It was impractical to obtain the individual permission of each person shown in the group photos within Chapter 20. As everyone shown in these photos was willing to be in each photo when it was taken I have assumed they would raise no objection to their inclusion in this publication. Similarly, I have assumed that those who attended such reunions would have no objection to their names being recorded, if only for posterity. Our descendants and later researchers will want to know we were there!

PREFACE

When I started out on my family history journey some 20 years ago I had no idea what a journey it would be. It has led to many lasting friendships and a wealth of understanding of the lives of my ancestors.

*At the time of writing my earliest known Pride/Pryde ancestor is James Pride who was born circa 1678. He was married to Helen Selkirk. Currently the known direct descendants of this couple number just under 8,000 spread over 13 generations, whilst the extended family tree, including spouses and connected individuals, amounts to over 22,000 individuals with over 3,150 different surnames. It would not be viable for me to include all these individuals so the contents of this book are an extract of my research, illustrating the life and times of some of the many descendants of James Pride and Helen Selkirk. The names of those kin included are shown in bold type and their kinship to James Pride and Helen Selkirk is also given. The line of descent from this couple is also shown for the main subject featured in any chapter, where appropriate.

Many generations of the Prydes were coal miners and the conditions in which they had to work form a large part of our ongoing life story, so this book contains a lot of information about how the men and women who worked in the coal industry were affected as it evolved.

I have deliberately told parts of the story of our ancestors by using transcriptions of original documents where available to prevent any bias, and to provide accuracy wherever possible. However, the poor condition of some of the original documents means that in a few cases some transcribed words may vary from the original, but the general meaning will still be correct.

Whilst I have made every attempt to be accurate in what is presented herein the reader should note that it is my interpretation of the records used and I take no responsibility for any errors or omissions.

In the old records there are many variations of surnames and I have utilised the version used most often. Pride and Pryde become interchangeable in many instances, even for the same person as is reflected in chapter content at times, but it seems it became generally standardised as Pryde from the middle of the 19th century onwards.

The events described have come from my own research and numerous other sources. I acknowledge the assistance of many fellow researchers, most of them cousins, too numerous to mention individually, who have contributed to my overall knowledge of the extended family, together with their provision of some of the photographs displayed. I trust I have reciprocated their contribution to my research with at least equal generosity.

However, I would like to extend my grateful thanks to the following persons who, although not being related to me, have been generous in their assistance with my research over the years:- Craig Ellery and William Gilbert Scott who both extracted a large number of records for me; Ronald Andrew Pryde, who did the same and who has also collaborated with me on the Pryde records for many years (latterly we found we have a DNA connection); and David Severs who has been of great help and encouragement to me in finally getting this book ready for publication.

Finally, last but not least, I thank my husband John for his loving support during all my research, without which this book would not exist.

Eve Pryde-Roberts
evepryderoberts@hotmail.com
June 2015

*   The latest figures as this book is prepared for online publication in the latter part of 2017 are as follows: -

known direct descendants of this couple number just under 10,000 spread over 13 generations, whilst the extended family tree, including spouses and connected individuals, amounts to over 30,000 individuals with over 3,685 different surnames. The remainder of the book and figures given remain the same as the original publication apart from minor amendments and revisions.

Eve Pryde-Roberts

October 2017

CHAPTER 1

OUR EARLIEST KNOWN PRYDE ANCESTOR

James Pride (circa 1678 – after 1748)
and
Helen Selkirk (1682 – after 1748)

James Pride (circa 1678 – after 1748) who was married to Helen Selkirk is at present the earliest known ancestor of the line of Pryde descendants featured herein. The records show his surname as Pride and this is the same for most of his many descendants until about 1840 when the spelling of Pryde came into regular usage. Whilst no surviving marriage record has yet been found for James Pride and Helen Selkirk she is referred to as his spouse on the baptismal records of their children. We can therefore be sure they married and it is very likely the marriage took place about 1703.

James Pride worked as a collier for the Laird of Prestongrange[1] in East Lothian, Scotland, and there were also another three likely family members of the same generation

---

[1] Prestoungrange is the older version of Prestongrange and in some cases both were used in the same document. In the interests of clarity I have used only the more modern version.

as him also employed by the same person. Two of these were **John Pride (circa 1673 – after 1716)** who married **Christian Pride (circa 1673 – after 1705**) at Prestonpans in 1694, so one of these two is likely to have been a sibling to James and the other a cousin of some degree. The third likely family member was **Elizabeth Pride (circa 1687 – after 1748)** who was married to Robert Lumsdale or Lumsden at Prestonpans in 1707; again it is likely she will have been a sister or a cousin. [The surnames of Lumsdale and Lumsden and other variants have been used in the records but for simplicity Lumsdale will be used herein.]

Records referred to below show a close-knit and inter-married group of men and woman all employed as colliers or coal bearers by the Laird of Prestongrange and these include, amongst others, the surnames of Ingles and Innes, Lumsdale, Hutchie/Hutchison and Selkirk/Selkrig.

That the workers were so close-knit and inter-married is not surprising as at this time colliers in Scotland were bound to the person who owned the mine by an Act of the Scottish Parliament passed in 1606 making Scottish colliers into serfs [slaves]. This Act declared [abridged and in modern idiom] *"that no person within this realm* [Scotland] *shall hire or conduce any colliers or coalbearers without a sufficient testimonial of their Master whom they last served, and the said colliers and coalbearers are to be esteemed repute and held as thieves and punished in their bodies for stealing themselves from their masters"*. Any person offering work to such colliers or coalbearers without sufficient testimony would have to pay a fine of £100 to their original Master.

2

This meant not only was the collier bound to his master, but that the whole family was compelled to work in the pits. During this period, when a child, boy or girl, was born to a collier, the parish minister, after conducting the baptism, would also stand as witness at the "arling" ceremony of the child being baptised. Arles were the coins given by the coalmaster to the father for the future labour of the child. Whole families worked together in the pits. The colliers would hew the coal from the face and women, usually their wives and daughters, became the bearers, carrying the coal to the shaft bottom and then up to the surface. Very young children became trappers, opening and closing underground doors to facilitate ventilation. Children also helped with the bearing of the coal until, in the case of the boys, they were strong enough to carry out hewing on their own accord.

Anyone who accepted work as a collier made himself a serf for life, so it follows that men would be loath to take up new employment as a collier. The reverse was also true, those already employed as colliers could not leave to follow other employment, nor could their children because of the tradition of arling, so resulting in the close-knit group evidenced as being in the employment of the Laird of Prestongrange in the 1700s.

So it was under these conditions of serfdom that James Pride and Helen Selkirk had eight children born between 1704 and 1721, all of whom were baptised at Prestonpans, East Lothian, Scotland. It is only on the last of these baptisms that the father's occupation of Collier is shown. As is usual for the time it appears not all of their children survived to adulthood.

A significant event took place in Prestonpans in 1745 and no doubt this Pryde group and their fellow workers would have been aware of it, and may even have become involved in it or affected by it. Initially known as the Battle of Gladsmuir, the Battle of Prestonpans[2] was the first significant conflict in the second Jacobite Rising and it took place on 21st September 1745 at Prestonpans on its borders with Tranent, Cockenzie and Port Seton.

The Jacobite Army was loyal to James Francis Edward Stuart and they were led by his son Charles Edward Stuart who was known in Britain during his lifetime as The Young Pretender, and afterwards as Bonnie Prince Charlie. With support from the French he landed on Eriskay on 23rd August 1745 with a few companions, and they rallied those still loyal to the Jacobite cause. With an army of 2,000 they eventually marched to fight against the government forces whose loyalty lay with George II, King of Great Britain and Ireland.

The government forces were led by Sir John Cope, who had 4,000 men under his command in Scotland, with around 2,300 being present at the battle of Prestonpans. Cope drew up his army with a marshy ditch to their front and with the park walls around Preston House protecting their right flank. He mounted his cannon behind the low embankment of the

---

[2] Further reading at the Battle of Prestonpans (1745) Heritage Trust at http://www.battleofprestonpans1745.org/heritagetrust/default.aspx

4

Tranent colliery waggonway which crossed the battlefield. The Tranent waggonway had been laid in 1722 to link the Tranent pits to the harbour at Cockenzie so it would have been in use by the colliers in 1745. During the battle hundreds of government troops were killed or injured whilst some 1,500 were taken prisoner; in contrast only around 100 Jacobite troops were killed or wounded. See Fig. 1 which shows the position of the troops either side of the Tranent waggonway, during the Battle of Prestonpans.

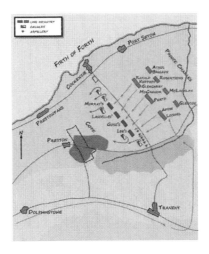

Fig. 1 – Plan showing the troops in relation to the Tranent waggonway[3]

[3] Author Hoodinski from Wikipedia Commons

William Pride (1704 – between 1741 and 1748), eldest son of James Pride and Helen Selkirk, died between 1741, when his last known child was baptised, and before 1748, when his brother Robert was listed in work records as the eldest child, so we can speculate William may have been involved in the battle in some way. Even if they were not physically involved in the battle anyone living in the vicinity would have been affected, with so many men killed or wounded needing attention and provisions needing to be garnered from the surrounding area for all those involved, some 6,000 men.

Although the Jacobite Army won this first battle they were eventually defeated at Culloden in April 1746.

Our knowledge of James Pride and his family is enhanced further as there is a surviving Journal of Management of the Coall [sic] and Salt Works of Prestongrange[4] which records details of the holdings between July 1745 and 2nd April 1748.

Within the Journal there is an "*Inventory of Coall* [sic] *and Salt Utensils and of Coaliers and Salters their Servants etc. belonging to the Estate of Prestongrange*" which is further described as a "*Narrative of some part of the Management of the said works from 15th of May 1745 to said 2nd of Aprile* [sic] *1748*".

---

[4] The following transcript extracts are shown with kind permission of the National Library of Scotland. (MS3720)

The same document lists the names of *"Coaliers, their wives & families now belonging to the works"* as at April 1748. Amongst the other workers listed it shows the following details [spelling as per document]:-

"Out of the Ground at present

At Pinkey James Pride Aged About 70 Married to Helen Selkrick 3 Sons All of Age & one daughter.

At Pinkey – Robert Pride his Eldest Son Aged About 45. Married to Christian Selkrick 4 Children All Sons whereof two Working.

At Gilmerton – Geo: Pride the 2^d Son About 40 married to Margaret Frizzell 5 Children

At Pinkey – Ja: Pride Youngest Son About 30 Married to Nancy Smith has 4 children.

At D^o. – William Selkrick Aged About 50 married to Elizabeth Pride has one Son working & 3 Daughters bearing"

Robert Pride (1710 – after 1755), George Pride (1716 – 1759) and James Pride (1719 – probably 1763) are the sons of James Pride as noted. Elisabeth Pride (1707 – after 1750), shown as wife of William Selkirk, is a daughter of James Pride and Helen Selkirk.

The reference to the colliers listed as being "Out of the Ground at present" means they were working in some other mine, i.e. in this case at Pinkey and Gilmerton. The following passage

7

from the journal shows what happened when the mine was flooded in 1748 and its effect on the colliers employed there.

"Disposal of Coaliers   Upon the stopping of the Works the Coaliers were ready to disperse and to engage themselves in different coalieries for bread. At the same time Mr. Baird of Newbyth and Mr. Adams at Pinkey and several other coall masters sent asking the favour of lending them to their Works but it was proposed by William Cadel & William Ingles that they should be allowed to go altogether to a pit of Tranent Coalerie (excepting so many as was necessary for sinking the New Pit and redding the Level) where they would be always at hand to come to their own beds at Prestonpans. As also that Mr. Cadel was willing to employ Wm. Ingles there which would save his wages meantime to Mr. Grant and yet he was evening and morning to visit the sinking of the Pit & what other work was adoing in Prestongrange Coalerie which proposal was agreed to accordingly the following coaliers with their wives and bearers were let go to Tranent Pit, viz. John King, John Lumsdale, Ja. Hutchie, R. Inniss, Wm. Hutchie and Wm. Inniss."

John King (1723 – after 1784) named above was the son of **Katherine Pride (1695 – after 1748)** and John King, and grandson of John Pride and Christian Pride. **John Lumsdale (1717 – after 1748)** was the son of Elizabeth Pride and Robert Lumsdale, all mentioned earlier as being part of the extended Pride family group.

As can be seen from the foregoing the colliers were owned by whoever owned the mine; they are listed in the inventory along with and in the same manner as the working utensils and other property belonging to the estate of Prestongrange.

There is much recorded evidence about the punishments suffered by those who fell foul of the rules of employment. These punishments included the placing of an iron collar around the neck of the offender and nailing him using the collar to a wooden support at the pit-bottom, where he was forced to remain for at least one day. Another punishment was being made to "go the round" which referred to the circular way in which a horse, by means of gearing, raised the coal from the bottom of the pit shaft, the offender being tied to face the horse and made to walk backwards, usually for the length of the shift.

James Pride is the eldest collier listed in the Journal being some 20 years older than the next eldest shown. The average life span at this time was 36 years so even allowing for the distortion of this figure because of the poor childhood survival rate, he was doing exceptionally well to be fit enough to be working in his seventh decade.

The importance of the survival of this journal cannot be over-estimated in the story of our Pryde family as it gives so much information and evidence about how they and the rest of the workers who toiled alongside them had to live their lives. Further evidence of the working conditions existing at that time is provided by a loose Petition[5] found in the same Journal This is shown in Figs. 2 and 3 and a transcription is as follows:-

---

[5] Reproduced by kind permission of the National Library of Scotland (MS3720)

Frontispiece

The Honourable ye Lord Prestongraings
Petitioned
Be Rott. Pride, James Pride,
Ja. Pride, Rott. Thomson
And William Ingles

INSIDE

Unto ye Honourable ye Lord Grang at Prestongrange
Ye petition of Robert Pryde, James Pryde his son, James
Pryde. Robert Thomson, and William Ines all Colzers [Colliers]
belonging to his Lordship

Humbly Sheweth
That we all are your Lordships Servants, and is willing to serve
your Lordship qn yt [when that] you have work for us, But since yt [that]
your
Lordships work is not goeing at Prestongraing, we at ye tyme
is at Pinky under Mr Robertson, and not far from your
Lordship so yt qn yt [that when that] you are pleased to fit your work in
Prestongraing we are near to be gotten qn yt [when that] your
Lordship pleases ------------
And at ye time John Birel, Oversman to ye Duke of Hameltown [Hamilton]
is hard upon us in stoping us of bread, where we now are be [by]
lifting us out of ys [this] work to place us in ye Lo [Lord] Dukes work at
Bowersstness [Borrowstounness]. --------------
And now ye workmen yt [that] is there sweres yt [that] if yt [that] we go to
yt [that] work
yt [that] they shall be our dead. --------------
And now we humbly Prey yt [that] you, out of your Clemency &
goodness will keep us from going to yt [that] place where our
life will be in so much danger, And we your Lordships
humble petitioners shall ever pray

SIGNED

Robet Pried
James Pryd [his mark - initials]
James Pride [his mark - initials]
Rott. Thomson [his mark - initials]
William Ines [his mark - initials]

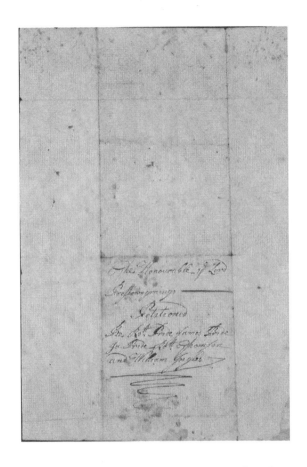

**Fig. 2 – Front of the Petition submitted to the
Laird of Prestongrange**

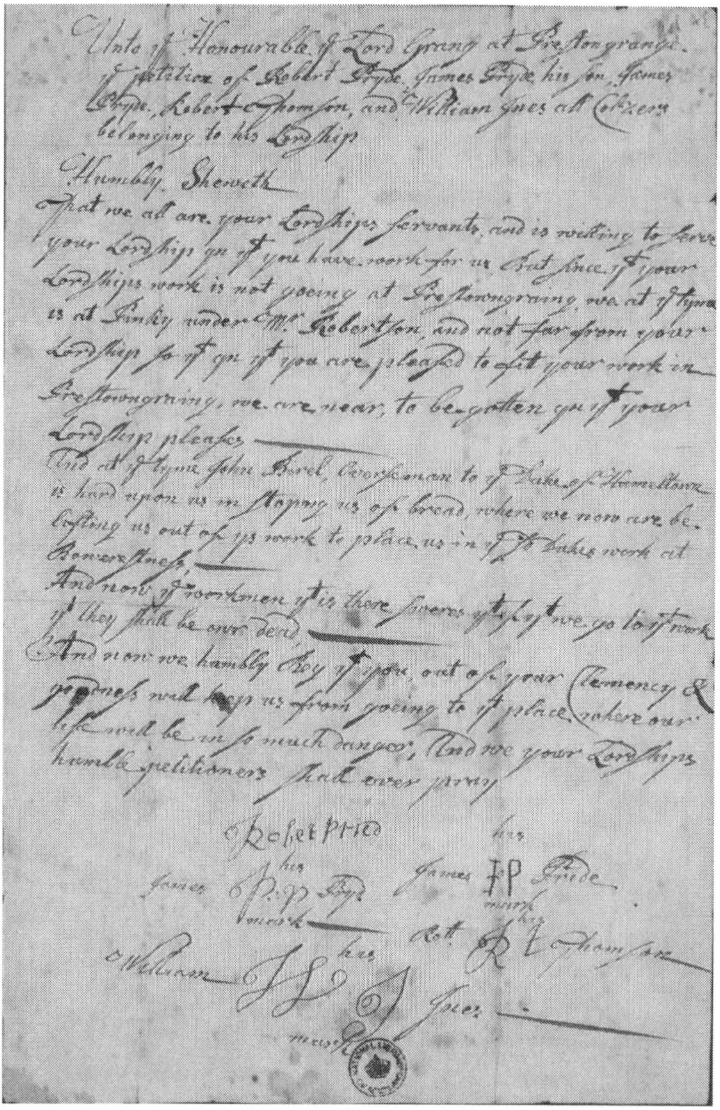

Unto ye Honourable ye Lord Grange at Prestongrange.
ye petition of Robert Pryde, James Pryde his son, James
Pryde, Robert Thomson, and William Gray all Coalziers
belonging to his Lordship

Humbly Sheweth

That we all are your Lordships servants, and is willing to serve
your Lordship yu if you have work for us But since yt your
Lordships work is not going at Prestongrange, we at yt tyme
is at Pinkey under Mr Robertson, and not far from your
Lordship so yt yu if you are pleased to sett your work in
Prestongrange, we are near to be gotten yu if your
Lordship pleases.
And at yt tyme John Burd, Oversman to ye Duke of Hamiltowne
is hard upon us in stoping us of bread, where we now are be-
lifting us out of ys work to place us in ye ye Dukes work at
Bowershness.

And now ye workmen yt is there swears yt yf yt we go to yt work
yt they shall be owr dead.
And now we humbly begs yt yow out of your Clemency &
goodness will keep us from going to yt place where our
life will be in so much danger. And we your Lordships
humble petitioners shall ever pray

Robert Pryde

            his
James   G.P.P. Pryde   James   J.P. Pryde
           mark   mark

William   J.G.   his   Rot.   R.T. Thomson
                   mark
                              Gray

Fig 3 – The Petition

12

Although there is some ambiguity caused by the way the names are listed it would appear that the Petition was instigated by James' son Robert, signed by him and his brother James and by James the Elder together with the other men named.

One can only imagine the conditions in which these men were being forced to work; they must have been bad even for the conditions prevailing at the time for them to take such drastic action as to get someone to write a petition for them, and for them to make such an appeal to the Laird of Prestongrange.

The Petition is undated but in the Franks Report of 1846, of which there is more in Chapter 3, it is referred to as being of 1746. Whilst there is no surviving record of a response, records show that neither Robert nor James Pride the Younger had any children born in Borrowstounness so I would like to think the petition had the desired effect and the men were withdrawn from working for the Duke of Hamilton at present day Bo'ness.

It is not unlikely that the Pryde men were amongst those considered as leaders amongst the small group of colliers, given the longevity and therefore experience of James the elder. This is further borne out by evidence of his son George being moved elsewhere to act as an Overseer.

As well as the Petition there is an heirloom from James Pride  that survives to this day. It is owned by his 6 x great-grandson, **Colin Marshall Pryde (Living)**, pictured, and it takes the form of a walking stick around the handle of which has been inscribed:-

JAMES♦PRIDE ♦1722♦

The walking stick is illustrated in Fig. 4 and as can be seen this is no rough hand-hewn stick, it is one that has been made by a craftsman and even the inscription is well done. It is possible the inscription was a later addition to the original walking stick which would therefore mean it predates 1722 – James Pride would have been about 44 years of age at this time.

One can only speculate as to how James Pride came to be the owner of such an object – since it is inscribed with his name it has to be assumed he obtained it by honest means, as he would hardly be likely to have it inscribed with his name if he was not the true owner. We can speculate he found it legitimately, or that it was given to him as thanks for a deed he did. It is highly unlikely we will ever know how James came to own such an object, but as it has been passed down eight generations we can be sure it was at that time a much treasured object and it has remained so through the following generations of the family.

Fig. 4

Images of the walking stick

15

James Pride and his family worked in an occupation in which men and woman were forced to remain by legislation, proof enough that it was one of the most difficult and onerous jobs of that time. However, we are extremely fortunate he left a legacy for future generations to find, in the form of the Petition and the walking stick.

We now know James Pride and Helen Selkirk left just under 10,000 known descendants and the true number is likely to be very much higher, so these members of the family are also their ongoing legacy.

The origins of Helen Selkirk have not been defined despite much research and debate by many interested parties.

Our Helen Selkirk seems most likely to have been born in the East Lothian or the Midlothian coal mining community, possibly in Prestonpans. Helen Selkirk's daughter, Elisabeth Pride married William Selkirk (born 19 October 1705 in Prestonpans) who was the son of William Selkirk (baptised 03 February 1678 in Prestonpans). It seems likely that Helen Selkirk and William Selkirk senior were related, possibly even siblings.

There was also a Helen Selkirk who was born on 04 May 1682 in South Leith parish to John Selkirk and Elizabeth Thomson. This John Selkirk was a merchant in Leith and a burgess in Edinburgh, and it would be highly unlikely that a daughter of a man of such standing would marry into the coal-mining community although all possibilities for her origin remain open at this stage.

CHAPTER 2

THE CHILDREN OF JAMES PRIDE AND HELEN SELKIRK

William; John; Elisabeth; Robert; James; George; James; and Marion Pride

Of the eight children born to James Pride and Helen Selkirk, only five are known to have survived infancy, as is evidenced in the Journal and other records of the time. These eight children were:-

William Pride (1704 – between 1741 and 1748) who was married to Helen Muir and this couple had at least seven children, mainly all born in the Prestonpans area between 1727 and 1741. No definitive records have been found for this couple or their children after 1741. As they are not mentioned in the Journal it may be that they were moved out of the area to work elsewhere. However in the Journal Robert Pride is referred to as James' eldest son, so it is possible William Pride died before 1748 as speculated upon in Chapter 1.

John Pride (1706 – before 1748) – as his younger brother Robert is referred to in the Journal of 1748 as the eldest son, it is assumed John died before this date. No marriage record found so he is likely to have died young.

Elisabeth Pride (1707 – after 1750) married William Selkirk and they had eight children between 1727 and 1750 who were baptised variously at Prestonpans, Inveresk and Tranent. In the 1748 Journal entry it is shown that their three daughters were working as coal bearers for their father – this would have been Helen aged 14 years, Christian aged 12 years and Elizabeth aged 9 years. Later baptism records indicate that their children remained working and living in the East Lothian area. Known descendants currently total just under 1,000 and later generations would settle in America, Australia, Canada, New Zealand and Norway.

Robert Pride (1710 – after 1755) married Christian Selkirk, who was sister to William who married Robert's sister Elisabeth. In addition to the previously-reported entry listing Robert and his family as being at Pinkey, elsewhere in the Journal it notes that in 1745 Robert had been working away at Longside for some six weeks.

Robert Pride and Christian Selkirk had seven children between 1732 and 1749, all baptised at Prestonpans apart from the last known child, David, who was baptised at Inveresk in October 1749. Bearing in mind this baptism date and location, together with the April 1748 journal entries stating that Robert, his sons, and his father James Pride, are at Pinkey, East Lothian, it would again seem the petition had the desired effect. Known descendants currently total just under 3,000 and later generations of Robert's family would settle in America, Australia, Canada, China, Malaysia and New Zealand.

James Pride (1715 – before 1719) Another child named James was baptised in 1719 so it is assumed this child died before then.

George Pride (1716 – 1759) married Margaret Fraser, and there is an entry in the Journal dated July 1745 which shows he and his wife had gone to Gilmerton to work some one and a half years previously at the desire of Mr. David Kinloch with a promise of being returned. The 1748 Journal entry confirms that they were still at Gilmerton and records show he was an Overseer at Gilmerton at least between 1740 and 1757.

George Pride and Margaret Fraser had 14 known children, three being baptised between 1737 and 1740 at Prestonpans; one at Inveresk in 1744, the following seven being baptised at Gilmerton, Midlothian, between 1745 and 1752, and the final three being baptised at Liberton, Midlothian, between 1753 and 1757. This confirms the move noted in the Journal became permanent. The baptism record of George in 1716 shows his surname being spelt as Pride but on the baptism record of their first child, Helen in 1737, George's surname is shown as Pryde.

Although George and Margaret had fourteen children burial or other records show eight of these children died young. No burial records have been found for three of the remaining children but no evidence of their survival by way of subsequent marriage has been found either. This leaves four children surviving to adulthood who went on to marry and produce families of their own.

A later inter-marriage would take place between a child of George Pride and Margaret Fraser namely **Thomas Pride (1753 – after 1796)**, and **Henrietta Maria Pride (1755 – after 1796)**, daughter of George's brother James Pride (see following) who married Agnes Smith.

Known descendants currently total just over 3,000 and later generations of George's family would settle in America, Australia, Canada, India, Malaysia and South Africa.

James Pride (1719 – probably 1763) married Agnes Smith at Duddingston, Midlothian, in 1739 and they had six children born between 1740 and 1755. Their first child, James, was born in 1740 at Prestonpans. The remaining children were born at Inveresk, Midlothian. This concurs with an entry in the Journal which noted that in July 1745 James Pride Younger and his wife had been away at Gilmerton above two years.

So far only three baptisms of children born to this couple before April 1748 have been found even though the 1748 Journal refers to four children. Known descendants currently total just over 2,800 and later generations of their family would settle in America, Australia, Canada (including the North West Territories), New Zealand and South Africa.

Marion Pride (1721 – died Unknown) No information apart from the baptism record has been found for this child.

As can be seen from the above and from the recurring instances of the same surnames both in marriages and confirmed within the journal, the colliers being bound to their owners meant they became and mostly remained a tight-knit group. In some instances the colliers were restricted to only travelling a short distance from their home, which further limited the marriage pool. Marriages therefore took place usually within the extended group as there was not much opportunity to meet others who were not part of the working group. Indeed, there is some evidence to suggest the colliers at this time were shunned by other people within the community, and referred to in a derogatory manner as the "brun yins" – the brown ones.

Those children of James Pride and Helen Selkirk who survived to adulthood appear to have not lived much longer than their fourth decade as far as can be ascertained, in the absence of burial records, from baptism records for their own children, or from the baptism records of their nephews or nieces for whom they stood witness. George died aged 43 years and it is likely James died aged 44 years, a normal life expectancy for colliers at this time. With their father James being so long-lived for that time it is probable they died within a few years of him. His grandchildren continued as colliers as they were bound to do, although over time they generally moved from Prestonpans in East Lothian to the coal-mining villages in Midlothian, as did many of their fellow workers.

The details on the baptism records for the children of just one of the grandsons of James Pride and Helen Selkirk are a very good example of how the men were moved from one area to another during this period under the control of their masters. **James Pride (1740 – after 1771)**, eldest son of James Pride and Agnes Smith, was born in Prestonpans, East Lothian, but moved to Inveresk, Midlothian, with his parents whilst still very young.

He married Agnes Cleland in 1761 at Borthwick, Midlothian, and they had five children together between 1762 and 1771. His first child John was baptised in Borthwick, Midlothian. Then James is listed on the remaining baptism records for his children as a collier at Oxfurdhall [sic] in 1764, at Blackside in 1766 and 1769 and by 1771 he was working at Vogrie. It is unusual in this era to have only five children but no further baptisms have been found for children born to this couple. It is possible James died some time soon after the birth of their last known child in 1771, when he would have been aged only in his early thirties. Conversely, the lack of further children may indicate his wife had died but a second marriage has not been found that can be attributed to James Pride and a second marriage usually took place fairly quickly when a widower had young children needing care.

Such were the lives of the children of James Pride and Helen Selkirk. However, as will be seen, times were slowly but inexorably changing in favour of the coal mining community.

CHAPTER 3

COLLIERS BECOME FREE

Walter Pride (1765 – 1843)
and
Isabel Thomson (1763 – after June 1841)

In 1775 an Act was passed freeing some Scottish colliers from serfdom. The Act was passed to make employment in mines more attractive to others because colliers and coalbearers were becoming scarce as no person wished to join employment where they would be bound to their master.

The Colliers and Salters (Scotland) Act 1775 stated [abridged] *"that whereas, by the Statute Law of Scotland, many colliers and coalhewers are in a state of slavery and bondage, bound to the collieries where they work for life...be it enacted, that on or after the First day of July 1775, any person, who begins to work as a collier in Scotland, shall be deemed free, and shall enjoy the same privileges, rights and immunities with the rest of His Majesty's subjects."*

However, the provisions of the Act were very restrictive to those already bound into coal working, in that they had to continue to be bound for between three and ten years, depending on their age and also on each collier having found and instructed an apprentice. If he failed to do this he was bound to serve for an additional three years.

The 1775 Act did little to improve the lot of the working collier and from then until the end of the century was a time of turmoil for them as they continued to agitate for greater freedom. Evidence of this was shown by a Proclamation to Coalmasters which was published in the Edinburgh Advertiser newspaper on the 21st October 1796 which read:-

"PROCLAMATION TO COALMASTERS

The following Bound COLLIERS having, in consequence, of a combination to raise their wages, deserted from the Coalworks at CRAIGHALL, it is hoped that no Coalmaster will give them any encouragement. Strict search will immediately be made after such of those who do not return: and as combinations of this sort may lead to the worst consequences it is requested that no Coalmasters will employ any of them but will give interaction concerning them by letter, addressed to Messrs. John Grieve or George Steel, overseers of the works at Craighall, by Musselburgh."

There followed a list of names of 70 men, including those of James Pride and Walter Pride. **James Pride (1766 – after 1802)** is likely to be the son of James Pride and Agnes Cleland as mentioned in the previous chapter. **Walter Pride (1765 – 1843)** was the son of Robert Pride and Janet Wemyss, with both men being great-grandsons of James Pride and Helen Selkirk.

LINE OF DESCENT FOR WALTER PRIDE
AND SOME OF HIS FAMILY AS FEATURED IN CHAPTER 3

James Pride (circa 1678 – after 1748)
and Helen Selkirk
|
|
Robert Pride (1710 – after 1755)
and Christian Selkirk
|
|
Robert Pride (1741 – after 1792)
and Janet Wemyss
|
|
Walter Pride (1765 – 1843)
and Isabel Thomson
|
|
and their son Robert Pride (1785 – 1862) and Agnes Lindsay
who had the following children:-

Walter (1808 – 1853)
John (1810 – before 1860)
George (1811 – before 1824)
Isabella (circa 1820 – 1889)
Robert (1823 – 1823)
George (1824 – 1889)
Brodie John Adamson (1826 – 1826)
Nicol (circa or before 1826 – 1826)
Jacka Adamson (1827 – Unknown)
Janet (circa or before 1828 – 1828)
Mary (circa or before 1830 – 1830)
Janet (circa or before 1830 – 1830)

Not surprisingly, the Act did little to attract new workers to the mines, and another Act was passed in 1799 stating that *"as from the date of 13th June 1799 all bound colliers and coalbearers should be free"*. This Act had the opposite effect to what was desired in that not only were new workers not tempted to join the industry, previously bound workers also left the industry, often working for half the wages they had earned previously. In an effort to tempt workers to remain working in the mine, or to rejoin, many employers offered a bounty, paying men in advance for their agreement to remain at their work in the mine for a fixed term, usually a year.

So in a complete turn-around, Walter's name not only appears on the 1796 document as reported above, where he had illegally left his place of employment, but he was also signatory to an agreement to work at Craighall and Cowpits Collieries for one year from 3rd July 1806. This agreement was signed by 138 colliers in return for bounty money they received on signing. The usual bounty payment was one guinea (£1 1s. 0d.). Some who were not old enough for the full payment received half (10s. 6d.).

The text of the agreement[6] stated:-

---

[6] The transcription of this document is reproduced by kind permission of Albert Russell and can be found at his website at http://www.hoodfamily.info/index.html. The transcription is taken from a copy of the original document held by and also shown by kind permission of the National Records of Scotland reference CS.34/1/99.

"We undersubscribing Colliers at Craighall and Cowpitts Collieries belonging to Sir John Hope of Craighall Baronet for and in consideration of the bounty money received by us from the said Sir John Hope as annexed to our subscription hereof, Do hereby each person for himself, Bind and oblige ourselves individually to continue working in the service of the said Sir John Hope as Colliers peacefully faithfully and honestly and that for all the days and space of one year certain from and after the third day of July Eighteen hundred and Six years (this not including any bargain or other agreement for longer time's service that any of us may have come under to the said Sir John Hope). In witness whereof these presents written by John Grieve are subscribed by us at Craighall and Cowpitts at the respective dates profixed to our signatures before these witnesses George Steel, Senr. Overseer of said Collieries, William Moffat, Cashier thereof, and the above John Grieve and Abram Moffat overseer of Cowpitts Colliery."

The colliers signed the agreement between 16th March 1805 and June 1806. Walter Pride signed on 30th March 1805 and received £1 1s. 0d.

Walter is later shown on the 1841 census, with his age rounded down to 75 years, born in the county of Midlothian, employed as Coal Miner, living at Smith Row, Craighall, with his wife Isabella, with her age rounded down to 80 years.

In 1842 a Children's Employment Commission was appointed by Parliament to enquire into the employment of children in mines and collieries, with Sub-Commissioners being appointed for each area. The Sub-Commissioner for the East of Scotland was Robert Hugh Franks and at the beginning of his report he presents a transcription of the Petition referred to in Chapter 1. He names this as Pride's Petition and dates it as being of 1746. He does this to illustrate that at that time the miners were literally "slaves of the soil". He then goes on to present the following statement taken from Walter Pryde [sic], who he records as being a grandson of the Petitioner, Robert Pryde. As there is almost 100 years difference in time between the issue of the Petition and the evidence given by Walter Pryde, one can only assume he must have been aware of the Petition's existence, and that it had been initiated by his grandfather.

The evidence statement is as follows[7]:-

No. 75   Walter Pryde aged 81 [sic] years, coal hewer [at New Craighall Colliery, Inveresk]:-

"I have not wrought for six years. Was first yoked to the coal work at Preston Grange when I was nine years of age: we were then all slaves to the Preston Grange laird.

Even if we had no work on the colliery in my father's time we could seek none other without a written licence and agreement to return. Even then the laird or the tacksman

---

[7] The extracts from the Report of R. H. Franks as part of the Children's Employment Commission 1842 are shown in this chapter with the kind permission of The Coal Mining History Resource Centre, Picks Publishing and Ian Winstanley.

selected our place of work and if we did not do his bidding we were placed by the necks in iron collars called juggs, and fastened to the wall, "or made to go the rown." The latter I recollect well the men's hands were tied in face of the horse at the gin and made run round backwards all day.

When bound the hewers were paid 4d. a tub of 4cwt. And could send up six to eight tubs, but had to pay their own bearers out of the money, so that we never took more than 8s. to 10s. a-week. The money went much further than double would do now.

There are few men live to my age who work below. My wife is 82 and she worked at bearing till she was 66 years of age. We are very poor, having had to bring up 11 children; five are alive. Sir John allows us a free house and coal and the Kirk Session allows us one shilling per week each. Should die if it were not for neighbours and son, who have a large family, and can ill afford to give".

The above testimony alone is confirmation of the conditions which the miners and their families had to endure. Walter was born some 20 years or so after the death of his great-grandfather James Pride and like him was long-lived, as Walter died on 3rd April 1843 at Inveresk, aged 78 years. He was born a serf and worked most of his life in servitude but did live to become a free man even though all his life he worked in coal mining. Once again like his great-grandfather he left a legacy of information for later generations to find which enables them to understand the conditions endured by him and his fellow workers. Known descendants of Walter Pride and Isabel Thomson currently total just under 700.

When giving his evidence for the Franks Report Walter stated he had 11 children and he made reference to a son who helped to support him. Records have only been found for eight of Walter's children, including five sons, three of whom reached adulthood but one of these predeceased him, making it likely it is his son Robert to whom he was referring, as he mentioned his son having a large family. **Robert Pride (1785 – 1862)**, 2 x great-grandson of James Pride and Helen Selkirk, married Agnes Lindsay at Inveresk, Midlothian, in 1807 and they had 12 children born between 1808 and 1830. Their lives are an illustration of how hard times befell many of the miners and their families in this period as the following outlines of what became of their children, all 3 x great-grandchildren of James Pride and Helen Selkirk, will show.

Walter Pryde (1808 – 1853) survived to adulthood and he married Christian Richardson at Newbattle in 1841, but predeceased his father, as he died aged 45 years in 1853. His death record states he was a Collier, of Chesterhill, Midlothian. No records have been found for any children born to this couple.

John Pryde (1810 – before 1860) also survived to adulthood and married Margaret Darling at Cranston, Midlothian, in 1844. They had five children born between about 1842 and 1852. The family are shown on the 1851 census where John is working as a Hawker of Delft Ware. The children are shown as scholars and paupers which would indicate the family are receiving some assistance from the parish authorities. John Pryde also died before his father, aged at the most 49 years, as he is listed as deceased on the death record of his daughter Margaret, who died aged 12 years in 1860. His wife Margaret lived until 1895 and as there were no children born to John Pryde and Margaret Darling after 1852 it is likely John died not long after this which would make his age at death more like 43 years.

George Pryde (1811 – before 1824), the third son, would seem to have died in childhood as another child born to these parents was baptised with the name of George in 1824.

The above three children were all born in Inveresk, Midlothian, and there is a big gap between the birth of George in 1811 and the next known child Isabella who was born in Cockpen circa 1820. It may be that the family moved from Inveresk after 1811 and any baptism records in another area for the years between 1811 and 1820 have not survived.

Isabella Pryde (circa 1820 – 1889) also survived to adulthood and she married William McKechnie in Cranston, Midlothian, in 1840. They had ten children together between 1842 and 1865 and she died in 1889 aged 69 years.

Robert Pryde (1823 – 1823), their fifth known child, lived for only two months being baptised in February 1823 and buried in April 1823.

George Pryde (1824 – 1889) also survived to adulthood and he married Marion Darling at Cranston, Midlothian, in 1844. (Marion was a sister to Margaret who had married George's brother John some nine months earlier). George Pryde and Marion Darling had 10 children born in Midlothian between 1846 and 1866 and he died in 1889 aged 65 years.

Brodie John Adamson Pryde (1826 – 1826) was born in Newton Village, Midlothian, in April 1826 and died in August 1826 aged just four months, some three months after the death of a brother who was the following...

Nicol Pryde (circa or before 1826 – 1826) who died in May 1826. No baptism record has been found for this child.

Another child, their ninth, was born in 1827 and baptised at Newton, Midlothian, named **Jacka Adamson Pryde (1827 – Unknown)** but there is no record for him apart from his baptism so it is assumed he too died young.

Janet Pryde (born circa or before 1828 – 1828) died in May 1828 so Robert obtained an order for burial for yet another of his children.

Robert's wife, Agnes Pryde née Lindsay, died on 3rd February 1830 aged 41 years. It is likely Agnes died whilst giving birth to twin daughters, their eleventh and twelfth children who were named **Mary Pryde (1830 – 1830)** and **Janet Pryde (1830 – 1830)** as their father Robert Pryde obtained an order for their burial, adjacent to their mother. The child Mary died on the 14th February 1830 and her sister Janet died on the 25th

February 1830. So out of twelve known children born to Robert Pryde and Agnes Lindsay only four survived to adulthood. Robert Pryde died in 1862 aged 77 years.

Following the publication of the Franks Report a Bill to prohibit the Employment of Women and Girls in Mines and Collieries, to regulate the Employment of Boys, and make Provisions for the Safety of Persons working therein was passed on the 22nd June 1842 [6 VICT]. To enforce this the following form of notice [8] was displayed at the entrance of every Mine or Colliery:-

BY ACT OF PARLIAMENT, VICTORIA, c

It is unlawful to employ any Woman or Girl in a Mine or Colliery: Penalty

It is unlawful to employ any Boy under Fourteen years of age in a Mine or Colliery: Penalty

It is unlawful for any other person than a Man between Twenty-one and Fifty years of age to have any charge of the Machinery by which persons are let down into or are brought up from a Mine or Colliery: Penalty

Every Indenture of Apprenticeship becomes null and void if the Apprentice is allowed to work in a Mine or Colliery.

---

[8] Details can be found at the Scottish Mining Website at www.scottishmining.co.uk and are shown in accordance with the terms of their copyright.

Once the above Act came into force, even though the underground work was so onerous to women and children, petitions were drawn up by the workers requesting that the ruling about women being employed in the mines be only applied to newcomers, not those already so employed. The petitioners believed that to deprive those affected of the right to work in the mines would lead to destitution for themselves and their families, not least because they would be considered unfit for other employment. The Petitions were not granted but there were instances of employers still giving work to women, and of women dressing up as men in order to gain work.

Sadly the new legislation did not come into force in time to improve the life of **David Weddel (1829 – before 1848)**, son of **David Weddel (1808 – 1870)** and Elisabeth Young. He was a 3 x great-grandson to James Pride and Helen Selkirk and he also gave the following evidence for the Franks Report in 1842 when he is listed as working at Edgehead Colliery, Cranston:-

"No.103. David Woddell [sic], 11 years old, picks and draws:-

I work 14 and 15 hours, and work every day except Monday, when I stay up because father does; sister and I work, and we are very sore wrought just now, as we have night and day work. Have not been to school for two months in consequence of the hard work.

Father cannot labour much, as he is nearly done in the breath; I don't know how old he is. Mother is clean done for; she can hardly breathe and has not worked for some years. Do not go often to kirk or sabbath-school.

(Can read well and write fairly his own name; very little knowledge of scripture or questions in catechism.)"

Despite David's concerns for the health of his parents they outlived him, as it seems David died after giving his evidence in 1842 and before 1848 when another child born to his parents was baptised with the name of David. Although his father moved away from coal mining and becomes a Toll Keeper, his time in the coal mines ultimately took its toll as his Cause of Death is later given as Chronic Disease of the Lungs (Miners).

As has been shown in this chapter the decades between the 1790s and the 1840s were a time of great change and unrest amongst the coal-mining communities in Scotland and elsewhere in other industries throughout the country and the changes were not welcomed by all. As is only to be expected our Pryde family were closely involved in all the different aspects of the changing times, sometimes to their personal detriment, as can be seen in the following chapter.

CHAPTER 4

TURBULENT TIMES – AN ASSAULT

George Pride (1790 – 1855)
and
Catherine Miller (1782 – 1868)

One person whose lifespan covered these times and who was directly affected by the unrest was **George Pride (1790 – 1855)**, son of **John Pride (1755 – after 1807)** and Mary Sharp. He was born in Gilmerton, Midlothian, and was another great-grandson of James Pride and Helen Selkirk. George and his wife Catherine Miller had seven children between 1810 and 1824 and at least six survived to adulthood.

The baptism record for their sixth child, **George Pride (1821 – 1881)** places the family in Gilmerton and this was the location of much unrest between the coal-mine owners and managers and the workers. The first indication of this is shown by a petition[9] made to the Sheriff in Edinburgh by John Marshall, Tacksman at Gilmerton Colliery, Midlothian, who wanted to eject the colliers from the homes provided by

---

[9] The transcription of the documents in this chapter reproduced by kind permission of Albert Russell and can be found at his website at http://www.hoodfamily.info/index.html. The transcriptions are also taken from copies of the original documents held and shown by kind permission of the National Records of Scotland reference AD14/24/259.

**LINE OF DESCENT FOR GEORGE PRIDE
AND SOME OF HIS FAMILY AS FEATURED IN CHAPTER 4**

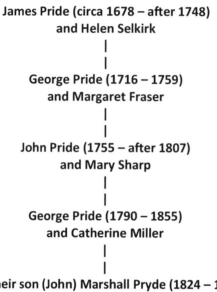

James Pride (circa 1678 – after 1748)
and Helen Selkirk
|
|
George Pride (1716 – 1759)
and Margaret Fraser
|
|
John Pride (1755 – after 1807)
and Mary Sharp
|
|
George Pride (1790 – 1855)
and Catherine Miller
|
|
and their son (John) Marshall Pryde (1824 – 1889)
who with Matilda Flockhart had 12 children including

David (1854 – 1879)
Mary (circa 1853 – 1930)

their employer because they had formed a union [referred to as a combination] and gone on strike.

The Petition to the Sheriff[10] is worded as follows:-

Petition for Mr John Marshall, Coal master, Gilmerton, to the Sheriff, 1823

29th October, 1823

To the Honourable the Sheriff of Edinburghshire, The Petition of John Marshall, Coalmaster, Gilmerton;

Humbly sheweth

That the petitioner is tacksman of certain parts of the coal on the estate of Gilmerton and gave employment at his coalworks there to the persons following, vizt.

David Penman, Alexander Brown, George Keddie, William Sharp, David Hoods, Thomas Hoods, Archibald Muir, John Richmond, James Hunter senior, William Hunter and James Hunter junior, David Armour, George Kerr, and William Crombie, Robert Frow, James Sharp, George Hoods, James Brown, James Irvine, and William Irvine, Robert Armour, George Pride, John Jack, Andrew Jack, Robert Patterson, William Patterson, John Smith, Thomas Sharp, Alexander Gibb, William Pride, William Wilson, James Jack, John Campbell, James Pride, Alexander Gordon, David Gordon, David Mason

---

[10] Outside of Scotland a Sheriff in this context would be recognised as a Trial Judge

*senior, David Mason junior, John Sneddan, Robert Blair, Robert
Blair and William Blair his sons, Benjamin Young, Alexander
Farm, Robert Pentland, Thomas Penman, John Sharp, John
Anderson, James Anderson, Robert Anderson, William Reid,
Burrell Sharp, David Pentland, James Miller, David Burnside,
Thomas Latta, Hunter Bowie, James Sharp, Thomas Waddel,
Charles Robertson, all now at Gilmerton; that the several
persons were merely labourers at will, the petitioner
employing them at his colliery, paying them according to their
work, and providing them with lodging in houses at the
colliery, while he was satisfied with their labour, and had
occasion for it; that these terms have been duly observed by
the petitioner towards the persons fore named; that
notwithstanding, the conduct of these persons has, of late,
been marked with the grossest irregularity, and with
determined contempt for the lawful commands of the
petitioner; so much so, that a combination has been entered
into, having for its object the direction of the work, which it is
their averred intention to usurp, and in furtherance of which
illegal combination, on the petitioner's refusal to comply, they
have struck work in a body, and entirely suspended the
petitioner's operations; that besides the unwarrantable nature
of particular instances of misconduct on their part, the
existence of such a confederacy is utterly destructive of the
relation of master and servant, and to countenance it by
complying with its demands would be of the most pernicious
tendency both to the petitioner and others, and would be
holding out nothing less than an inducement to the repetition
of similarly illegal acts; that the petitioner has resolved*

therefore to dismiss, and has accordingly dismissed as labourers at his colliery, and from his service, all and each of the foresaid persons, and he now applies for the interposition of your Lordships authority to recover possession of the houses and pertinents occupied by them and their families at Gilmerton Colliery.... "[the rest of the petition states they are no longer employed etc. and asks for them to be removed.]

George Pride is mentioned above along with other members of the extended Pryde family. In November of the same year it would appear George Pride attended an illegal union meeting and was ejected from this because he refused to agree to join with others in a strike. A few days later he was badly assaulted during two days of serious rioting. He refused to give evidence against his attackers who were incarcerated in Edinburgh Tolbooth but subsequently freed. There was a great deal of correspondence and evidence produced about this case, most of which was considered by the Sherriff of Edinburghshire and the Procurator Fiscal. Much of the evidence is repetitive but part of it is as follows:-

"Fiscal Edinr Recd 27th Novr 1823
Precognition as to an assault on George Pride - no one in custody
note within
29th Novr 1823

Dear Sir

I hand you a precognition relative to an assault committed on George Pride a collier at Gilmerton -- from the statement contained in the information from Mr Burnett WS [11] . - certificate of Mr Peacock Surgeon and report of an officer who was sent to enquire into Pride's situation, the Sheriff thought it proper to go and examine him and others at Gilmerton.

As Pride was then in a way of recovery some time was allowed to elapse before any further examinations were taken, to see if any information should be obtained as to the aggressors, but none has been got which appears to warrant any proceedings with a view to punishment - Pride is now recovered and at work - if any directions are received from the Kings Council they will of course be attended to. - I remain

Dear Sir
Your m ob ser
Arch Scott
Edin 27 Nov 1823
The Papers are
Information from Mr Burnett WS
Report of Mr Thomas Peacock
Petition for a Precognition
Declaration of George Pride
Do _____ Margt Naismyth and others
Letter of Mr Peacock
Adam Rolland Esq, Crown Agent."

---

[11] WS signifies membership of the Society of Writers to Her Majesties Signet, a private society of Scottish solicitors.

This was soon followed by:-

"Opinion on Precognition for assault on George Pride
29 Nov 1823
Precogn for Assault on George Pride
Edinr.

This being a very aggravated case of assault committed by an unknown number of persons in company upon one, it is very desirable that some person should be punished for it.

There is little doubt that Pride could identify some persons who assaulted him if he was not afraid to speak out. Endeavours should be made to dispel his fears, and he should be particularly examined if he was turned out of any committee a few days previous to the assault, and if so, who were present on that occasion.

James Brown seems to be the person against whom there is most evidence. He and Alexander Brown should both be examined as accused persons and if they declare to an alibi some persons shd be got to identify them as being among the crowd who committed the assault.

If another witness could be got to identify James Brown and he was proved to be one of the committee who turned Pride out of doors on Saturday evening preceding the assault it would authorise a prosecution.

Charles Robertson should be examined as to what passed at the committee.

29th Novr 1823
A Alison"

 And another:-

"Petition
of
The Procr Fiscal
agt
George Kerr and others
8 December 1823
Edinr 8th Decr 1823

Unto the Honourable the Sheriff of Edinburghshire, the petition of Archibald Scott Procurator Fiscal of Court for the public interest.

Humbly sheweth

That during the last six months an illegal systematic combination, concert and conspiracy has existed among the colliers in the employment of John Marshall tacksman of North Green Coaliery on the lands of Gilmerton, Parish of Liberton, in order to compell him to agree to certain regulations with regard to working the coals and conducting the works as well as paying their wages and other matters which they have no right or title to regulate or control, and with a view to carry

44

their purposes into effect the said colliers have held private meetings, entered into illegal resolutions and all struck work the more effectually to concuss or compell the said John Marshall to go into their measures and further a great number of them did not only threaten some who were desirous of continuing to work, but did actually beat and severely wounded them and in particular George Pride and the persons so illegally combined have made collections of money to support some of those associated with them and money has also been collected at other Coallieries and in particular at Easthouses, and transmitted to the persons aforsaid.

That from information received by the petitioner it appears that George Kerr, Archibald Muir, James Brown, Charles Robertson, John Campbell and David Armour all now or lately employed by the said John Marshall at the said Coalliery and residing at or near Gilmerton or Carthall have been guilty Actors or art and part in promoting, managing and carrying into effect the whole object and purpose of the said illegal combination and conspiracy and other offences before stated and seeing that it is necessary to have the said persons dealt with according to law, the present application to your Lordship is made to the effect aftermentioned.

May it therefore please Your Lordship to Grant Warrant to Officers of Court to search for and apprehend the said George Kerr, Archibald Muir, James Brown, Charles Robertson, John Campbell and David Armour and bring them before you for examination respecting the premises and thereafter to incarcerate them in the Tolbooth of Edinburgh or Canongate therein to remain until liberated in due course of law and also Grant warrant to cite the said John Marshall and all others that can give information to appear to be precognosed or do otherwise as may seem meet.

According to Justice
Signed Archd Scott P.F."

The response was:-

"Edinr 8th Decmr 1823

The Sheriff having considered this Petition Grants Warrant to officers of Court to apprehend and bring before him the therein designed George Kerr, Archibald Muir, James Brown, Charles Robertson, John Campbell and David Armour for examination, also grants warrant to cite for precognition as craved

Signed Ad: Duff

Edinr. 13 December 1823 [and similar dated 20th December 1823]

The Sheriff having resumed consideration of this Petition with the Declarations of the therein designed James Brown and Charles Robertson Grants Warrant to Officers of Court to apprehend and incarcerate them in the Tolbooth of Edinburgh. The Keepers hereby ordered to receive and detain them for further examination. [The entry dated 20th December 1823 is identical except that 'for further examination' is replaced by 'until liberated in due course of Law'].

Signed Ad: Duff"

An almost identical petition dated 6th January 1824 was issued and approved, but it contained the following additional information:-

Petition against David Pentland

"... but did actually beat and severely wounded them and in particular George Pride and the persons so illegally combined have made collections of money to support some of those associated with them and money has also been collected at other Coallieries and in particular at Easthouses and transmitted to the persons aforsaid and moreover the Colliers so illegally combined have attacked houses in Gilmerton in which the colliers who do not go into their measures live, and in particular on the night of Sunday the fourth current that in which John Weir or Wear lives was attacked with a view to assault him and they threw stones at the door and window of said house, the latter of which they broke and a large stone came into the house to the great damage of the said John Weir or Wear and Helen Waldie the occupier thereof.

That from information received and circumstances and discovered it appeared that David Pentland, Collier, residing at

Gilmerton had been guilty Actor, or art and part in promoting, managing and carrying into effect the whole objects and purposes of said illegal combination, and conspiracy and in particular of attacking the house of the said Helen Waldie and other offences before stated - in order therefore that he may be dealt with according to law the present application is made to the effect aftermentioned.

May it therefore please your Lordship to grant warrant to two officers of court to apprehend the said David Pentland and bring him before you for examination respecting the premises and thereafter to incarcerate him in the Tolbooth of Edinburgh therein to remain until liberated in due course of law and also grant warrant to cite the said Helen Waldie and all other it may be found necessary to examine to appear to be precognosed or do otherwise as may seem necessary.

According to Justice
Signed Archd Scott P.F."

The response was:-

Edinr 6th Janry 1824

The Sheriff having considered this petition grants warrant to officers of court to cite the therein designed David Pentland to appear before him for examination also grants warrant to cite for precognition as craved. Signed Adam Duff"

Then also a further response on the same date states:-

"Edinbr 6 Janry 1824

The Sheriff having resumed consideration of this petition with the declaration of the therein designed David Pentland this day emitted grants warrant to officers of court to apprehend and incarcerate him in the Tolbooth of Edinburgh. The keepers hereby ordered to receive and detain him for further examination.

Signed Ad: Duff"

Two of the men listed above, i.e. David Pentland and David Armour, were married to two sisters, namely Isobel Sharp and Helen Sharp, respectively. These two women were second cousins to George Pride through his mother Mary Sharp, so there is no doubt that a great deal of family disharmony would be brought on by this case. There would also be a great deal of bad feeling between fellow workers.

The rioting which took place in November 1823 was not the end of the matter. There is another petition dated 14th January 1824 which shows colliers from other pits were also becoming involved in the general unrest, including named colliers from Gilmerton who *"did along with about one hundred more assemble at Gilmerton last night with fire arms and bludgeons in a riotous and tumultuous manner and assault and abuse a number of well disposed persons, discharge firearms at them and their dwelling houses and enter the houses of the inhabitants of the said village whom they threatened if they did not agree to comply with their measures, in consequence of which the most of the inhabitants were much alarmed and a gross breach of the peace was committed and with a view to prevent detection they were disguised in their dresses."*

Further papers dated April 1824 show no prosecutions were pursued in respect of the assault on George Pride, viz:-

"Dear Sir

I send you a Precognition relative to certain illegal proceedings and combination on the part of the Colliers at Gilmerton, which were so alarming at one time that a party of Sheriff officers and a number of men were sent out for some day and nights to protect the inhabitants, as to which the Sheriff had communications with the Lord Advocate at the time - the Precognition was commenced in consequence of a recommendation of the Solicitor General, before whom a memorial was laid by Mr Marshall the tacksman of the Coalliery and the Sheriff had some communication with Mr Dundas on the subject. As matters were now adjusted between Marshall and the men who he continues to employ at the works, it is thought the Crown Counsel would not judge it necessary that any further proceedings should be taken, the more especially as it is so very difficult, if at all possible to get direct evidence against any individual, and those who were most likely the principal aggressors, suffered some imprisonment.

No further information can be obtained with regard to the assault on George Pride, the Precognition as to which was formerly with you and returned for further inquiry - it is put up with the other papers - I remain

Dear Sir
Your mo O S
Archd Scott
Edin 14 April 1824
Adam Rolland Esq Crown agents"

The response was:-

"Fiscal Edinburgh [Start of paper appears to be obliterated]
Recd 15th April 1824

Precognition as to the Combination amongst the Colliers at Gilmerton

Mr R has only sent the letter in this case, as matters seem to have been adjusted - But if Mr Solr wishes to see the Precogn, which is voluminous, it will be immedly sent – [this entry has been crossed through and it continues as follows:-]

Perjury of Mason
Assault on Pride
Recd April 17.

I understand that no person is in custody on any charges arising out of this case. – The investigation and inquiry may *perhaps have done good. At present I think the proceedings may lie over.   April 18. John Hope"*

During the period of the strike and assault George's wife Catherine was pregnant, and on 3rd March 1824 she gave birth to their last child, a son, who was baptised as Marshall Pride. On various records throughout his life this son was named either as Marshall Pride or John Marshall Pride. George Pride and Catherine Miller had already named their eldest surviving son **John Pride (1811 – 1864)**. The naming of the son born after the assault as Marshall and the usage of his name as John Marshall means there is little doubt he was so named in recognition of the tacksman's involvement in the events of November 1823, and most probably acknowledging his support in this matter, the tacksman's name being John Marshall.

Later generations of the extended family maintain the use of John Marshall or Marshall as Christian names. I have approximately 20 recorded instances of this even into modern generations which can only attest to the seriousness of the incident which took place in 1823 which has been retained in the consciousness of the family to the present day. **Marshall Pride (1824 – 1889)** was baptised at Whitburn and the baptism register notes that Marshall was born at Greenrigg so after the tumultuous events at the end of 1823 George and his family moved from Gilmerton, Midlothian, to Greenrigg, West Lothian.

The family later moved back to Midlothian as George Pride is shown on the 1841 Midlothian census working as a Coal Miner, and living at Whitehill, Dalkeith, with his wife Catherine, together with their children Isabel, George and Marshall. By 1842 the family move to Loanhead, Midlothian where they were to remain for the rest of George's life.

On the 1851 census of Loanhead, Lasswade, Midlothian, George is shown aged 62 years, employed as a Collier living at 63 Collier's Close with his wife, daughter Isabella and two of his granddaughters.

George died in 1855 which was the year that Scottish records were made compulsory and for that first year more information was required to register a death in Scotland than at any other time. The death record shows George Pride was aged 65 years at the time of his death and that he was born in Gilmerton. It records he was the father to seven children, two of whom had predeceased him and also states that prior to his death he had been living at Loanhead for 13 years. His death was registered by his son Marshall.

A sad postscript is that George's last-born child (John) Marshall Pride, as mentioned previously, married Matilda Flockhart in Cockpen, Midlothian, in 1845 and they had 12 children together. They were married for 44 years before Matilda died aged 65 years, on 17th May 1889. On 18th June 1889, Marshall committed suicide by shooting himself in the head. A local newspaper reported the event and it stated *"He had been in low spirits, it seems, since his wife died about a month ago."*

Marshall's son, **David Pryde (1854 – 1879)** had also committed suicide by shooting himself in the head when he was only 24 years old. He had married Margaret Paterson at Liberton in 1876 and his death left her with a two year old son, **John Marshall Pryde (1877 – 1925)** and a six month old son, **William Pryde (1879 – 1929).**

The suicide of her brother, the death of her mother and subsequent suicide of her father were not the only calamities to befall another child of (John) Marshall Pride and Matilda Flockhart. Their daughter **Mary Pryde (circa 1853 – 1930)**, pictured, was a 3 x great-granddaughter of James Pride and Helen Selkirk. She married Lawrence Ferrier Baxter at Cranston, Midlothian, in 1873 but sadly he was to come to an untimely end, as he was killed as a result of an accidental explosion of gunpowder at Clayfield Limeworks, in the parish of Newbattle, Midlothian, in 1887. Mary was aged 34 years at this time and left on her own with seven children to raise, plus she was pregnant at the time of husband's death.

Less than two years after the death of her husband and just three days before the death of her mother, Mary and Lawrence's son **Andrew Baxter (circa 1878 – 1889)** died aged 11 years, from congestion of the lungs. Then after coping with these two deaths very close together, her father committed suicide a month later, as had her brother some 10 years earlier. She was also to lose another son as her eldest son **Thomas Baxter (1873 – 1899)** died in early 1899 from a fever, aged only 25 years.   Thomas's death was registered by his brother **Marshall Pryde Baxter (1876 – 1967)**, whose name is yet another example of the continued use of the name Marshall and its integration into the family as a Christian name.

Despite this tragic chain of events Mary lived until the age of 77 years; she died in Dalkeith in 1930.

CHAPTER 5

LIGHT IN DARKNESS

George Pride (1820 – between 1860 and 1873)
and
Margaret Marshall (1817 – 1846)

Most readers will already be aware of the dangerous working conditions experienced by coal miners through the centuries and into the present day and there are numerous incidents of work-related death and injuries suffered by the descendants of James Pride and Helen Selkirk. However it is rare to get such a complete account as the following event considering that it occurred in 1839.

George Pride Jnr. (1820 – between 1860 and 1873) was born in Newton Village, Midlothian, and was a double 2 x great-grandson of James Pride and Helen Selkirk, as George's grandparents were Thomas Pride and Henrietta Maria Pride who were first cousins, both being grandchildren of James Pride and Helen Selkirk.

George's parents were **George Pride Snr. (1779 – 1832)** and Elizabeth Pettigrew and oral family history recounts that George Snr. emigrated to America during the 1820s and settled in Albemarle Co., Virginia, but he later returned to Scotland. **John Pryde (1811 – 1894)**, another son of George Snr., remained in America after his father returned home and

LINE OF DESCENT FOR GEORGE PRIDE
AND HIS BROTHER WILLIAM AS FEATURED IN CHAPTER 5

James Pride (circa 1678 – after 1748)
and Helen Selkirk
|
|
George Pride (1716 – 1759)
and Margaret Fraser
|
|
Thomas Pride (1753 – after 1796)
and Henrietta Maria Pride (1755 – after 1796)
(Granddaughter of James Pride and Helen Selkirk
and daughter of James Pride and Agnes Smith)
|
|
George Pride (1779 – 1832)
and Elizabeth Pettigrew
|
|
George Pride (1820 – between 1860 – 1873)
and Margaret Marshall

and his brother William (1815 – 1871)
and Agnes Marshall

he married in Richmond, Virginia, in 1834, further details about his family are shown in Chapter 7. After his return to Scotland George Snr. died in Newbattle, Midlothian, in 1832 aged 53 years.

Some seven years after the death of his father, when he was aged 18 years, George Jnr. was trapped in a fall of rock, earth and rubbish at the High Pressure pit, on Whitehill Mains Grounds with eight other men and four women, on 9th March 1839. It took the group two nights and part of three days before they found their way out by way of the Back Dean Pit. The story of their experience was published in the form of a book "Light In Darkness or The Miner's Tale, A True History" which was published in 1846 and it is transcribed in part here. Although the publication is out of copyright I acknowledge the work of the Editor, James Bridges, W.S., and the publishers Johnstone, Hunter and Co. of 4 Melbourne Place, Edinburgh from whose 1877 publication this extract is mostly taken although some parts are from a transcription of another earlier edition. The words of Peter Hay, the narrator, are as much as possible, taken from the 1877 edition as these are stated to be shown verbatim therein. It is of necessity a partial and not totally literal extract as the condition of the copy is very hard to read in places. However, enough survives to get a clear understanding of what took place that night. I have omitted parts where the words of prayers or hymns, or the thoughts of the editor were shown in the original. Please note that John Nic[h]olson mentioned in the following account was brother-in-law to George Pride Jnr., having married his sister Jean in 1828.

Light in Darkness.

(a miners tale of comradeship and faith).

Edited by James Bridges from short hand notes narrated by Peter Hay. In the year 1846.

Where there is a rise in the ground near a small rail junction on the permanent road from Musselburgh, Dalkeith and Edinburgh a coal mine called High Pressure Pit had been in operation for some time.

Underground was mostly a low narrow tunnel undulating as it followed the coal drifts, where a great deal of the work was done lying on a side. The roof seldom allowed a man or woman space to stand was supported by Fir staves and freestones. Light was supplied by a little oil lamp fixed on the forehead yielding only what the dark narrow cavern permitted.

Coal wagons were dragged by a harness on all fours in a close heat and continual drip of water threatening on all sides.

On an early Saturday morning 9th March 1839 a crowd of people gathered after hearing a hollow rumbling and saw the sides of the pit had given way. The night shift workers of Men, Women and Children had only just went underground when midway down the earth shot rubble dust and stone thundering downwards.

To over thirty fathoms it choked the mine trapping thirteen fellow mine workers in its dark depth.

News soon spread and help came from all over in a desperate hope of saving as many of the thirteen lives as possible. The pit being old had underground roads in several directions and it was hopeful an air supply may be had from an outlying abandoned Back Dean Pit.

Labourers worked intensely to clear away the rubbish and dirt that had accumulated in enormous quantities. To get workers down a large wooden drum was constructed fitting close to the pit walls that fortified them as it slowly descended.

The owner of the pit Messer's Stenhouse worked in kind and gave encouragement where possible. In fact all became kinsfolk in a bid to help. The acquaintances of those trapped were visited by the editor who found tidiness and a good fire burning with precious coal amid an air of sounding grief and quiet resignation. They considered it was their place to hold out hope while underground workers wrestled with the heavy earth.

The day had now advanced and parties who worked on felt hope had now diminished as the air underground would become foul and light would soon vanish. Speculation grew from not so favourable to imagining them still alive and waiting for them to appear.

Miner Peter Hay later remarked "Our pit was called the High Pressure Pit and, according to the regulations, we went down at about eight o'clock at night on that awful Friday, to engage in our lawful employment, which was that of preparing roads for carrying the coal to the pit bottom.

There were of Adam's Row men, John Nicolson, the gatesman, whose business was to see that the work was done to his mind, and he makes everyone do as he thinks proper; George Campbell; Thomas Reid; Jamieson Bennett; James Reid; George Pride; and Betsy Campbell, George's wife. And of Millerhill there were myself; John Reid; Ellen Reid his daughter aged 15; Janet Shaw, 30; James Reid, of the Old Engine, and his daughter Margaret Yedom, aged about 12.

The four women were carrying rubbish. I was taking it from them, and putting it in the waste - that is, filling in the vacancies where coals had been taken away before. The men were building biggins for holding back the road, saving two, who were cutting down stone to make the road higher. George Pride was filling water, of which there was about two foot at the foot of the pit. Now, while we were all thus engaged in our lawful employment, as I said, between nine and ten at night, George Pride arrived among us, in great agony, with the fearful tiding that our pit was giving way!

His good-brother, John Nicolson, would not at first believe that the thing was so very disastrous and continued at his work for a while. …. length he went to see for himself taking with him George Pride; Jamieson Bennett and James Reid.

To our awful dismay the …. at that time gave way with three awful …. which exactly closed off every avenue whatever at the pit bottom, and threw John Reid against the wall, cutting his face much and knocking down one or two more. I ceppit [caught him in my arms], his face streaming with blood; and says he "Peter, Peter what is to become of us…? We'll never see our wives and bairns again."

Says I "John, there is no fear; I hope we shall see them yet."

But truly, I must say, we had much consternation at coming to think we were just buried three hundred and sixty feet down in the earth, and seemed as if shut up to a certain death. We resolved, however, to go to the Back Dean air-gate thinking to ourselves that, if we could not make our escape there, we were indeed completely gone!

The air-gate, you must know, was a low, crooked passage, about three quarters of a mile in length, cut through the rock and cut from the High Pressure Pit to the Back Dean.

It was in most places only two or three feet high though in some as high as six and generally between two and a half feet wide. It was merely for the passage of air, and it was closed by a strong door near the place where we sat.

The door was broken open and we tunnelled into that old air-gate. But we had not advanced far when a mass of rubbish stopped our progress. We commenced to get this cleared; and this occupied four or five of our men for three or four hours. Some of us got wedges and a punch and mell; but we had to cut a foot off the mell shaft, the working place was so small.

I had remained behind; but after a time, going to see how they were getting on; John Nicolson said to me, "Go away and tell the men yoke to the pit bottom, and see and get it cleared, for this place is completely choked up. It will never do, there is no air in here." I stood for a moment and appealed, "Oh" said I, "is there no appearance of any opening?" "No Peter," said he "it is as close as the wall face." We therefore commenced at the pit bottom and continued until word was brought back that they had got an opening in the air-gate.

This was glad news, and by this opening (as little as it was) we proceeded till we came to the water's edge. The opening was so little we had to go carefully, but we progressed to the water's edge. John Reid went to the chin in it. But the air became exceeding bad. It put out four or five of our lamps. It was necessary, therefore, to leave it. Those behind were told to move back, taking good care of their lights; and we all returned to the High Pressure Pit bottom, and began again to work at the stuff there and here we continued till the bad air extinguished every light we had at the pit bottom. Still, however, we had light out o'er at the place we were originally working at, and that was some comfort to us. We called this our headquarters for we always returned to it.

"Well", said Peter, "the women were sitting here, for they did not engage in the clearing of the rubbish; the men only did that. Here we all gathered together, and this place became a kind of Bethel to us; for after we had sat down and become composed, John Nicholson proposed that prayer should be offered up, for they saw nothing but evidently death before them. We placed ourselves all down in a composed manner, for I asked them all to be sedate; and so they were, you may believe. There were some amongst them who knew the Scriptures. Jamieson Bennett in particular showed great faith, and was full of the promises. Poor Betsy Campbell was very composed too but whiles broke out into raptures saying, 'she should never see her twa bairns mair!"

All, however, were quiet and composed, and we sung the first four verses of the 20th Psalm and I prayed.

We then sat and crackit a while, and afterwards sent a deputation to the Back Dean Pit, to see if there was any relief from that quarter, for we thought they might get down from above there and work their way towards us by the auld air-gate. But they returned and said they had gone as far as they could for air, and halloed and shouted to see if there was anybody coming, but they heard none, and it was concluded that we certainly must die, for we thought the High Pressure Pit was filled to the daylight, and hence that there was no hope.

A great deal of us were in highly low spirits at this time, because we saw nothing but death evidently before us. We fell a'cracking, however, and it was observed that 'while there was life there was hope'. Let us rejoice that we have a God that can hear and answer prayer wherever His people are; for though we are shut up in the bowels of the earth, yet He is able to hear us, and He can both hear us and deliver us. He is the same God yesterday, to-day, and for ever, without variableness or shadow of turning. Let us remember the wonderful deliverance He wrought for the Israelites, when, for their escape from the land of Egypt to Canaan, He opened a way for them in the Red Sea; and when there was nothing but insurmountable mountains on both hands-the roaring ocean before and the enemy pursuing behind-when all refuge seemed to have failed them, and they thought, many of them, that nothing could deliver them, it was that the very next thing that they heard was the Lord speaking to Moses, and saying, Speak unto the people that they go forward. Man's extremity is God's opportunity. Let us not despair. Let us resign ourselves entirely to His will and pleasure. Let us be putting ourselves in a posture fit for death, and with the highest resignation, submit ourselves to whatever seems to Him best for us.

Now, you must know that by this time our lights were altogether gone out. The air was too bad to support them. So we were left quite in the dark; and I must tell you that this turned out, as you will see, a happy thing for us, though we liked it not at the time.

It was then observed, that though we should never behold each other in the face on this side of time, we hoped the next time we met would be in the light of the New Jerusalem, where the sun should never go down, nor the moon withdraw her shining.

One of the men said if he survived he would make amends and turn over a new leaf. ....The girls at first cried with hunger; but the hunger wore off. Hunger never touched any of the older ones. At least we had plenty of water to support us and we believed in the Lord and his mercy. It was the sweetest and shortest Saturday night I ever passed.

During the night we began to feel low and I sang a hymn to them where the second last line was 'Let the wings of time more hasty fly.' From this we were consoled and led to talk of our families and our lives at this pit. A pit that had gave us employment and good people as neighbours. Once again we sent men to look to see if relief was on the way but they returned after hearing no helpful sound. We felt like Jonah in the whales belly and his cries for help, and why not us, were we not enclosed in the belly of the earth?

It may have been around six o'clock at night we decided to write our names on a stone, and say on it we were at least alive at that hour, so that our friends might know something about us when they came to find our bodies, if ever they found them. On the completion of two names the lights went out so I could write no more but we were sure God our maker would know who we were. While talking we became a little gloomy on discussing if there was a way to find us and the consequences if this proved impossible. Another party returned from the air gate with no news and this made us feel the same way as before so we sang heartily and talked of the Scriptures.

By this time we were beginning again to consider about making another trial, and seeing whether any relief was coming to us from above by the Back Dean Pit. Three accordingly were sent out-myself, Jamieson Bennett and James Reid. I went first, till we came to the water's edge, and there we sat down and consulted; when it was agreed amongst us all that we thought the air was better, and indeed that it was tolerably good. We had no lights to prove it, but judged only from our breathing, and we were all of this opinion. We therefore agreed to return with the tidings that there was no relief appearing from the Back Dean Pit; but that the air was better in the air-gate, and that we proposed to make a trial of it, if they all were agreeable. So we returned and told them. But they were refractory, and unbelieving. One, indeed, said he had made up his mind to die where he was, and if any of us escaped with life, we might give intimation to his friends where they would find his body. It was replied that, to be sure, if we sat there, it was inevitable death,.........to sit there was little else than suicide.

It was no wonder that there was some difficulty about trying; for since then I have seen the place again, and I can truly say that, if we had had light at the time to see the hole into which we had to creep, I scarcely think we would have ventured to *go. But see how good God was. We grieved when our lights went out; but God put them out in mercy, that we might not fear to enter into the narrow places for our life. The loss of our light was just the means of our life.*

So it was agreed that three should make a trial, and the rest follow half an hour afterwards. The three appointed to go were, Jamieson Bennett, John Reid and George Pride. But they would not go without me; so, of course, four were sent away. Half an hour was allowed for removing the obstacles in the way, and making a clear passage. So we four went on until we came to the water's edge. Then we sat down, and prayer was offered to the prayer-hearing and prayer-answering God, who heard our cry and answered our request.

After prayer, we went into the water. At our very first entrance we crept on our bellies for perhaps four or five yards so low was the roof, and all in the dark. Then we proceeded onwards a while with noticeable ease on our feet.

The roof had sitten down in the place where we crept, and the water was floating around our mouths, so that we had to turn the back of our heads round to keep our mouths out of the water. We pressed on and on, however, and with a little more comfort, till we came to a broad flagstone. Bennett and Reid called back, that if they did not get picks they could proceed no further, for they had got a stone here which lay across the whole way. Well, we had had the good presence of mind the day before to leave two picks on the dry ground a little distance from the water. So George Pride and I returned and found them and carried them to Bennett and Reid, and they were enabled to remove the flag in a very short time.

Just as they got the flag removed, the back parties were making an advance; but they had to stop a little till we were ready. So, all things being clear for the march, we proceeded onward, everyone following the other, and aye naming each other out loud as we marched on in our journey to see if all were on the move. We continued thus on our march till we met with another disagreeable bit; but it was soon overcome. The rubbish had fallen down and was raised about the level of the water, and the passage was very high. We soon surmounted it, however, creeping on our hands and feet. But there was no water here, and we got through the rubbish and marched on. After this we came to a place where we walked on our feet; but the water was very high; in some places higher, in some lower. It was sometimes up to our waist, at other times to our shoulders, touching even our chins; and the women had to hang to our necks, and just float and swim as they best might, for it would have drowned them, the young ones at least, to walk. We carried on, however, the best way we could, getting through the water, till we observed that we had left some of the party behind, and I waited till the last came forward.

By this time I thought that George Pride had found the dry ground, and had escaped away with great joy to the pit mouth; for I cried several times to him, but received no answer. So, when the rest came up, and were following me, as I thought, I moved up a road or avenue. But it was to my great joy that

70

they did not follow me. For I soon found, to my dismay, I had gone wrong! I went over a mass of rubbish just twofold; the road became impassable with rubbish, and the air so extremely bad that one of my ears gave a loud crack and a ring, and the streamers flew from my eyes, and there was excessive heat. Then, thought I, I am certainly wrong here! However, I must be as cool as possible, for I know there are two ways behind, a right and a wrong; and I have heard of people's brain turning in such situations. So, if my brain were to turn and I took the left road instead of the right I might just go back the way I had come and be lost! With as much coolness of mind, then, as possible, I returned backward, and turning to the right hand, I again went to the shoulder in water; but at last I reached the dry ground.   Then I began to feel the smell of sulphur and reek; and as I knew that a lamp hung constantly burning in the Back Dean Pit to help the purity of the air, I thought it must be this that was causing the smoke and the smell. I was right, and immediately found myself just were we had so long desired to be, hard by the bottom of the Back Dean Pit! And that, you may believe, was no small comfort unto me!

To my great joy the rest were all safe arrived before myself, and they had not missed me at the time, every one was so excited with his own case. For my own part, before I went up the air gate I was like a lion for strength, but after I came out I was weak enough. We found the air extremely bad; our sides blew, the same as if we had been running a race, for want of breath, and that made us weak.

However, we shouted up from the bottom of the pit, and, to our great joy, we were quickly heard and answered. A bucket was sent down; but, as we were so weakly, a man was sent down with it to help us. So the man descended about half way down the pit. To use his own words, however, he soon did not know if he was coming down or going up, and he called to them to take him up, for he was not able to live in the air of the place. We who had come from a closer neighbourhood were able to stand it; but he had come from the fresh air was not able. So the bucket was again let down, and we were drawn up in the following order:-

Ellen Reid, James Reid, Janet Shaw, first; then Jamieson Bennett, John Reid and Margaret Yedom; then George Campbell, James Reid and John Nicholson; and Thomas Reid, George Pride and Betsy Campbell and myself.

So we reached the Back Dean Pit head, and we saw the pleasant light of day; and as I did look on the Sabbath morning and my first words were "Glory be to God in the highest that I am once more on the earth safe alive." And glory be to His name I now say, and shall say to the end of my life."

Such is the narrative of Peter Hay and we are most fortunate that once again such a record involving the Pryde family has survived to this day.

Two years later, at Newton Church in 1841, George Pride Jnr., Collier of Adamsrow, married Margaret Marshall of Millerhill, both in Newton Parish. George's brother William had married

72

Agnes Marshall, sister to Margaret, also in Newton in 1834. William Pride and Agnes Marshall emigrated to America sometime between 1847 and 1854.

Only one child has been found for George Pride Jnr. and Margaret Marshall, namely **William Pryde (circa 1845 – 1934)** who was born in Newton Village, Midlothian. George's wife Margaret died at the beginning of 1846 from consumption, so the care of baby William is likely to have passed to another female family member whilst George continued working. This may account for the fact that although George Jnr. later emigrated to America his son William stayed behind in Scotland, and on the 1861 census William, by then aged 16 years, is shown living with his first cousin **John Pryde (1835 – 1905)** and his wife Margaret Ratcliffe at Millerhill, Midlothian.

George Pride Jnr. is next found on the 1860 census for Placerville, California, America, living near to his brother William and his wife Agnes but no record has yet been found to show when he left Scotland. Nor have any death details been found for George Jnr. but when his son William married in 1873 his father is listed as deceased.

As mentioned earlier, George's brother **William Pride (1815 – 1871)** had married Agnes Marshall, sister to George's wife Margaret Marshall, in Newton, Midlothian, in 1834 and they had six children born in the local area between 1835 and 1845. The family were still in Newton in March 1847 when William obtained an Order for Burial for his daughter Helen and in fact four of their six children had died before William left for America. His wife Agnes and their only surviving daughter Louisa followed him to America in 1854. Their eldest and only surviving son **John Pryde (1835 – 1905)**, 3 x great-grandson of James Pride and Helen Selkirk, had married Margaret Ratcliffe at Millerhill, Midlothian, at the end of 1853 and he stayed behind in Newton when the rest of the family emigrated. It is that John Pryde with whom William Pryde, son of George Pride Jnr., is shown living on the 1861 census. It is worth noting that John Pryde together with his first wife Margaret Ratcliffe and second wife Elizabeth Penman had 19 children between 1854 and 1893. He died in 1905 aged 70 years and known descendants currently total just over 300.

Prior to William Pride being joined in America by his wife and daughter he obtained land in Kentucky Flat, near White Rock, California, by means of a Pre-Emption Notice which was recorded in 1853 as follows:-

"William Pryde

Know all men by these Presents That I William Pryde have located and hereby claim a certain piece or parcel of Land (for Agricultural and Grazing purposes) lying and being in the County of Eldorado State of California and situated about ¾ of a mile from White Rock and including upper and lower Kentucky Flat more particularly described as follows to wit commencing at the head of Garden Flat below the South Fork canal at a Pine tree blazed constituting the S. East corner thence running North of East along a line of blazed trees 160 rods to an Oak Tree blazed thence West of the North 160 rods to a Pine Tree blazed thence South of West 160 rods to a Pine tree blazed thence East of South to the South Fork Canal at the place of beginning.   Dated 5th March 1853

Filed 5th March 1853 @ 7AM

Recorded March 5th 1853 @ 8AM

Geoff Ingham

Records of Eldorado Co.

By James Durant Deputy"

The above document means that William had marked boundaries on land which had previously not been in the possession of anyone else, and by claiming the pre-emption rights he was obtaining the right to buy the land for himself.

After he had been joined by his wife and daughter in 1854, William and Agnes had at least two more children, both of whom survived to adulthood. William Pride died in Placerville, California, in 1871, aged 55 years and his wife died in 1886 aged 71 years.

 Their daughter **Louisa Glass Pryde (1845 – 1916)**, pictured, 3 x great-granddaughter of James Pride and Helen Selkirk, was born in Newton Village, Midlothian, and was named after the wife of a Midlothian Minister, the

Revd. John R. Glass. His wife Louisa was held in high esteem in the general locality as she tried to ease the lives of those in her parish. Louisa Glass Pryde married Albert Adams at El Dorado Co., California, on 25th May 1859 when she was aged only 14 years and 3 months – it was legal at this time for girls to marry from the age of 12 years. Albert Adams was some 11 years her senior and they had three children together between 1862 and 1868. Louisa Glass Adams née Pryde died in Placerville, California, in 1916 aged 71 years, her husband having predeceased her by some 11 years. The following Obituary Notice appeared in the Mountain Democrat Newspaper dated 30th December 1916:-

"PIONEERS RAPIDLY PASSING AWAY

"Mrs Louisa Pride Adams, a well known and highly esteemed pioneer woman of this county, passed away at her home in Blair's district, last Wednesday, Dec. 27th, from general debility, being confined to her room but a few days.

Louisa Pride was born in Edenston [sic], Scotland, February 27, 1845, and came to California with her parents in 1854, who located near White Rock Canyon, in this county. In May 1859, she was married to Albert Adams, and for sixty years lived in the neighborhood where she died. Her husband preceded her in death eleven years, and one daughter, Mrs G I Akin, who passed away about two years ago. She is survived by two daughters, Mrs W I Hartwick and Mrs J E Hassler, of this country, and a sister, Mrs B Purcell of Sacramento.

The funeral took place at the family home, Friday, at 1p.m. with services by Rev. E E Clark and interment in the White Rock cemetery."

It is proper that the obituary acknowledges the part that Louisa, and by default her parents and her uncle George, had to play in the settlement of the area. Her uncle George Pride certainly travelled a long way from the depths of the High Pressure Pit in Scotland in 1839 to the west of America – a distance of some 5,000 miles (8,000 kilometres) in terms of distance, but in practical terms a different life even though it would appear he still earned his living as a miner.

CHAPTER 6

AN ORDINARY MINING FAMILY

John Pryde (1811 – 1864)
and
Helen Lawson (1809 – 1870)
and their family

Before delving into the lives of the above family it may help to try and understand the day-to-day life of the Scottish colliers in the early to mid-1800s. As has already been seen the years following freedom from serfdom were hard ones for the colliers with much agitation and hard times generally in the country as a whole. Not only were colliers fighting to establish acceptable working conditions but they were often paid in kind only, receiving tokens which could only be spent at the Company shop which resulted in inflated prices. A cholera epidemic swept the country and reached Scotland between 1831 and 1832. In the environs of Edinburgh and the surrounding districts just under 2,000 persons succumbed to the disease and just over half of these lost their lives. The poor living conditions generally including those endured by the colliers contributed to the spread of the disease.

Just one example from the Pryde family of how this affected the miners and their families is that cholera is given as the cause of death for **Helen Pryde (1805 – 1832)**, daughter of

George Pride and Elizabeth Pettigrew and 2 x great-granddaughter of James Pride and Helen Selkirk. She was sister to George and William Pryde whose lives were featured in the previous chapter. She had married Andrew Brown in April 1831 at Newton Parish, Midlothian, and given birth to a daughter, **Elizabeth Brown (1832 – 1853)** in Newton, Midlothian, in February 1832. Just eight months later, by October 1832, cholera had claimed Helen's life, aged just 27 years. Her husband Andrew Brown also died in 1834 aged just 25 years leaving their daughter Elizabeth an orphan. Newton Kirk Session Minutes dated 26th December 1842 shows one shilling weekly was to be paid to Elizabeth Brown residing with her grandfather in Millerhill.

Between 1834 – 1845 a New Statistical Account for Scotland was undertaken which included detailed reports for each parish; this was collated by Church Ministers and other local figures such as schoolmasters and doctors. A set of planned questions dealing with subjects such as the geography, climate, natural resources and social customs of each parish produced the format for the accounts. These show that after 1830 the population in some of the coal-mining villages was diminishing, as in Gilmerton, and yet in others, as in Newbattle, the population was increasing and this was because of the availability and accessibility of coal for working in each area. The New Statistical Account for Newton, written by the Revd. John Adamson, shows that in 1831 the population stood at 2,272 yet by 1841 the population had reduced to 1,743. He puts this decrease down to the collieries not being worked to the same extent as formerly and notes

Sheriffhall colliery belonging to the Duke of Buccleuch is nearly worked out and that in a few years Edmonstone colliery, belonging to John Wauchope, Esq., will also be worked out unless a more powerful engine can be employed. There is a later note dated 1845 which confirmed Sir John Hope, who had taken a lease for Edmonstone Colliery, had erected one of the most powerful engines in the country, it having been constructed in Cornwall, and it was believed the installation of this engine would give employment to the collier population for the next 50 years.

The following is an extract from the New Statistical Account of Newton[12] which is useful in giving not only an account of how the Pryde families and their neighbours were living and working, but also how they were viewed by others outside of the coal-mining communities.

"The collier population is subject to a peculiar disease which is vulgarly called the black-spit, and by the faculty is dignified with the Greek term melanosis. It is a wasting of the lungs occasioned, as is supposed, by the inhaling of the coal-dust while working, and the expectoration is as black as the coal itself. Many strong men are cut off by it before they reach the age of forty, especially if they have, for any length of time, been engaged in what in opposition to coal-hewing is called

---

[12] By their kind permission the transcription is from images at the Statistical Accounts Online Service © University of Glasgow and University of Edinburgh. The Statistical Accounts of Scotland are available online at http://edina.ac.uk/stat-acc-scot/

stonework, (sinking of pits, driving of mines, &c). Almost all the men are affected by it sooner or later, so as to be rendered unfit for any active exertion for years before they drop prematurely into the grave, between the ages of forty and sixty or sixty five. The vicissitudes of temperature to which they are daily exposed on issuing from the pits throughout a great part of the year, coupled with irregular habits in the case of too many, no doubt contribute to this mortality.

Though their earnings are such that the collier population might enjoy the comforts of life in a superior degree to agricultural labourers, yet, from want of management, this is far from being generally the case. In too many instances, this happens from excess in eating and drinking followed by the necessary abstinence imposed by exhausted resources, the wages being no sooner got than with many they are spent in sensual indulgence, as they know no other. It is their custom, also, to procure everything upon credit, which makes their expenditure much more and their enjoyment much less than they would be, if they were in the habit of husbanding their resources. Instead of independent action, according to what prudence may dictate as for the best, they are entirely regulated by custom; and hence there is little hope of their being speedily elevated from the degraded condition indicated by such a state of things. To this, however, there are honourable exceptions, and there are individuals and families that, for character and the manner in which their households are conducted, may stand a favourable comparison with those of their own rank in any other sphere of life. When the parties are free from indolent, and, above all, intemperate habits, the actual condition, in respect of food, clothing, and other comforts, is exceedingly good, the working classes connected with the collieries earning very good wages, so that it is only intemperance, vice, and mismanagement that render it otherwise. Indeed those who have tastes and inclinations elevated above the prevailing sensuality and vice have it in their power to gratify them, and hence in their dress and household equipment are distinguished for cleanliness and comfort; while in the very next dwelling, and with an income no way inferior, there may be nothing but squalor and hardly a seat to sit upon.

While habits are dissolute, intelligence and morality are low. Ignorance and ungodliness go hand in hand. Nor can it well be expected to be otherwise. The young, even when not previously neglected as to their education, are taken from school often as early as eight years of age, to be set to work in the pits, and soon forget any smattering they may have acquired, and being, from so early a period of life, daily exposed to the most corrupting influences, nothing else can result but that the tastes and habits they acquire should be of a vitiated nature, and their notions of morality perverted and debased.

It is pleasing to record, however, amid so much that is unfavourable, that a marked improvement has been going forward, and that means that have been used to render them as a class more intelligent, moral, and religious, have not been altogether unavailing, so as perhaps to warrant the expectation that by perseverance therein, still more cheering

83

results may yet be produced, and a reformation be gradually affected, alike happy for the individual and profitable for society. These, however, are prevented from taking effect with numbers, who are continually shifting from place to place, removing whenever they can get no more credit, and in order to get quit, it may be feared, of the debts that have been contracted. This mode of life they can all the more easily follow, that coalmasters generally make no inquiry as to character, and if they have need of workmen, give employment to the first that offers. As far as obtaining employment is concerned, good and bad are on equal footing. In this respect, it is no advantage to have a good character, while a bad one subjects to no penalty, so that self-interest does not require that the latter should be avoided or maintained; and thus one of the salutary influences which men are subjected to in their dependent relations in society is rendered inoperative. This is a very great disadvantage,--must have contributed not a little to make them what they are, and renders more hopeless their ever being raised out of it while such a state of things continues."

It was during the period so described in the Statistical Account that John Pryde brought up his own family.

John Pryde (1811 – 1864) was born in Liberton, Midlothian, and he was a 2 x great-grandson of James Pride and Helen Selkirk. He was the second eldest son of George Pryde who was married to Catherine Miller, whose life has been described in Chapter 4. However, his elder brother William

LINE OF DESCENT FOR JOHN PRYDE
AND HIS FAMILY AS FEATURED IN CHAPTER 6

James Pride (circa 1678 – after 1748)
and Helen Selkirk
|
|
George Pride (1716 – 1759)
and Margaret Fraser
|
|
John Pride (1755 – after 1807)
and Mary Sharp
|
|
George Pride (1790 – 1855)
and Catherine Miller
|
|
John Pryde (1811 – 1864) and Helen Lawson
who had the following children:-

George (1833 – Unknown)
David (1835 – 1910)
John (1838 – 1915)
James (1840 – after 1861)
Mary (1842 – 1924)
William (1845 – 1891)
Alexander (1847 – 1927)
Robert (1849 – 1930)

seems not to have survived to adulthood so John would have been looked upon as the eldest son.

On the face of it, John Pryde seems to have lived an unremarkable life; he was brought up in the coal-mining village of Liberton with his five younger siblings. He was 12 years of age when the assault on his father took place and in all probability would have been working alongside his father for a number of years by then. He would have known all the men involved and would have moved out of the immediate area with his parents and siblings following the assault.

John Pryde married Helen Lawson at Liberton in 1831 and their first three children were born there, between 1833 and 1838, but by 1840 the family had moved to Dalkeith and this is where their next five children were born. As John and Helen would have been bringing up their family during the time described earlier in the Statistical Account we are easily able to imagine their day-to-day lives.

According to the census returns for 1841 and 1851 John worked as a Coal Miner but on the 1861 census he is listed as a Colliery Contractor – a Colliery Contractor would undertake to supply a number of men to work the coal face. The practice of using a Colliery Contractor to be responsible for supplying men to work began after the 1799 Act and continued in some parts up to Vesting Day in 1947 when coal mines were nationalised. The system clearly suited the coal masters, making recruitment, and firing, simpler.

On his 1861 census entry John was shown aged 49 years and he was living at 37 Cowdenfoot Village, Dalkeith, with his wife and their children, John, James, Mary, William, Alexander and Robert. An older son, **David Pryde (1835 – 1910)** had married a month previously and it was David who later registered the death of his father in April 1864. The cause of death was Miner's consumption of Lungs - 6 years; Asthma as certified by L R Thomson L.D. John Pryde was aged 52 years at his death which was caused by what is referred to as black-spit in the New Statistical Account quoted previously. Indeed, it may have been the onset of this illness that forced John Pryde into becoming a Colliery Contractor instead of labouring on his own account as a miner.

Although there is nothing of any great compulsion about the life of John Pryde, this chapter about him is included to illustrate how coal mining continued to shape and affect the lives of the family from one generation to the next. Almost 200 years after the birth of James Pride (who married Helen Selkirk) we see his great-great-grandson still labouring in the mine and dying because of the effects of doing so. Eleven generations after James Pride his descendants were still working in the coal mines as was the case with my own father. However, the children of John Pryde and Helen Lawson are a good example of how some of the later generations were able to change their lives from the mid-1850s onwards as can be shown by the following précis of their lives. They were 3 x great-grandchildren of James Pride and Helen Selkirk.

GEORGE PRYDE (1833 - after 1841) no trace after the 1841 census when he is shown living with his parents and siblings aged eight years so it is assumed he died in childhood.

DAVID PRYDE (1835 – 1910) shown as a Colliery Clerk when he married Margaret Rutherford at Dalkeith in 1861. By 1875 he was living near Wrexham, North Wales, where he sank a local pit called Gatewen Colliery and he stayed on to manage this until 1888. See further details in Chapter 18.

JOHN PRYDE (1838 – 1915) was working as a Miner's Assistant at the age of 13 years according to the 1851 census but by 1861 he was working as a joiner. He married Violet Flockhart at Dalkeith in 1866 and after the birth of two sons, the first of whom, **John Pryde (1867 – 1869)** died in infancy, the family moved to Falkirk. His wife died there in 1881 and his second son **Robert Pryde (1868 – 1884)** also died there aged 16 years after succumbing to Scarlet Fever. John Pryde had been working in Glasgow since 1881 and after the loss of his first wife and second son he remained there where in 1888 he married Elizabeth Rodger. At various times in his life his occupation was given as joiner, wagon builder and [wheel]wright. He died in Glasgow in 1915 aged 77 years, his second wife having predeceased him in 1898.

JAMES PRYDE (1840 – after 1861) was living with his parents and employed as a Coalminer Roadman according to the 1861 census but no definite trace of him has been found after this. According to family lore James travelled to America with one or more of his brothers to prospect for gold and died there. A small amount of documentary evidence has been found to support this but no definitive proof has been found. See also the following notes for his brother William Pryde.

MARY PRYDE (1842 – 1924) married Adam Paterson in Edinburgh in 1873 and they had one daughter and three sons. Mary Paterson née Pryde died in Edinburgh in 1924, aged 81 years, her husband having predeceased her by some 33 years.

After the death of his mother, one of her sons, **David Pryde Paterson (1879 – 1936)** emigrated to Australia in October 1927, as a single man. When he was about 50 years of age he married Janet Kemp in 1928 at Canterbury, New South Wales. Sadly he was to die there just six years later, in 1936 aged 57 years. Throughout his life he earned his living as a Brass Moulder.

WILLIAM PRYDE (1845 – 1891) went to America to prospect for gold and silver and in 1874 and 1875 he was in Silver State, Humboldt, Nevada. William was then shown on the 1880 American census working at Candalaria, Esmeralda, Nevada. Records show that Candalaria, see Fig. 5, was a silver mining village which was dry i.e. it did not have its own water supply and at one time it was cheaper to buy whisky than water. The shortage of water in the mining and milling process led to a high incidence of 'miners' consumption'. William Pryde must have returned to Scotland in the late 1880s, possibly because of failing health, as he died in 1891, aged 46 years, at the home of his sister Mary, at Balfour Street, Leith, and the occupation on his death record was given as Gold and Silver miner. He did not marry.

**Fig. 5 - Candelaria, Nevada in 1876
– now a ghost town**
(Source unknown)

ALEXANDER PRYDE (1847 – 1927), pictured, would appear also to have travelled to America in the late 1860s, from oral family history confirmed by ship's manifest but little has been confirmed of his time there and he later returned to Scotland. He visited his brother David in Wrexham in 1878 and married, in spite of family opposition, a

90

servant who was employed by his brother. Her name was Harriet Powell and they subsequently had 11 children together. Alexander started off his working life as a Clerk but then was mostly employed in various minor supervisory roles in the local coal and steel making industries. He did not have a good employment record as again, according to oral recollection within the family and surviving work records, he was unreliable and liable to go off wandering, sometimes for months at a time. He died in 1927 aged 80 years, some four months after the death of his wife.

ROBERT PRYDE (1849 – 1930) joined the Royal Horse Artillery on the 11th August 1870 when he was aged 20 years. By 1886 he was stationed in India where aged 37 years he married Margaret Mabel Milner Prager who was aged 21 years. They lived the rest of their lives in India where they died at Bangalore within a fortnight of each other in 1930. They had eight children, five of whom died soon after birth or in infancy. One daughter and two sons grew to adulthood, but one son, **Robert William Pryde (1893 – 1923)** died unmarried aged 30 years, having succumbed to the tropical disease of Sprue whilst working for Bombay Police. Robert's other surviving son, **Arthur Walter Pryde (1896 – 1986)** became Inspector General of Police, in Sind, India. See also the entries in Chapter 18. It is worth noting that in 1984 Arthur Walter Pryde gave a tape-recorded interview, which recalled his times living and working in India, and these are held, on four tapes, in The National Archives, as part of the British Library, Asia, Pacific and Africa Collections, under reference Mss Eur K490 – IOR Pos 12033. This carries on the tradition inadvertently started by his 4 x great-grandfather, James Pride, in that in the 18th century he left information in the form of the 1746 Petition for future generations to find, as did Walter Pryde, in the 19th century, when he gave evidence to the Franks Commission in 1842.

As can be seen from the above, although the majority of Prydes stayed in the Midlothian area in the 1850s and afterwards, where their descendants are still to be found today, some also travelled throughout the world in the hope of building a better life for themselves and their families. The following chapters tell a few of the stories of their many varied lives and fortunes.

CHAPTER 7

EARLY EMIGRATION TO AMERICA
- AND CIVIL WAR

The family of John Pryde (1811 – 1894)
and
Mary Ann Knowles (1814 – 1885)

As described in Chapter 5, George Pryde, who was trapped underground in the fall of coal at the High Pressure Pit in Whitehill, Dalkeith, in 1839, had a brother John Pryde who had travelled to America in the 1820s with their father George Pride Snr. and John remained in America when his father returned to Scotland. This is the earliest known mention of attempted emigration that I have found for our Pryde family.

After travelling to America in the 1820s with his father, **John Pryde (1811 – 1894)**, 2 x great-grandson of James Pride and Helen Selkirk, and son of George Pride Snr. and Elizabeth Pettigrew, subsequently married Mary Ann Knowles in Richmond, Virginia, in 1834. They had 15 children born between 1834 and 1858; the first 14 children were born in various locations in the state of Virginia, and their last child was born in 1858 in Granger Co., Tennessee. John worked at various occupations mostly connected with the railroad industry.

**LINE OF DESCENT FOR JOHN PRYDE
AND SOME OF HIS FAMILY AS FEATURED IN CHAPTER 7**

James Pride (circa 1678 – after 1748)
and Helen Selkirk
|
|
George Pride (1716 – 1759)
and Margaret Fraser
|
|
Thomas Pride (1753 – after 1796)
and Henrietta Maria Pride (1755 – after 1796)
(Granddaughter of James Pride and Helen Selkirk
and daughter of James Pride and Agnes Smith)
|
|
George Pride (1779 – 1832)
and Elizabeth Pettigrew
|
|
John Pryde (1811 – 1894)
and Mary Ann Knowles
and some of their 15 children:-

John Carlyle (1842 – 1877)
William George (1843 – 1900)
James Simpson (1845 – 1864)
Robert B. (1848 – 1864)

However, by 1880 he was a farmer living at Burnetts, Hamblen County, Tennessee. He and his wife and children lived through the troubled times which erupted in America in the 1860s as shown as follows, in the following extracts of the lives of a few of their children.

William George Pryde (1843 – 1900), pictured, was the

 seventh child of John Pryde and Mary Ann Knowles and 3 x great-grandson of James Pride and Helen Selkirk. He was born on 1st December 1843 at Buffalo Gap, Virginia. During the American Civil War on 12th March 1862 he enlisted as a Confederate soldier at Goodson, Tennessee, as a Private in Company A, Virginia 37th Infantry Regiment.

After his Civil War service William George became a Detective in Memphis. He married his first wife Sallie Bayless-Telford in 1870 but it is probable she died soon after as William George married Mattie F. Smith circa 1875. It appears he had a child, **Mary Henrietta Pryde (circa 1875 – after 1952)** but which person was her mother is as yet unsure as details about his early marriage and fatherhood are very sketchy.

It is known however that he and his second wife Mattie had a son, **William H Pryde (July 1877 – December 1877)** who was born in Memphis, Tennessee, where William George lived and worked as a Detective for 27 years. The following extracts from contemporary newspapers illustrate not only the cases in which he was involved, but also how tragedy was to strike the family.

Extract from Daily Inter Ocean Newspaper (Chicago, Illinois) dated Wednesday, 24th January, 1877:-

"RESISTING AN OFFICER

MEMPHIS, Tenn, Jan. 23 - This afternoon, while attempting to arrest a colored burglar named Williams, on Linden Street, Detective Pryde was shot by the burglar and mortally wounded, the shot entering the left breast above the heart and ranging downwards. Williams escaped."

Extract from the New York Herald (New York, NY) dated Wednesday 31st January, 1877 states:-

"MURDERS IN MEMPHIS
(From the Memphis Appeal, Jan 27.)

...... Tuesday afternoon Mr. L. Kaufman's residence, on Exchange Street, was robbed of $3,000 in jewelry and $3,400 in money. The thieves were pursued next day by the police and detectives, and one of them, Jack Williams, colored, traced to a house at No. 209 Linden Street. The thief resisted arrest and shot Detective Pryde in the shoulder, producing an ugly wound. Williams then fled the city, but was captured on the Charleston Railroad train when near Bunton station and brought back to this city."

Then the first personal tragedy which was to strike William George Pryde is as shown in the following extract from the Cleveland Leader Newspaper, Page 5, Wednesday 2nd January, 1878 [this was a re-publication from another earlier dated newspaper report as was normal practice at that time – see footnote about the date on next page]:-

"A Terribly Sad Tragedy

The saddest of all sad accidents was that which occurred in the house of William G. Pryde, a Memphis (Tennessee) Detective, early Monday [13] morning. He had returned home about midnight and two hours after was aroused by what he thought was a noise at the window. Rising in bed, he attempted to draw his revolver from beneath his pillow. It became entangled in the bed-clothes, and, given a nervous jerk by Pryde's hand, the hammer fell upon the cartridge, and it exploded. A babe of 5 months of age was lying by its mother's side, both peacefully sleeping, and the bullet passed through the abdomen of both mother and child. Springing up, Pryde struck a light, and before him saw the picture from whose horrible spellbound contemplation the speedy entrance of neighbours alone aroused him. At first he could not speak as many voices asked the cause of the dreadful scene, and kind hands raised the heads of his dying wife and child, but at last he almost shrieked out his heart-rending story. "Don't cry, poor Will", said his wife an hour later, just before she breathed her last. "I know how it was; you didn't mean to do it, my husband". In a few minutes the baby spirit too, passed over the river. Between Pryde and his wife there existed a tie, the tenderness of which was frequently a matter of comment among their friends. Pryde, is an unusually useful detective, a man of gentle manners and quiet, gentlemanly bearing. His wife was a modest little woman, whose good influence, acting as a check on the detective's naturally degrading life cannot be calculated. The unfortunate man was almost crazed, and only kept from self-destruction by the close watch of his friends."

---

[13] The Monday referred to in the newspaper report was Monday 24th December 1877, this was also the date of the inquest.

An extract from Times-Picayune (New Orleans, LA) Newspaper dated Tuesday, 25th December, 1877 states:-

"MEMPHIS Dec 24. - The coroner's jury in the case of Detective Pryde, who accidentally shot and killed his wife and child, this morning, exonerates him, his wife having repeatedly stated it was an accident before her wound proved fatal."

Immediately after this William George Pryde was faced with another tragedy as an extract from Daily Inter Ocean, Chicago, Illinois, Newspaper, Friday, 28th December, 1877 states:-

"PRYDE'S MISFORTUNES

Memphis, Tenn. Dec 27 - The wife and child of Detective Pryde, who were accidentally shot Monday morning, were buried today, and this morning a telegram was received stating that Pryde's brother John had been found murdered Monday morning near Town Creek, Ala."

William's brother, **John Carlyle Pryde (1842 – 1877)**, pictured, was also born in Buffalo Gap, Virginia. He had a relationship with Rachel Elizabeth Mozingo who gave birth to a son,

 Benjamin Pride (circa 1862 – circa 1872) and she was pregnant again when John Carlyle left to join the Confederate Army where he became a 1st Lieut. of Company-C 59th Tennessee Infantry Regt. John Carlyle Pryde was taken prisoner-of-war and paroled at the end of the conflict when he was aged 23 years of age.

He never returned to Rachel Mozingo and in 1866 he married Mattie J Roddy with whom he had two children, **Lillian Gay Pryde (1867 – 1948)** and **Charles Albert Pryde (1868 – after 1880)**.

I have not been able to find any other details about the murder of John Carlyle Pryde which occurred when he was aged 35 years.

Rachel Mozingo gave birth to a son who was named John Carlisle Pride (1863 - 1917), his birth being registered by his mother with an incorrect version of the name of John Carlyle Pryde. The surname continues in use as Pride within this line to the present day. Rachel Mozingo and her sons lived with her parents until she married John A Robertson in 1871.

To continue with the life of William George Pryde, after the tragic death of his second wife he married his third wife Elizabeth Lawless circa 1880. William George is shown on the 1880 census aged 35 years, born Virginia, of a Scottish father and an Irish mother, working as a Detective and living at Shelby, Tennessee, with his wife Lizzie and her two brothers John and Walter. William George and his wife had a son together, **John Walter Pryde (1881 – 1931)**.

Detective William George Pryde continued his career and was involved in many interesting cases which is evidenced from the following newspaper extracts.

An extract from Wheeling Register (Wheeling, WV) dated Monday 14th May, 1883 states:-

"AT PISTOL'S POINT

A Memphis Woman Tries to Persuade a Doctor to Marry Her.

Memphis May 13 - Quite a sensation was created yesterday at noon by Mrs. Ella Ennis, a handsome widow of about thirty years of age, who went in the office of Dr. H.W. Purnel, a well-known physician in this city, and demanded of him that he should at once proceed to the County Court Clerk's office and procure a license to marry her, as he (so she alleges) had promised to do. This demand was backed up by a navy six shooter, which the woman held in a threatening manner. Dr. Purnell had no alternative but to

Accede to the Demand

He however, discreetly sent a friend who was in the office and witnessed the affair, to notify the police to be on hand at the Clerk's office. Mrs Ennis followed the Doctor up Main Street towards the Court House, where the Clerk's office is located. She kept about six feet behind him, and held conveniently in her hand, covered with her handkerchief, her trusty weapon. On arriving at the Clerk's office, Detectives Pryde and McCune, who had been sent post haste to the scene, seized her hands and wrested from her the pistol. She at once realized the trap that had been laid for her, but

Boldly Demanded of the Doctor

to fulfil his promise, saying "You have wronged me and must marry me." Protected as he was by the officers, Dr. Purnell declined to go any further in the matrimonial way, but was himself taken under arrest, as he, too, had a pistol upon his person. The two were soon after admitted to bail in the sum of $500 each to answer the charge of carrying concealed weapons. While going to the station house Mrs. Ennis told Detective Pryde that Dr. Purnell might just as well die today, as she intended to kill him if it was the last act in her life. The cause of this little episode in the hitherto peaceful career of the lady, is alleged to have been due to the failure of the doctor to keep

His Pledge of Marriage With Her

which dates back to last September. At that time Dr. Purnell left the city, but was followed by the lady to Denver. He however, succeeded in eluding her. She afterward found him in New Orleans and brought the subject matter to a crisis today in the manner mentioned. She has been a widow for five years, her husband having died during the epidemic of 1878. She has some property besides about $7,000 in bonds. The doctor and his friends claim him to be the victim of either a crazy or designing woman. It is known that several days ago she went to his office

Armed With Two Pistols

and made the same demand of him as was made today. On that occasion the doctor displayed more courage and quietly disarmed her.

Mrs. Ennis has four children, and has always borne a good reputation. The escapade of today has set the gossips going, and there is a general feeling of sympathy for the woman. It is understood tonight that the affair will not be prosecuted, but be permitted to disappear from public gaze.

Mrs. Ennis, however, has two brothers residing here and in all probability they will see that justice is done her."

Another case is reported as follows:-

An extract from Daily Baton Newspaper (Baton Rouge, LA) dated Friday, 13th February, 1885 states:-

Detective Pryde, of Memphis, arrived here last night with the two negroes who are suspected of having murdered Mrs Judge Cole recently in the town of Plaquemine and robbed her of valuable jewelry. They were offering for sale a pair of diamond earrings, when Detective Pryde came across them. They told several stories about how they got them, all of which was taken cum grano salis by the detective. After reflecting over the matter awhile he concluded to arrest them and telegraph to various points for information about them, as he felt sure the jewelry was too valuable to have been honestly obtained by the negroes.

Word came from Plaquemine to hold them, and the next day the Deputy Sheriff Sam Bigley reached Memphis, identified the earrings as being a pair owned by Mrs. Cole, and he also identified one of the negroes, Geo. Wilson, as being a notorious and brutal character well known to the officers as a very bad character. He is to leave here today for the scene of the murder with the captured negroes. It was rumoured in town this morning that one of them had made a confession."

An extract from the Daily Advocate (Baton Rouge, LA) Newspaper dated Monday, 15th June, 1885 states:-

"Messrs. Pryde and Barnum, of Memphis, Tenn, called on the Governor and obtained payment of the State's reward for the capture and conviction of the murderers of Mrs. Henrietta Cole. Mr. Barnum is the jeweler to whom Mrs. Cole's diamond rings were offered for sale, and Mr. Pryde is the detective to whom Mr. Barnum confided his suspicions about the matter, and who arrested the criminals."

Three months later Detective Pryde was again in the news:-

An extract from Tombstone Epitaph Prospector Newspaper dated Wednesday 16th September, 1885 states:-

"AN ESCAPING CONVICT SHOT

MEMPHIS, SEPT 16

About two weeks ago Gen McNeal, colored, and escaped convict from the Arkansas Penitentiary, at Little Rock was discovered in Memphis. At the time he was serving a sentence

103

on the chain gang, having been arrested for trespassing. He was being conveyed back to Little Rock by two private detectives who thoughtlessly removed his shackles before they had handcuffed him. McNeal seeing his opportunity for escape was not slow to take advantage of the situation, and lit out at a break-neck speed and soon distanced his pursuers. This afternoon Detective Pryde, of the Memphis police force met McNeal on Main Street near Madison and attempted to arrest him. McNeal saw the officer just as he was in the act of grasping his arm and he turned to flee. Pryde made a grab at him, but the negro eluded him and started on a run out Madison towards Front Street. Several passers-by attempted to catch him but he was too quick from them and he was in a fair way to again escape, when Pryde, who was pursuing with his pistol in his hand, took deliberate aim and fired at the fleeing convict. McNeal dropped at the report of the pistol and was taken to the station house where he was given medical attention. The bullet entered his right side about two inches from the back bone and the wound is doubtless mortal. The shooting was witnessed by several hundred people."

And as a final illustration of his exploits:-

An extract from State (Columbia SC) Newspaper dated Tuesday 2nd December, 1891 states:-

"CHARGED WITH 27 MURDERS

Tall Hall Thirsts for the Gore of Three More Men

MEMPHIS DEC 21 - Six officers, armed with Winchesters and a requisition, arrived in Memphis this morning and took Tall Hall, the Kentucky murderer, in charge, and left with him for Virginia. John Wright of Knox County will try to intercept the train, and in order to avoid him the officers took a circuitous route. It is thought the mob will take charge of Hall at Norton, Virginia, where he killed his last man.

United States Marshall Taylor says that twenty-seven murders have been traced to Hall. He cheerfully informed the officers that he would return to Memphis and kill Detectives Hedrick and Pryde and a reporter.

After he was taken in charge by the Virginia authorities, a requisition charging Hall with four murders arrived, but it was not honored."

A partial Extract from the Times-Picayune (New Orleans LA) Newspaper dated Friday, 12th February, 1892 states:-

"KILLED ONE HUNDRED

The Bloody Record of Desperado Talton Hall, now on Trial in Norton, Va.

HE CONFESSES HE HAS MURDERED NINETY-NINE BEINGS, BUT DENIES THE HUNDRETH

A dispatch from Richmond, Va., of Feb 8, says: As the trial of Talton Hall, the tri-state desperado, has been in progress during the past week at Norton, in south west Virginia, a sketch of his career will be of interest at this time. He was but

18 years old when he started upon a life during which he has lost count of how many lives he has taken.

He says it's not 100, but won't say it's not 99. Thirty victims are named and charged by him by the authorities of Virginia, and Kentucky. He freely discusses the possibility of getting out of his present "scrape" and as long as he keeps making the incriminating confession of his guilt he freely discusses his history and his life, and everything except his faithful wife, whose name is never profaned by discussion amid his surroundings.

On the 9th day of December last Detectives Pryde and Hedrick of the Memphis police force, arrested him, and it now seems probable that his career will shortly end. The officers found their man in a room on Front Street, where he was quietly eating his supper in company with his wife. Hall was armed with a rifle and revolver, but the officers took him unawares, and he quietly submitted to arrest. .... "

The article continued listing the crimes known to have been committed by Hall including first killing the murderers of two of his brothers; the first husband of his wife in order that they could marry; and he also shot the Triplett brothers, who were his wife's brothers. After killing the sheriff of Floyd County who was attempting to arrest him, Hall joined the John Wright band of outlaws. He was responsible for the killing of Dick Vance, another notorious criminal who was jealous of the infamy being given to Hall and during this exchange Hall also shot three of his own cousins who had defended Vance. Talton Hall was found guilty and hanged on 3rd September 1892 at Wise Court-house, Virginia.

William George Pryde died at home at 28 Mulberry Street, Memphis, Tennessee, on 3rd May 1900 being survived by two children and his wife Elizabeth. He had been in work the day before his death but had had to be taken home in a buggy by his colleague Capt. O'Haver as he was in great pain. He had suffered from Bright's disease for many years but the condition had worsened in the previous 18 months. He had been connected with the Police Department for 23 years, and his red hair and prowess as a detective had earned him the byname of "The Red Fox".

As an example of how divisive war can be it is worth noting that William George Pryde and John Carlyle Pryde had two other brothers who also fought in the American Civil war. **James Simpson Pryde (1845 – 1864)** fought on the side of the Confederates, like his two older brothers, but was killed towards the end of the war near Midway, Greene Co., Tennessee, when aged only 19 years of age. See also Chapter 17.

Another brother, **Robert B Pryde (1848 – 1864)** fought on the Union side, the opposite side to his brothers. There can be little doubt this caused bad feeling between the brothers, and this is confirmed by oral recollection within the family that Robert was afraid of his brothers, thinking they would kill him. He had enlisted in the 13th Regt. of the Tennessee Cavalry

Volunteers, joining Company G under the command of Captain S.M. Scott. An excerpt from the history of the 13th Regiment, Tennessee Volunteer Cavalry provides us with the following information:-

"....On the 29th [September 1864] *the Brigade moved slowly as far as Jonesboro, skirmishing with the enemy and driving them through the town... The remainder of the Brigade remained at Jonesboro while the Thirteenth advanced towards Johnson City, driving Gen. Vaughn's brigade... The Fifteenth Pennsylvania drove another force of rebels as far as Devault's ford and across the Watauga River. We were now fighting the Confederate forces of Generals Williams and Vaughn.*

(The following event, which happened during the night of the 28th had been overlooked in the confusion of advancing towards Johnson City during the 29th.)

On the morning of the 30th we learned of the death of Robt. Pride, who had been killed by accident the night before at Jonesboro. He was a member of Company G., and had been detailed as Orderly at Col. Miller's headquarters. He had remained at Jonesboro, with Adjutant Stacy, and at night had laid a little gun that Col. Miller had given him on the ground, and laying his saddle on the gun, spread down his blanket and went to sleep. In the night he was awakened by an alarm of the enemy, and reaching for the gun, it was supposed he caught it by the muzzle, the lock catching some part of the saddle, discharged, the bullet struck him in the face and killed him instantly. "Bob" as he was called, was a brother-in-law of

Alfred M Taylor. He was a bright, brave boy and a general favourite in the Regiment. We would note here that young Pride had a brother killed in this same campaign who was fighting on the other side."

Military Discharge Papers relating to Robert B. Pryde state:-

"I certify, on honor, that Robert B. Pride, a private of Captain S.M. Scott's Company-G of the 13th Regiment of [the] Tennessee Cavalry Volunteers, of the State of Tennessee, born in Richmond, State of Virginia, aged 18 years; 5 feet 4 inches high; fair complexion, blue eyes, dark hair, and by occupation a student, who joined for service and was enrolled on the 24th day of September, 1863, at Carter Co., Tennessee by C.C. Wilcox, for the period of three years, and mustered into the service of the United States on the 28th day of October, 1863, at Knox Co., Tennessee, by M.L. Ogden; and having served honestly and faithfully with his company to the present date, is now entitled to a discharge by reason of death by an accidental shot through the head near Jonesboro, Tennessee, September 29th, 1864."

Although the discharge papers state he was 18 years of age at the time of his death, it is likely that when Robert enlisted for service he lied about his age, as when he died he was aged only 16 years.

As stated for their brothers at the beginning of the chapter, James Simpson Pryde and Robert Pryde were 3 x great-grandsons of James Pride and Helen Selkirk. It is impossible to imagine what their father, John Pryde, must have felt having

109

left Scotland in his teens and deciding to stay and make a new life in America after his own father had returned to Scotland, only to then see two of his sons die in tragic circumstances in the bitter battles between the Union and Confederate Armies, which led to the loss of over 600,000 men in only four years.

Add to that the reported murder of his son John, and the accidental killing of his daughter-in-law and grandson by his son William and we begin to realise how John Pryde and Mary Ann Knowles must have grieved for their children through their long marriage. At least 10 of their 15 children predeceased their father and nine of these were adults when they died.

John Pryde died in Grainger, Tennessee, in 1894 aged 83 years, his wife Mary Ann having predeceased him by some nine years. Known descendants currently total just over 1,100.

CHAPTER 8

ESCAPE FROM THE MINES TO THE MINES

Robert Pryde (1795 – 1878)
and
Mary Brown (1794 – 1865)

Once freed from their bondage at the end of the 18th century the poor living and working conditions tempted many to emigrate in the 1800s but it will come as no surprise that many miners emigrated only to work in coal mines abroad. They were prepared to uproot their families in the hope of finding a better life and my research has shown that, although times were hard, many achieved their aim of a better life, particularly for their children and grandchildren.

One of these was **Robert Pryde (1795 – 1878),** 2 x great-grandson of James Pride and Helen Selkirk. He was born in Cockpen, Midlothian, in 1795, a natural son of Robert Pride and Isobel Smith. He was a nephew of Walter Pride who gave testimony to the Franks Report in 1842 as shown in Chapter 3.

LINE OF DESCENT FOR ROBERT PRYDE
AND SOME OF HIS FAMILY AS FEATURED IN CHAPTER 8

James Pride (circa 1678 – after 1748)
and Helen Selkirk
|
|
Robert Pride (1710 – after 1755)
and Christian Selkirk
|
|
Robert Pride (1741 – after 1792)
and Janet Wemyss
|
|
Robert Pride (1765 – after 1841)
and Isobel Smith
|
|
Robert Pryde (1795 – 1878)
and Mary Brown
and some of their 7 children:-

John (1827 – 1855)
Isabella (1829 – 1902)
William (1832 – 1912)
Robert (1837 – 1912)

Robert Pryde married Mary Brown at Newbattle, Midlothian, in 1820 and they had five children born at Newbattle between 1821 and 1829. No details of their first three children have been found, apart from their baptism records, so it may be that these children died whilst still young. However their fourth and fifth born children survived to adulthood and they and their parents must have emigrated from Scotland to America between 1829 and 1832 as they had a further two sons, the first being born in Pennsylvania, America, in August 1832.

Vital records i.e. birth, marriage and death records, are scarce to non-existent for this time period in Pennsylvania so we have to refer mainly to the various census records available for further information. Robert Pryde is listed as Head of the Family on the 1840 census for Norwegian, Schuylkill, but no additional details of who comprised his family by name were recorded.

Listed adjacent to the Robert Pryde household in 1840 was the household of George Brown, who had married Robert's half-sister **Alison Pryde, (1803 – before 1895)** in Newbattle, Midlothian, in 1822. The household of George and Alison Brown is also listed on the 1830 census for Norwegian, Schuylkill, so Robert Pryde and his half-sister Alison and their respective families may have emigrated together or Robert and his family followed later. When **Elizabeth Brown (1823 – 1909)**, the first born child of George Brown and Alison Pryde, who was born in Newbattle, Midlothian, in 1823, died in Laramie, Wyoming, in 1909 her obituary heading is "OLD

PIONEER LADY GOES TO REWARD" and a further obituary stated she had survived her five brothers, all of whom had served in the Civil War.

By 1850 Robert Pryde and his wife Mary, had left the Browns in Norwegian as they and their son William are shown living at Schuylkill Township and Robert's occupation is listed as a miner. By 1860 Robert and Mary are settled in Minersville, which is also in Schuylkill County, Pennsylvania, and he is listed as a coal miner, aged 65 years. Also living with the family is another son, also called Robert. All three places where the families resided according to each census are near each other and part of the same coal field.

Coal was first discovered in the area in 1799 and mining in Minersville started in 1814. The town was originally nothing more than a log cabin, saw mill and tavern but many immigrants from all nations came to the area looking for work, and on 1st April 1830 Minersville was incorporated as a borough. Typical homes for the mine workers were built from rough-hewn timber, although by the mid-1850s, about the time that Robert and his family settled in Minersville, a regular mail service and Minersville Water Company had been established so the community were able to enjoy the amenities becoming available.

Robert and Mary's son, **John Pryde (1827 – 1855)** who had been born in Newbattle, Midlothian, died and was buried in Minersville in 1855 aged 28 years, so it is likely Robert Pryde and his family settled in Minersville prior to this.

114

Robert Pryde Snr. is on the 1870 census still living at Minersville, near his daughter Isabella and her family, and still working as a miner. His age is shown as 70 years, but as he would have been 75 years of age at this time it is possible he had not given his true age so that he would continue to be employed. Robert Pryde died in Minersville in 1878 aged 82 years, his wife Mary Pryde née Brown having predeceased him in 1865. Known descendants currently total just over 60.

His two sons born in Pennsylvania did not marry although they were long lived. **William Pryde (1832 – 1912)** who is listed on the 1850 census as a Mechanical Engineer aged 17 years, living with his parents in Schuylkill Township, was by 1883 living in Tacoma, Pierce, Washington State, working as a Blacksmith. By 1900 he is aged 67 years and working his own farm at Elias, Chehalis, Washington State, where he died in 1912 aged 80 years.

As briefly noted previously, his brother, **Robert Pryde (1837 – 1912)** was shown living with his parents at Minersville on the 1860 census. He was listed as being 21 years old and working as a Coal Miner. By 1880 he was lodging at Gold Hill, Storey, Nevada, and engaged in mining, and he was in the same place on the 1900 census, aged 62 years, working as an Ore Miner.

By 1910 he was still working as a miner, and still in lodgings, but he had moved to Oakland Township, Alameda, California, and he died there in 1912, aged 75 years, some 3 months before the death of his brother William.

Isabella Pryde (1829 – 1902) was the only surviving daughter of Robert Pryde and Mary Brown. She was born in Newbattle, Midlothian, in 1829 so would have been a baby or young infant when the family made the trip to America.

In 1859 she married William George at Minersville, Pennsylvania, and they remained living in Minersville for the rest of their lives. In 1860 William George was working as a coal miner, but by 1870 he is shown as a Store keeper, and he and Isabella have two children, **William George Jnr. (1862 – 1918)** and **Mary George (1868 – after 1895).** The mining tradition carried on through the family as William George Jnr. is shown on the 1900 census working as a Mine Labourer in Minersville as is his son, **William George III (circa 1886 – 1944)** aged 15 years. By 1910 another son **Robert Pryde George**

 (1888 – 1950), pictured, is also shown working as a Coal Breaker, in the coal mine in Minersville, believed to be at Oak Hill Colliery. A Coal Breaker was one of the first jobs a youth could expect to have in Minersville.

They would spend the day sitting in front of troughs and they would hand-pick extraneous materials from the coal which had been brought up from underground.

All the miners who lived and worked hereabouts made an important contribution to the growth and prosperity of the area and this was acknowledged by the installation in 1997 of a Miner's Memorial Statue, see Fig. 6, at Minersville.

Fig. 6. Miners Memorial Statue, Minersville.[14]

[14] My sincere thanks to Tom D. Symons of Minersville for his efforts and kindness in obtaining this photograph for use in this book.

A plaque adjacent to the memorial states:-

COAL MINERS' STATUE

MINERSVILLE

SCHUYLKILL COUNTY, PA

The Miner

———————

As a boy he worked in the breaker picking slate out of the coal.

As an adolescent he worked the doors, or led the mule teams, or threw spragues between the wheels of the coal cars.

As a young man, he helped the miner dig the coal, and he loaded it into the cars supplied by the mule drivers.

As a Miner he drilled into the coal, set the charges, and blasted the coal loose.

As an old man, as a miner with injuries, he returned to the breakers to work beside the boys picking slate.

Twice a boy, they said, and once a man when you worked inside the mines.

Anthracite – hard coal – was known and used by the Indians and local settlers well before Necho Allen "discovered" coal on Sharp Mountain outside of Pottsville in 1790. The discovery by those outside the region that anthracite would actually burn led to boom times in Schuylkill County starting in the 1820s and 1830s.   Locally mined coal heated the homes of Philadelphia, fuelled the Industrial Revolution, and helped win the Civil War and two World Wars.   Although there are not as many mines as there were years ago, the industry continues to be a vital part of the region's culture and economic life.

Schuylkill County and the nation would be a different place today if the miner had not toiled above ground and in the depths to extract anthracite from where it formed so many millions of years ago.   Many lost their lives and even more were injured over the years. This monument is dedicated to the memory of all who have worked in the mines.   Let us thank these miners, for they have touched our lives.

Dr. Thomas B. Graves, President 1996 – 1997
Rotary Club of Minersville, Pennsylvania

Robert Pryde (1795 – 1868) and his descendants are amongst those miners whose work in the local coalfields is acknowledged by the memorial.

CHAPTER 9

WAGON TRAINS AND MORMONISM

John Pryde (1854 – 1930)
and
Janet Young (1855 – 1920)

and his brother and her sister

Robert Pryde (1867 – 1955)
and
Christina Young (1870 - 1907)
then Marion Young (1883 – 1966)

John and Robert Pryde were brothers and 3 x great -grandsons of James Pride and Helen Selkirk. Their father was **George Pryde (1821 – 1881)** who married Isabella Young at Lasswade, Midlothian, in 1852. Before his marriage to Isabella George had had two children with Marion Brown, he then he had eight children with Isabella Young, but out of these ten children it appears only John and Robert left Scotland. Their grandparents were George Pride and Catherine Miller, whose story is told in Chapter 4.

LINE OF DESCENT FOR JOHN PRYDE
AND HIS BROTHER ROBERT PRYDE
AS FEATURED IN CHAPTER 9

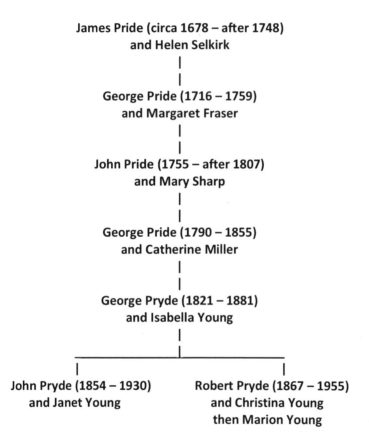

James Pride (circa 1678 – after 1748)
and Helen Selkirk
|
|
George Pride (1716 – 1759)
and Margaret Fraser
|
|
John Pride (1755 – after 1807)
and Mary Sharp
|
|
George Pride (1790 – 1855)
and Catherine Miller
|
|
George Pryde (1821 – 1881)
and Isabella Young
|

| |
John Pryde (1854 – 1930)   Robert Pryde (1867 – 1955)
and Janet Young   and Christina Young
                            then Marion Young

John Pryde (1854 – 1930), pictured, was born in Gorebridge,  Midlothian, and he married Janet Young there in 1881. Janet's father was George Young and her mother was Catherine Black, who had been baptised into the Mormon Church (now known as the Church of Jesus Christ of Latter-day Saints) in 1867 by George Crookston. Mormonism began in Scotland in 1839 when two expatriate Scots returned to Scotland to proselytize their faith. By the end of the 19th century some ten thousand Scottish people had joined the church, and almost half the converts had left Scotland as part of the Mormon gathering to Zion.[15]

The initial success of the conversion was helped in part by the poor working and living conditions prevailing in Scotland at this time, especially in the Lowlands. George Young converted to Mormonism in June 1883 some 16 years after his wife, when he was 57 years of age and it appears this was the catalyst for the whole of the extended family to go to America; John Pryde travelled there on his own in July 1883 and his wife and her parents and siblings joined him at Braidwood, Illinois, within a year or so.

John Pryde and Janet Young later moved to Colorado, where John was injured in a coal mine blast which led to him having ill health for about three years. After this he moved to

---

[15] See The Ebb and Flow of Mormonism in Scotland, 1840 – 1900 by Frederick S Buchanan at Brigham Young University Studies. Vol. 27:2 (1987) – extract by their kind permission.

Rocksprings, Wyoming, where he ran a bakery business for 17 years. Janet Young had been baptised into the Mormon faith before leaving Scotland and on 5th September 1902, some 20 years after his wife, John was also baptised into the Mormon faith. In the spring of 1906 he and his family decided to join his brother Robert who had settled in the area of Big Horn, Wyoming. John bought himself a forty-acre farm and town lot and he worked the farm until his death in 1930 when he was 76 years of age. John and Janet had 10 children and known descendants currently number just over 100.

Robert Pryde (1867 – 1955), pictured, emigrated from Scotland to America in the late 1880s, when he was aged about 20 years and still single. He initially joined up with his elder brother as he married Christina Young, sister of Janet Young, in Huerfano, Colorado, in December 1888 and they had seven children born in Colorado, Montana and Wyoming between 1889 and 1903. Robert's wife Christina was also a member of the LDS Church and in 1903 Robert was also baptised into this faith. It may have been this which prompted their move in 1904 from Rock Springs, Wyoming, to Byron, Wyoming, a distance of some 300 miles (approximately 480 kilometres). The journey was made by covered wagon, and took about a month. See Fig. 7.

Fig. 7 The Pioneers – Image supplied by the LDS Church

They were also joined in the Big Horn area by John Pryde and Janet Young as reported above. Sadly, Christina died in 1907 at Byron aged 37 years, when her youngest child was four years old.

About three years later Robert wrote to the family in Scotland and asked if there was anyone who would come over to take care of the children. Marion Young, who was second cousin once removed to Robert's late wife Christina, came over from Scotland, arriving in Billings, Montana, on 4th March 1911. Robert met Marion's train and they were married in Billings on the day of her arrival. She became step-mother to the younger children still in the family home and by all accounts was much loved by them.

Robert had worked in the coal mines in Colorado and Rock Springs, Wyoming, before settling in Byron, Wyoming. He then worked as superintendent of Allen Oil Co., for 27 years in the Byron - Lovell area. Marion Pryde served as Mayor of Byron from 1925 to 1927.

The town of Byron is named after Byron Sessions who led the first group of settlers to this location in May 1900. He did so at the request of the leaders of the LDS Church with the hope of helping the Mormon people settle there. The members of the original Mormon scouting party, or Pathfinders as they were also called, met and took advice from Colonel Cody, better known to most as Buffalo Bill. He had previously secured a permit to irrigate nearly all of the lands from the north side of the Shoshone River from Eagles Nest to the Big Horn River. However, when the Mormon scouting party had completed their task and identified the area they wished to settle, Buffalo Bill, in view of the Mormons' wish to build a canal and irrigate the land lower down, relinquished the land and water to them, free of charge, in the firm belief they would accomplish what they had set out to do.

Marion Pryde née Young, second wife of Robert Pryde was baptised into the Mormon faith on 29th June 1918 in the river to the south of the town of Byron.

Ellis Island records show that Robert and Marion Pryde visited Scotland in the early 1920s, returning to America on the 28th February 1921 on the ship *Algeria*, departing from Glasgow.

Records also show they became citizens of America in 1920 prior to leaving the country.

On the 1930 census Robert is shown living at Byron, Big Horn, Wyoming, aged 62 years, working as a pumper in an Oil Field. Also shown living with him is his wife Marion, aged 46 years, daughter **Margaret Louise Pryde (1903 – 1998)** aged 23 years, who is listed under her married surname of Crowder, and her two children **Jennie [nickname for Janet] Elaine Crowder (1927 – 1995)** and **Catherine Doris Crowder (1929 – 1995)**. Robert's daughter Margaret Louise Pryde, as shown on the 1930 census, was born in 1903 and died in 1998 and she was one of the children who made the long journey by covered wagon to Byron in 1904 with their parents.

Her sister **Mary Pryde (1897 – 1997)**, pictured, was born in 1897 and died in 1997 aged 100 years and 30 days. She also made the journey to Byron in the covered wagon and liked to boast that not only had she ridden in and driven a covered wagon but she had also flown on jet planes.

Robert Pryde died in 1955 aged 87 years and his wife Marion died in 1966 aged 83 years. They had been married for 44 years, from the day when Robert met Marion's train as it arrived in Billings, Montana. Although they had no surviving children together, they brought up six children from Robert's first marriage to Christina Young. Known descendants currently total just over 70. See also Chapter 20.

CHAPTER 10

EMIGRATION AND ENTERPRISE IN NEW ZEALAND

John Pryde (1840 – 1921)
and
Jane Goodlet (1842 – 1908)

John Pryde (1840 – 1921), pictured, was born in Ormiston, East Lothian, the third child of seven but first son of **John Pride (1802 – 1864)** and Mary Jeffrey. He was a 3 x great -grandson of James Pride and Helen Selkirk. It appears he was the only one of the siblings to emigrate, as although his sister **Mary Pryde (1842 – 1926)** together with her husband John Mutter travelled to America in the early 1870s they soon returned to Scotland.

It is not clear exactly when John Pryde emigrated from Scotland to Dunedin, Otago, New Zealand, but he became a partner in the Otago Antimony Mining Company in 1872. Antimony is a type of metalloid which is used mainly as an alloy for lead and tin which is then used for the production of solders, bearings and bullets. The Antimony reefs had been discovered in the area around Bannockburn, Central Otago, by Thomas Hall; it was he and another man, named George

129

LINE OF DESCENT FOR JOHN PRYDE
AND HIS SONS AS FEATURED IN CHAPTER 10

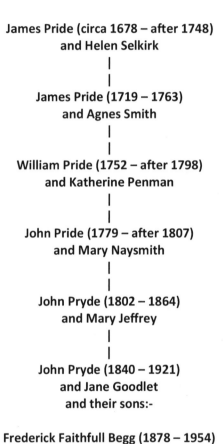

James Pride (circa 1678 – after 1748)
and Helen Selkirk
|
|
James Pride (1719 – 1763)
and Agnes Smith
|
|
William Pride (1752 – after 1798)
and Katherine Penman
|
|
John Pride (1779 – after 1807)
and Mary Naysmith
|
|
John Pryde (1802 – 1864)
and Mary Jeffrey
|
|
John Pryde (1840 – 1921)
and Jane Goodlet
and their sons:-

Frederick Faithfull Begg (1878 – 1954)
John Menzies (1881 – 1954)

Wilson who became partners with John Pryde. The men did not have the necessary funds to open the lode fully but they did manage to extract 10 tons which after smelting and being sent to London only managed to achieve £12 a ton.

John Pryde met Jane Goodlet in Dunedin and they married in 1876. By that time work had ceased on the mine but it was reopened in 1882 with John Pryde being put in charge of 12 men. In the hope of a successful outcome a smelter was erected at Slaughteryard Hill above Bannockburn Bridge where John Pryde also had other mines including his Excelsior Mine, see Fig. 8, which supplied coal for the Smelter. Work did not go as planned and the antimony mine closed by the end of year, even though by then the owners of the antimony mine had already bought Excelsior Mine from John Pryde.

John Pryde continued with several other mines, see Fig. 9, and projects and by 1889 he was the chief coal miner in the area with 12 men working under his direction. However, business was not always good and at one time he offered three leases for sale but was unable to find a buyer. He continued in his endeavours and on 6th July 1892 the following "MINERS RIGHT" was issued, No 68430 Fee 10 shillings. District and place in which issued: Otago; Cromwell

"Issued to John Pryde of [illegible] under the provisions of "The Mining Act 1891" No. 33 to be in force until 5th July 1893.

Signed James Fleming, Mining Registrar, Not Transferable."

In June 1899, one lease was purchased by a syndicate and in 1900 the Cromwell & Bannockburn Colliery Co. was formed. They took over two further Pryde leases at Adam's Gully and Shepherd's Creek. It would appear also that by 1906 John Pryde had three mines in operation with 50 men working but by 1914 these enterprises were wound up.

John Pryde died in Oamaru, New Zealand, in 1921 and known living descendants currently amount to just over 20. In 1951 John Pryde was recalled in a local publication [16] as *"a man of dour enterprise, never particularly popular but persistent, hard-headed and hard-working and often capable of success where others failed."*

Note for Fig. 9 - It is highly likely the man standing to the left of the group in the picture is John Pryde, as there is in existence a portrait-style photo of him with a spaniel at his feet. The two children to the right of the group are likely to be his sons, John and Frederick. This would date the photograph at circa 1885.

---

[16] Heart of the Desert – J.C. Parcell – Otago Centennial Publication 1951

Fig. 8 - Pryde Excelsior Mine, Bannockburn, New Zealand

Fig. 9 - Pryde Mine, Bannockburn, New Zealand

John Pryde and Jane Goodlet had two children, **Frederick**

Faithfull Begg Pryde (1878 – 1954), pictured, who was born in Otago, New Zealand, but he was shown on the 1901 census aged 23 years, working as an Assurance Agent and lodging at Shotts, Lanarkshire, Scotland. In 1906 he married Christina Sutherland in Edinburgh, and after service in WW1 he stayed in the UK. He died in Edinburgh in 1954, having reversed his father's earlier emigration by returning to the family roots in Scotland.

The second son of John Pryde and Jane Goodlet was **John Menzies Pryde (1881 – 1954)**, pictured in photo taken in his childhood. He enlisted to fight in the Great War in 1916 and joined the Canterbury Infantry Bn., C Company. On enlistment

his occupation is given as Miner and his father, John Pryde, of Bannockburn, Central Otago, is shown as next of kin. John Menzies Pryde returned to New Zealand at the end of the conflict and was involved in the coal and gold mining industries. He married Helen May Curline in New Zealand in 1922 and they had three children. He died in New Zealand in 1954, the same year his brother passed away in Scotland.

CHAPTER 11

BOUNTY EMIGRATION TO AUSTRALIA

The children of John Tait (circa 1795 – after 1830)
and
Helen Armour (1795 – after 1830)

From about 1825 onwards the settlement of Australia by the British was outgrowing its convict origins and at the same time there was a great deal of poverty in Britain. Workmen and tradesmen were needed in Australia whose towns and cities were expanding. Whilst many British people wished to migrate to Australia few could afford the fare, so the Australian government paid to assist the migrants' passage to Australia. This suited many parishes in Britain as they were able to reduce the number of paupers who were a charge on their rates. Ships' masters were paid a bounty per head on safe arrival of their passengers in Australia.

It was on such a "bounty" ship, the *India,* that siblings Charlotte, Andrew and Catherine Tait travelled, departing from Greenock in Scotland on 4th June 1841. They were 3 x great-grandchildren of James Pride and Helen Selkirk, being three out of the four eldest of seven children born to John Tait and Helen Armour between 1818 and 1830.

**LINE OF DESCENT FOR THE CHILDREN OF
HELEN ARMOUR AND JOHN TAIT
AS FEATURED IN CHAPTER 11**

James Pride (circa 1678 – after 1748)
and Helen Selkirk
|
|
George Pride (1716 – 1759)
and Margaret Fraser
|
|
Helen Pryde (1737 – after 1775)
and James Armour
|
|
George Armour (1765 – after 1817)
and Charlotte Sharp
|
|
Helen Armour (1795 – after 1830)
and John Tait
|
|
and their children
Charlotte (1818 – 1911)
Helen (1819 – after 1846)
Andrew (1821 – 1841)
Catherine (circa 1822 – after October 1841)
Alison (1823 – Unknown)
John (1826 – 1906)
Margaret (circa 1830 – 1898)

It would seem that both John Tait and his wife **Helen Armour (born 1795 – after 1830)**, for whom no surviving death records have been found to date, had died between 1830 and 1841 and they may well have succumbed to the cholera epidemic mentioned in Chapter 6. This would have resulted in their children being taken into care, with the unmarried older children being offered a bounty passage to Australia when the scheme came into operation.

At the time of sailing **Charlotte Tait (1818 – 1911)** would have been 23 years of age, **Andrew Tait (1821 – 1841)** was 19 years old and **Catherine Tait (circa 1822 – Unknown)** was aged about 18 years.

About a month into the voyage the ship had an encounter with pirates, who hove to and enquired as the contents and destination of the *India*. After being satisfied the ship was carrying bounty immigrants who were not likely to be carrying anything of much value they were left to continue their voyage without any molestation. The same pirate ship was captured a few days later by H.M. brig *Acorn*. No doubt the passengers felt much relieved that this incident passed by without causing them any harm but much worse was to befall them.

Some six weeks into the voyage, on 19th July 1841, the ship *India* caught fire and sank. By all accounts it would appear two members of the crew were drawing off spirits, when the candle they were using fell on some spilled spirit which immediately caught fire, see Fig. 10.

A French whaler ship, the *Roland* which was in the vicinity came to give aid once they were aware of the tragedy which was unfolding. It was due in a large part to the efforts of its crew that so many lives were saved.

Fig. 10

Painted in 1841 by Samuel Elyard, this watercolour depicts the burning of the barque *INDIA* with the whaler *ROLAND* in the background coming to their aid[17]

---

[17] Original held in the collection of The Australian National Maritime Museum under whose Terms of Use this image is reproduced.

Numbers reported vary slightly but it would appear that there were 21 crew on board the *India* and only one of these, a boatswain, Charles Cummings, lost his life. There were also 193 emigrants on board, 17 of whom lost their lives and one of those who died was Andrew Tait.

None of the passengers were able to save any of their possessions and some had lost even the clothes they wore due to the severity of the fire. The crew of the *Roland* clothed them as best they could and the ship made for Rio de Janeiro, Brazil, some 1,200 miles from where the *India* had sunk. Upon arrival those rescued were given every assistance possible. A collection was made from the British residents and merchants who gave very generously as did the crews of American ships in the port. The survivors were housed awaiting the arrival of another ship, the *Grindlay*, which had been hired by the British Government to continue the voyage and transport them to their original destination of Port Phillip in Australia.

The *Grindlay* left Rio de Janeiro on 22nd August 1841 arriving at Port Phillip on 22nd October 1841, some 4½ months after the passengers had set sail from Scotland.

The fire encountered on the voyage of the *India* was widely reported in the newspapers of the time, both in Australia and back in Britain, with a report being published in the London Times on 21st September 1841 and The Greenock Advertiser on 8th October 1841, to name but two, and these reports contained a list of the names of those who had lost their lives.

Helen Tait (1819 – Unknown), the second eldest child of John Tait and Helen Armour had married John Chambers in 1838 in South Leith, Midlothian, and she and her husband and baby son remained in Scotland, when her siblings, Charlotte, Andrew and Catherine emigrated.

One can only imagine the distress of Helen Chambers, née Tait, who was heavily pregnant with her second child when the news of the fire and the death of their brother reached her and the other siblings who remained behind in Scotland.

After her arrival in Port Philip in October 1841 nothing is known of what happened to Catherine Tait.

Her sister Charlotte Tait married William Baldy at Melbourne in 1848. There is a William Baldy on the Passenger List for the *India* and it is likely he is the same person that Charlotte Tait married. William Baldy and Charlotte Tait lived in the Pitfield area until their business was wrecked by a State-wide flood in 1851 so they eventually moved to Geelong. They had four children together, born between 1848 and 1854 but in April

1854 William Baldy died at Geelong. Charlotte Baldy née Tait subsequently gave birth to two more children, **Henry Baldy (circa 1859 – 1947)** and **Charlotte Baldy (circa 1860 – 1941)**, pictured. Although these children were given the surname of Baldy, William Baldy

was not their natural father as he had died some four to five years earlier. Nevertheless, through their mother they are both 4 x great-grandchildren of James Pride and Helen Selkirk.

Charlotte Baldy née Tait died in 1911 aged 92 years having lived a long and eventful life, being one of the early settlers in the Port Philip/Melbourne area of Australia. During her lifetime she had experienced the loss of her parents whilst still young; emigration from her homeland; an encounter with pirates; the sinking of the ship in which she was travelling which also resulted in the drowning of her brother; her home and business being lost due to flooding and the early death of her husband with the subsequent births of two additional children. However, Charlotte Baldy née Tait was also witness to another unusual occurrence in her lifetime although it is likely that she was not aware of it and this concerns her fourth child.

Out of the four children born to William Baldy and Charlotte Tait, the first three married and raised their own families, the  majority of whom remained resident in the state of Victoria, Australia. The last born child of their union was **Alice Allan Baldy (circa 1854 – 1928)**, pictured, 4 x great-granddaughter of James Pride and Helen Selkirk. She married Thomas Cleveland in 1876 at Skipton, Victoria. Although they had no known children together their marriage was a long one, as the following report in The

Advocate Newspaper [18], Burnie, Tasmania, Saturday 28th August, 1926 states:-

"MR. AND MRS. THOS. CLEVELAND, two of the oldest residents of Skipton (Vic) have celebrated their golden wedding anniversary. They were married at Skipton in 1876 and have resided there ever since. Mr. Cleveland, who is 80 years of age, has been churchwarden and bellringer at the Presbyterian Church for 40 years."

However, all was not as it seemed, because recent research has revealed that prior to his marriage to Alice Allan Baldy, Thomas Cleveland had been married to Anne Hubbard in Leicester, England, in March 1866. It has now been possible to prove the truth of the family story handed down through the Hubbard family which recounted that Thomas Cleveland had disappeared soon after his marriage to Anne. The recollection within the family is that in August 1866 Anne and Thomas were at a train station in London. He left her for a few minutes, supposedly to make a purchase from a local shop, and never returned. Anne Cleveland née Hubbard was heart-broken and never knew what happened to Thomas but finally in 1884 she had his will probated after having him declared dead. Anne Cleveland née Hubbard married again in 1885 and no one

---

[18]   MEN and WOMEN Personal Paragraphs. (1926, 28th August). *Advocate* (Burnie, Tas. : 1890 - 1954), p. 2. Retrieved 18th April, 2014, from http://nla.gov.au/nla.news-article67526378

within the Hubbard family knew what had happened to Thomas Cleveland.

Only recently a Hubbard family researcher[19], found an entry for a Thomas Cleveland, arriving at Port Philip, Australia, on 27th November 1866, after departing from the port of London on board the ship *Golden Sea*. Subsequent comparison of Thomas's signature on each marriage certificate confirms they were one and the same person. It is not known if Alice Cleveland née Baldy was aware that Thomas was committing bigamy when he married her; it could be speculated this was the reason why their marriage remained childless for any children born would be considered illegitimate as their marriage was bigamous.

So not only did Alice's mother Charlotte Baldy née Tait experience all the events already listed, she was also witness to the marriage of her daughter to a bigamist, albeit almost certainly unknowingly.

As mentioned earlier in this chapter, when Charlotte, Andrew and Catherine left to sail to Australia in 1841, they left behind their sister Helen and up to three younger children. One of their siblings, **Alison Tait (1823 – Unknown)** who was born in Lasswade, may not have survived to adulthood as no record can be found for her after her baptism.

---

[19] Janice Cassani, Massachusetts, USA – to whom I am grateful for sharing this information for inclusion in my book

However, Catherine must have maintained contact with her other two remaining younger siblings as both later joined her in Australia. Her brother **John Tait (1826 – 1906)**, pictured,  was born in Lasswade, Midlothian, in 1826. He married Margaret Coyne in 1858 in Victoria, Australia, and they had seven children born there between 1859 and 1879. Those that survived to adulthood remained living in Skipton and brought up their own families there. John Tait died in Skipton in 1906, his wife Margaret having predeceased him.

Catherine's sister **Margaret Tait (circa 1830 – 1898)**, pictured,  travelled to Australia in 1852 on the ship *Runnymede.* Contemporary accounts report that instead of arriving at Melbourne as planned, the ship unexpectedly ended its journey about 170 miles from its original destination, at Portland Bay, an area which had been settled by the Henty family in 1834. Margaret Tait married James Madden in Portland on 23rd July 1852 about one month after their ship had arrived in Australia. Margaret Tait and James Madden had eight children together, born between 1854 and 1870.

An extract from the diary kept by Margaret Madden née Tait illustrates the difficult times experienced by these early settlers, as follows:-

"We sailed from England in the 'Runnymede' (450 tons) in 1852, with 400 immigrants on board and a crew of thirty. With our ship becalmed for a fortnight on the equator, the journey occupied four and half months during which time there were four deaths and four births. The seas through the Bay of Biscay and around the Cape of Good Hope were very rough, whilst we narrowly escaped being wrecked on King Island. Portland at last in June 1852, but our only means of communication with the mainland were two small boats, so that a further lengthy period awaited us before we had all disembarked.

Our reception on land was as cold as the weather, for there was nothing to buy as all the male population had drifted to the diggings. Our accommodation was provided by the government, simply a large bark hut, with our only provisions a large fore-quarter of beef set up against the wall. There was neither knife nor tomahawk, pot nor pan, so all the womenfolk adjourned while the menfolk did what they could. As Portland could supply no bread, we had to depend upon a supply of ships' biscuits.

The Henty family had a whaling station at Portland and strewn along the beach were the skeletons of dozens of whales, the whale oil producing a most disagreeable odour. Just previously the Hentys left Portland to take up land at Merino Downs. I fell in love with a respectable young man named James Madden, who possessed a fine team of bullocks and a dray, and we were married forthwith. Imagining ourselves quite rich with such an outfit we set out for Merino Downs, *with a most trying journey ahead of us. One spot, the "Glue Pot", was appropriately named, for the mud was so deep the bullocks almost sank from sight. The following morning we peeped out from the dray, to behold thick snow falling - and this was our welcome from a land we had been told was warm and hospitable. Our 'possum rug helped to keep out the cold, and after a fortnight of hazardous journeying we arrived at Merino Downs. One of our companions speculated in a ton of flour which he sold in Ballarat later at £11 per bag.*

We settled at Merino Downs for three or four months, when, in spite of the protestations of Mr and Mrs Henty, Mr Madden felt the urge of the diggings at Ballarat, two hundred miles away. On the bullock track once more we woke one morning to find the bullocks had escaped and almost two weeks transpired before they were recovered. Our next stop was The Grange (Hamilton) then Mt. Rouse (Willaura), Wickliffe, Lake Bolac and Streatham. At Streatham we veered to the left and headed for the Fiery Creek diggings (Beaufort). South to Lake Goldsmith, where we met the blacks, a big fine fellow who proudly assumed his kingship stepping out to threaten us if we did not leave his terrain. The bullockies cracked their whips, and the blacks almost cracked their skulls as they fled headlong for the neighbouring timber. Carngham was our next port of call, and as my sister, Mrs Baldy, lived at Pitfield, I decided to reside there. My husband and I lost our way on one of our journeys from Carngham to Pitfield, but arrived safely about 11 o'clock at night.

A State-wide flood in 1851 had wrecked Mr. Baldy's place of business, so he eventually sold out and left for Geelong. After a sojourn of eight months with my sister, my husband returned to convey me to Ballarat, a journey of fifty odd miles that occupied three weeks in a horse dray. Strange sights confronted us - German women yoked up in a little cart with two dogs in the lead and the husband pushing behind - and a swamp with many drays hopelessly bogged. We had no luck at Ballarat and lost our bullocks. My husband then took a job sawing timber where Ballarat station now is, and our bark hut was on the present site of the Town Hall Hotel in Armstrong Street.

Ballarat seemed to be on the wane and we set out for Mt. Cole for timber for the homestead at St. Enochs. The timber was there but no means of bringing it down from the steep mountain slopes. Here we arrived on Christmas Day, 1853, and were entertained by about two hundred and fifty blacks at a giant corroboree at night.

We set south again, shot a wild turkey at Mt. Emu, put out our fire, as we thought, and finally arrived among the timber at Madden's Flat. A spark remained, however, and fired the grass, so we found ourselves most unpopular for a time. Here we remained, and built a four roomed house, while the men commenced a saw pit. Mr Madden came into Skipton and bought a piece of ground. He arranged with a stonemason to build a four-roomed cottage. Skipton was on the direct route to Geelong, as there was no traffic to Ballarat. Vrarat, Pleasant Creek and Fiery Creek diggings were all then in full swing, and

Skipton was a camping place for all traffic from these places to Geelong. We decided to open a store in Skipton - a large tent - at the end of the bridge, and I sold the goods as fast as Mr. Madden brought them from Geelong. There was a hotel where Morgan's store now is, this hotel being the only important place in Skipton when we arrived.

Crowds of Chinese passed through from Portland to Smythe's Creek and Ballarat. They traversed this route to escape the immigration dues on Chinese immigrants. Two or three hundred came here at .... the site of the present Jubilee Park. They bought their ... about fifty at a time, cooked and ate it and away they went.

A man named Stephens built a little church of bricks manufactured by himself. It accommodated about fifty persons."

In 1863 James Madden, who gave £10, and John Tait, who gave £1, were subscribers along with many others, to funds raised to provide what came to be Skipton's First Common School. This opened in 1864 and amongst the thirty-two Foundation Scholars were siblings **David Andrew Madden (circa 1854 – 1944)**; **William Baldy Madden (circa 1856 – 1932)**; **James Madden (1858 – circa 1934)** and **Margaret Madden (1860 – 1930)**, all children of James Madden and Margaret Tait and 4 x great-grandchildren of James Pride and Helen Selkirk.

Margaret Madden née Tait died in Melbourne, Victoria, in 1898, aged 68 years, her husband having predeceased her by some three years.

Known descendants of Helen Armour and John Tait currently number just over 200. As can be seen by the foregoing, the Tait siblings were amongst the first pioneer families to settle in this part of Australia, exhibiting, like many others, the will to survive, multiply and prosper despite many setbacks in this new land.

CHAPTER 12

EMIGRATION AND UNIONISM

James Pryde (1858 – 1929)
and
Jane Drysdale Russell (1861 – 1928)

and his brother and her sister

George Pryde (1865 – 1923)
and
Margaret Drysdale Russell (1865 – 1939)

James Pryde (1858 – 1929), pictured, born in Tranent, East

Lothian, was another 4 x great-grandson of James Pride and Helen Selkirk. He was an illegitimate son of **Mary Pryde (circa 1834 – 1911)** as was his brother George (see below), Mary being the daughter of **Peter Pryde (1806 – 1872)** and Catherine Wilson.

James Pryde married Jane Drysdale Russell at Tranent, East Lothian, in 1881 and on the marriage record it was stated that the father of James was James Whitelaw. James Pryde and his wife Jane lived in East and Mid Lothian for the first eight years of their marriage and he worked as a Coal Miner.

LINE OF DESCENT FOR JAMES PRYDE
AND HIS BROTHER GEORGE PRYDE
AS FEATURED IN CHAPTER 12

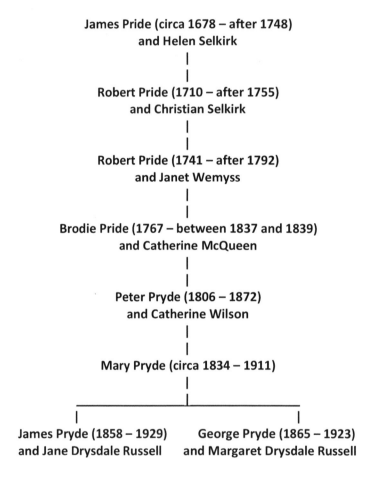

James Pride (circa 1678 – after 1748)
and Helen Selkirk
|
|
Robert Pride (1710 – after 1755)
and Christian Selkirk
|
|
Robert Pride (1741 – after 1792)
and Janet Wemyss
|
|
Brodie Pride (1767 – between 1837 and 1839)
and Catherine McQueen
|
|
Peter Pryde (1806 – 1872)
and Catherine Wilson
|
|
Mary Pryde (circa 1834 – 1911)
|

James Pryde (1858 – 1929) and Jane Drysdale Russell	George Pryde (1865 – 1923) and Margaret Drysdale Russell

Whilst still living in Scotland they had five children, four of whom were surviving when the family emigrated to Australia travelling on the ship *Merkara* from London leaving on 26th September 1889 and arriving in Brisbane on 12th December 1889. The ships passenger list shows that James, aged 30 years, was a miner, born in Haddington, and that he was able to read and write and was a Presbyterian.

The family settled in the Ipswich area of Queensland, Australia, where they had three more children. James was a founder member and later President of the Queensland Colliery Employees Miners Union which was founded in 1908, and he also served on the first Coal Mining Industry Wages Board in Queensland, in 1925. Given his involvement in the Union, looking after the welfare and working conditions of the miners, the death of his brother George (as described below) was no doubt a bitter irony as well as a family tragedy.

James died in Booval, Queensland, in 1929 aged 70 years, some nine months after his wife had passed away and known descendants currently total just over 250.

George Pryde (1865 – 1923), pictured, was born in Gladsmuir,

East Lothian, and was another illegitimate son of Mary Pryde and therefore at least a half-brother to James Pryde above, but by family recollection they referred to each other as brothers, so they may also have had the same father. However, as they were also

sometimes referred to as step-brothers it is impossible to be certain if they had the same father.

George emigrated to Australia whilst still single, travelling some five months after his brother, sailing on the ship *Tara* from London, leaving England on the 8th February 1890, to Brisbane, where he arrived on 1st April 1890. He joined his brother at Ipswich, Queensland, where he married in December 1891, Margaret Drysdale Russell, who was sister to Janet Drysdale Russell who had earlier married George's brother James.

It appears George and Margaret had only two children, **Margaret Drysdale Pryde (1893 – 1983)** and **Alison Tait Isabella Pryde (May 1902 – November 1902)** both of whom were born at Ipswich. George died in a pit accident in 1923, the cause of death being shown on his death certificate as 'Fractured Skull (accidental); cerebral haemorrhage and heart failure'. [See also Chapter 17.]

The subsequent Inquest into his death was held at Ipswich Court House on 4th June 1923 and was reported as follows:-

"Sir

I have the honour to advise that on the 30th ultimo at the Court House, Ipswich, an inquiry was held before me as Warden and Messrs. Shelton, Gray, Davidson, and Scott, four experienced miners, into the cause of an accident which occurred at the New Chum No. 4 Colliery on the 14th. Idem whereby

George Pryde the pitheadman at the said colliery was killed.

The witnesses examined were:-

Alexander Bell Jeffrey, engine driver; Robert Jeffrey, assistant pitheadman; William Robert Robinson, engine driver; George Mathieson, Manager New Chum No. 4; and Samuel Ellis Carter, police constable.

It appears from the facts adduced in evidence that on the date in question, George Pryde was in the act of placing an empty waggon on the cage which was few inches above the level of the landing. The engine driver lowered the cage and it was let down several inches below the level; the front wheels of the waggon went down on to the cage floor and Pryde overbalanced falling into the waggon and through to the ground, a distance of about 20 feet, the waggon falling on top of him. He sustained a fractured skull which caused death. The deceased was an experienced pitheadman and on that account he was engaged for the work he had in hand on this new mine.

Yours obediently

Stewart ------------ (Signature)

Warden

Annotated "No Action" and signed C.J.C. for C. Vale 8/6/23 The Under Secretary, Justice Department.

Certificate of Particulars - Inquest of Death

I hereby certify that on that on the thirtieth day of May 1923 I held an Inquest of Death at Ipswich and that the following particulars were disclosed:-

Name of deceased:- George Pryde

Profession or calling: Pitheadman

*Height, colour of hair, peculiar clothing
and any other means of identity   } Fully Identified*

Where found and when: New Chum No. 4 Colliery on 14th May 1923

Date of death: 14th May 1923

Supposed cause of death: Fractured skull

Persons last seen in the company of deceased and names of suspected persons} Alexander Bell Jeffrey and William Robert Robinson, and Robert Jeffrey.

Accused: Nil

Names, residences and callings of witnesses} Alexander Bell Jeffrey, engine driver, Bundamba and William Robert Robinson, engine driver, Booval

Robert Jeffrey, asst. pitheadman, Dinmore

George Mathieson, Dinmore, Mine Manager

Samuel Ellis Carter, Booval, Police Constable

Suspicious circumstances: Nil

Detailed notes of the evidence given were as follows:-

Court House, Ipswich

30th May 1923

BEFORE The Warden and Four Assessors

Mining Inquiry into the cause of an accident which occurred at New Chum Colliery on the 14th May 1923 whereby George Pryde was killed.

Mr. Stafford appears to examine the witnesses.

Mr. Kilpatrick appears on behalf of the Queensland Collieries Employees Union.

Mr. Mathieson appears on behalf of owner of New Chum Colliery.

Alexander Bell Jeffrey sworn states I am an engine driver and resident of Station Hill Bundamba; was at the New Chum Colliery on the 14th. May last I remember an accident to George Pryde on that day; I was present when the accident occurred which was between 9 and 9.30a.m. At the time I was driving and Engine driver Robinson was standing by my side; After the cage had come to the top, the cage was slightly too high but Pryde was able to get the waggon off (was between one and two inches too high).

159

On the suggestion of Robinson, I lowered the cage and on doing so I lowered it to my knowledge about 6 inches too low; while the cage was in that position Pryde came to put the waggon on with a result that the cage being too low it upended, and Pryde went through the waggon on to the waggon down below. I had intended to put the cage in its usual position but Pryde came on too quickly. Pryde fell to the ground a distance of twenty feet; the waggon fell also, but after Pryde; I am unable to say if the waggon struck Pryde or not. After the accident I went to Pryde and he appeared to be seriously hurt and I have heard that he has since died. When Pryde was being attended to, I heard him saying, "Don't hurt me". and he was not able to give me any opinion himself as to how the accident occurred. I was employed by the New Chum Colliery on the 14th May last but that was not my usual place of employment. I was sent down to the engine on this occasion to enable myself to learn to drive the engine so as I could drive it on the afternoon shift; I have a General Winding certificate and prior to this day, I was employed at No. 3 New Chum Colliery on the Tunnel Winding Engine. Had been on the winding engine about half an hour prior to the accident; the engine was not difficult to control and had a clear view of the pithead, my brakes were satisfactory, and they were tested the morning after the accident, and they were tested by a full unbalanced load on the cage by Driver Robinson. There was a board across the end of the shaft opposite to where Pryde put the waggon only don't know what the board was there for. When asked did he have any idea why the board was there, witness refuses to answer. I believe the board would stop the

160

waggon falling if the cage were level and the waggon come on slowly; I couldn't say if the waggon would be stopped if it came on fast; the board would stop it if the board would not break I did not notice if the board had broken after the accident or not. I saw a waggon being placed on the cage after the accident, when the cage was in the same position as it was that morning. I noticed that an attempt was made to push the waggon off when the cage was in that position, but the attempt was unsuccessful. When the waggon came, it came quickly and upended and went straight through underneath the board. I couldn't say if the waggon would have to slide along the cage and not run on the wheels. I don't think the cage was lower down that, the distance which I have previously stated; I judged the distance to be 6 inches. The cage was stationary when Pryde put the waggon on; there were no stoppers on the shaft at the time. I cannot say if had there been stoppers on the shaft the accident would have been averted. I have driven No. 3 shaft and there are "shuts" on there. To my idea if there had been similar shuts on the No. 4 shaft as there are on No. 3 the cage could not have got down again after once coming through and then the waggon would not have dropped or upended and the accident might possibly have been averted under those circumstances. Have held a winding license over 15 years.

No questions by Mr. Kilpatrick and none by Mathieson.

161

Taken and sworn at Ipswich this 30th day of May 1923 before me. Signed by the witness Alexander B Jeffrey and also the Warden."

George Pryde was aged 57 years when he died and he was buried at Ipswich Cemetery on 15th May 1923. There are 15 descendants currently known.

There is no doubt the involvement of James in the affairs of the Queensland Colliery Employees Miners Union and the first Coal Mining Industry Wages Board in Queensland would have led to improvements in the working conditions of the coal miners in the area and this is perhaps a fitting legacy after the loss of his brother George in a mining accident.

CHAPTER 13

EMIGRATION, HARD TIMES,
A CHILD LEFT BEHIND

James; Alexander; Janet; Thomas Alexander and Brodie Pride – some of the children of Alexander Pryde (1823 – 1898) and Janet Davidson (circa 1822 – 1893)

There is another group of 4 x great-grandchildren of James Pride and Helen Selkirk who emigrated to Australia, no doubt full of hope and not a little trepidation, and their story is one which illustrates the hard times that can befall any of us.

They were some of the 11 children of **Alexander Pryde (1823 – 1898)** and Janet Davidson, and brothers Alexander Pryde and Thomas Alexander Pryde and their sister Janet Pryde, by now known by her married name of Janet Kerr, all arrived in Sydney, Australia in February 1884, aboard the ship *Stirlingshire*. The price for the journey per adult was £13 7s. 6d. which would have meant a considerable amount of money had to be found to pay for the travel costs of each family. However, their passage to Australia was made under the Assisted Passage scheme, so some or all of the cost would have been subsidised or totally paid for by the Australian Government or by prospective employers through one of the several schemes which operated at that time.

LINE OF DESCENT FOR SOME OF THE CHILDREN OF ALEXANDER PRYDE AND JANET DAVIDSON AS FEATURED IN CHAPTER 13

James Pride (circa 1678 – after 1748)
and Helen Selkirk
|
|
Robert Pride (1710 – after 1755)
and Christian Selkirk
|
|
Robert Pride (1741 – after 1792)
and Janet Wemyss
|
|
Brodie Pride (1767 – between 1837 and 1839)
and Catherine McQueen
|
|
James Pride (1795 – between 1834 and 1841)
and Janet Leitch
|
|
Alexander Pryde (1823 – 1898)
and Janet Davidson
|
|
and some of their children
James (1847 – 1914)
Alexander (1849 – 1898)
Janet (1855 – 1892)
Thomas Alexander (1857 – 1931)
Brodie (1860 – 1895)

Due to a measles epidemic 23 people died on the voyage and the ship was quarantined on arrival. After being released from the ship the families eventually made their way to Lambton, New South Wales.

Alexander Pryde (1849 – 1898) was born in Newtongrange, Midlothian. He married Jane Kerr in 1872 at Arniston, Midlothian, and they had five children born between 1872 and 1882 in that general area, although sadly one child died soon after his birth. Census records show that Alexander Pryde worked as a coal miner. On 16th February 1884 Alexander aged almost 35 years and Jane aged 31 years, together with three of their four surviving children, namely **Isabella Pryde (1872 – 1885)** aged eleven years, **Jessie Pryde (1875 – 1937)** aged eight years and **Joan Johnstone Pryde (1882 – after 1904)** aged almost two years, arrived in Sydney, Australia. Their four year old son, **John Kerr Pryde (1879 – 1950)**, remained in Scotland and according to oral family history the plan was that he was to join his parents and siblings at a later date.

The family settled at Lambton, New South Wales, which at that time was a coal-mining township with a population of around 3,000 and it appears Alexander was employed as a coal miner. The first misfortune to befall the family was that Isabella, their eldest daughter, died in January 1885 aged just 12 years. Only a fortnight later her mother Jane gave birth to another daughter who they named **Isabella Merton Pryde (1885 – 1968)** in tribute to her recently deceased sister. Three further daughters were born to Alexander and Jane, namely

Jane Kerr Pryde (1887 – 1973), **Lilly May Pryde (1889 – 1969)** and **Margaret Dickson Pryde (1893 – 1974)** all of whom were born in Lambton.

Whilst the majority of the children were still young it appears Alexander began to suffer ill-health, commencing early in 1893 as is evidenced by the following newspaper article[20]:-

Report on Monday 7th May 1894 states:-

"THE WALLSEND MINERS

The usual monthly meeting of the Wallsend Miners was held on Friday evening, Mr. R Punton in the chair.

An appeal for assistance on behalf of Mrs. Pryde, was considered. The husband had been unable to work for 12 months, and there were six children. As the meeting considered this a needful case, it was decided to donate the sum of £5."

Following the onset of Alexander's ill-health, his wife Jane worked to keep the family as best she could and it would appear the people of Lambton held her and Alexander in good regard; they also had a charitable spirit as is shown in further newspaper reports viz:-

---

[20] Newspaper reports shown in this chapter are, unless otherwise stated, extracted from issues of the Newcastle Morning Herald & Miners' Advocate (NSW : 1876 - 1954) freely available from http://nla.gov.au

Article dated 30th March 1895 states:-

"LAMBTON

CHARITY SERVICE

On Sunday a charity service is to be held on the park, when a sermon will be preached in the afternoon by the Rev. D. Fraser, of Newcastle, for the purpose of raising funds to assist Mrs. Pryde, who unfortunately has been almost totally deprived of the means of earning a livelihood by the death of her horse, used for dealing purposes. The case is one deserving of practical sympathy, as this poor woman has for some considerable time maintained her husband, a confirmed invalid, and a young family by selling fruit and vegetables round the district. A good choir will be in attendance, and should the weather prove unfavourable the service will be held in the Star Theatre."

The service went ahead and was well attended and successful as reported as follows:-

"1st April 1895

Lambton - Charity Service

Yesterday afternoon a charity service was held on the Lambton Park for the purpose of obtaining funds to assist Mrs Pryde and family. There was a fairly large attendance. Alderman G Noble presided, and opened the proceedings by explaining the object of the meeting. Mrs Pryde, who supported her sick husband and family by dealing, some time ago had her cart

167

damaged by the tram, and in this matter she was assisted by Mr A Griffith, M.P., who sent a guinea; but on Saturday week Mrs Pryde's horse had to be destroyed in consequence of a broken leg, which deprived her of the opportunity to go round and earn a livelihood. The committee has requested the Rev. Donald Fraser of Newcastle, to assist, and he readily consented to preach on that day. The choir, conducted by Mrs C Noble, then sang some Sankey's hymns, and after devotional exercises the Rev. D Fraser spoke, taking his text from the words, "Take ye away the stone," St. John, 11th Chapter, 39th verse. Following this a collection resulted in the sum of £7 10 shillings being realised, which in view of the depressed times is considered an achievement beyond expectations. In conclusion, Mr E Hardy moved a vote of thanks to the preacher, also all who had in any way rendered assistance, which included Mr H J Noble (organist), and others who helped in the choir. This was seconded by Mr Pritchard and carried with acclamation. The service concluded with the doxology."

Less than a year later in early 1896, **Jessie Pryde (1875 – 1937)**, pictured, 5 x great-granddaughter of James Pride and Helen

Selkirk and the eldest surviving daughter of Alexander and Janet gave birth to an illegitimate son. The father refused to support the child, no doubt putting further strain on the already stretched finances of the family. Jessie charged her erstwhile partner with deserting his child and in the Police

Gazette for New South Wales dated 19th February 1896 there appears the following entry[21]:-

"LAMBTON - A Warrant has been issued by the Lambton Bench for the arrest of Robert Hetherington, charged with deserting his illegitimate child. He is 21 years of age, 5 feet 8 or 9 inches high, stout build, full face, dark hair, gray eyes, wore dark clothes and soft felt hat. Complainant, Jessie Pryde at North Lambton."

In 1898 Jessie married John Burnley, and there was another court case in early 1899 as Robert Hetherington contended that now Jessie was married he was not liable to contribute to the cost of the upbringing of their son. This was overturned by the court in what was called a Landmark case as the ruling concluded that the Poor Law in England, which stated that any man marrying the mother of illegitimate children became responsible for their upkeep, did not apply in Australia. Robert Hetherington died in 1911 aged 36 years, and his son with Jessie continued to be brought up by her and his stepfather.

The difficult times continued as Jane Pryde née Kerr died on 9th March 1898, from apoplexy, aged 46 years, leaving behind her ailing husband and their remaining children, aged between 16 years and 4 years. As Jane was the main breadwinner this had a catastrophic effect on the family finances but once again the residents of Lambton came to the assistance of the family.

---

[21] State Records Authority of New South Wales; *Police Gazettes 1862-1930*; Roll: *3142*; Year: *1896*; Page: *65*. Via Ancestry.com

A newspaper report dated 16th March 1898 states:-

"A DISTRESSED FAMILY

A public meeting convened by the Mayor was held in the Council Chambers on Monday night to devise the best means of raising funds to assist Mr. Alexander Pryde and family, who are in distressed circumstances. The Mayor (Alderman Burg) presided, and there were about 15 gentlemen present.

Mr. W Kerr [half-brother to Jane Pryde née Kerr] *reported that the family were now receiving as relief of 10s per week from the government, and 5s. a week from the Newcastle Benevolent Society; 2s 3d of this sum had to be paid for rent. There were six of a family to keep. Mr. Pryde had been unable to work for years, and the family had been supported by the efforts of the mother until her death recently.*

Messrs. J Turnbull, G Hardy, and W Conn spoke in favour of the movement."

Following further discussion it was agreed that a limelight entertainment be given in the park in aid of the family and for the provision of such a committee was formed.

The planned benefit went ahead and once again was successful as can be shown in the following newspaper article dated 16th April 1898:-

"Lambton

Limelight Entertainment

The limelight and concert entertainment in aid of the Pryde family, given by Messrs. Hall and Simon, of Newcastle, and assisted by a local committee, was held in the park on Thursday night. The attendance numbered upwards of 600, including adults and children. The Mayor (Alderman H. Burg) presided and said that the large attendance was very gratifying for the committee. Mr Henry Williams then conducted the meeting through an excellent programme of lantern views, interspersed with singing and recitations."
Further details of the entertainment then followed.

However, only five months after the death of his wife, Alexander Pryde succumbed to consumption and passed away on the 3rd August 1898. He was 49 years of age.

Although there are no further details regarding what happened to the remaining children before they reached their majority and married, it is probable they made their home with their sister Jessie and her husband John Burnley. There were other extended family members living in the area but they were also experiencing troubled times of their own as will be shown in the following pages. Known descendants of Alexander Pryde and Janet Kerr currently number just over 50.

Alexander's brother **Thomas Alexander Pryde (1857 – 1931)** and his wife Margaret Dickson married at the end of 1880 at Stobhill, Midlothian.

They had had three children born in Gorebridge, Midlothian, between 1881 and 1883, but sadly these had all died before they made their way to Australia.

They arrived in Lambton in early 1884 and within four months of their arrival Margaret gave birth to a daughter, **Margaret Pryde (1884 – 1959)**. She was followed by **Jessie Pryde (1886 – 1959), Jane Ann Pryde (1888 – 1951), William Alexander Pryde (1898 – 1981)** and **Thomas Alexander Pryde (1902 – 1962).**

All these children were born in Lambton and survived to adulthood, with William and Thomas later going into a building business together as the Pryde Brothers.

By 1890 Thomas Pryde (Snr.) was the licensee of the Marquis of Lorne Hotel in Lambton, see Fig. 11. From 1890 the licence for the hotel was granted to Thomas Pryde as a matter of course each year until 1896.

However, it would seem that from 1896 onwards the renewal of the licence each year became less certain, no doubt due to Thomas's conduct as reported in the local newspapers at the time, as follows.

Fig. 11 – Marquis of Lorne Hotel, Lambton [22]

The following newspaper article appeared dated Friday 26th June 1896:-

"LICENSING COURT.

THURSDAY, JUNE 25

(Before W. E. Henry, P.M., T. Fryar and T. Croudace, J.P.)

The following renewals were granted: ..... Thomas Pryde, Lambton. In this case an objection was lodged that Pryde had been indulging. Mr. Sparke appeared for the applicant, who

---

[22] Image courtesy of the Newcastle Museum, New South Wales, Australia and shown with their permission.

promised to reform. Sergeant Salter said that with the exception of Pryde getting too much of his own beer, the house was well conducted, and on the promise just made, he would withdraw the objection."

However, there does not appear to have been a sustained change in Thomas's behaviour as a report dated Tuesday 20th October 1896 states:-

"WALLSEND POLICE COURT

MONDAY, OCTOBER 19TH

(Before Mr. H. J. Chisholm, P.M. and Messrs. Fletcher and Rushton, Js.P.

"SUNDAY SELLING

Thomas Pryde, landlord of the Marquis of Lorne Hotel, Lambton, pleaded guilty to selling liquor on Sunday, the 11th instant, and was fined 40s. Paid."

"DRUNK

Thomas Pryde pleaded not guilty to being drunk in his licenced premises on Sunday, the 11th instant. Sergeant Salter deposed that about 2 p.m. on Sunday, the 11th instant, the defendant's wife sent for witness, who proceeded to the hotel, and found him in a room off the bar. Defendant appeared to be drunk. The case was dismissed with a caution."

The above events and perhaps others not reported may have been a factor in the transfer of the licence of the Marquis of Lorne Hotel from Thomas Pryde to John Donnelly, which took place on 6th December 1897.

It is also obvious from the foregoing that Thomas's behaviour caused the marriage between him and Margaret to be a stormy one and matters continued in the same vein. On 6th January 1905 the following report appears in the local newspaper:-

"LAMPTON POLICE COURT

THURSDAY JANUARY 5TH

(Before Mr. G.F. Scott, S.M)

Thomas Pryde for being drunk was fined £1, in default 14 days' hard labour."

And then on Friday 3rd August 1906:-

"LAMBTON.

175

At the Police Court on Thursday. before Mr. G. P. Scott. S.M., Thomas Pryde was proceeded against by his wife for assault. Defendant pleaded not guilty. After hearing the evidence of Mrs. Pryde, the Bench sentenced the defendant to a month's hard labour."

It appears Margaret and Thomas stayed together as there have been no further such reports found. Margaret died in 1925 aged 65 years. Her obituary refers to her being in business, first in Dickson Street, which is the location of the Marquis of Lorne Hotel, and then in Chinchen Street. Thomas Alexander Pryde died on 12th January 1931 aged 73 years and it would appear that after leaving the Marquis of Lorne Hotel, he and his wife traded as storekeepers, because on 22nd December 1931 the following newspaper advertisement appears:-

"THIS DAY, AT 10.30.

Under instructions from L.E. Thompson Esq. Trustee Assigned Estate T Pryde, Chinchen-street, Lambton

LANG, WOOD AND CO. LTD., will sell by auction, AT THE ROOMS, Croasdill House, Thorn-street,

THIS DAY, AT 10.30

(Removed to the rooms for convenience of Sale),

THE WHOLE OF THE

Stock of a Storekeeper,

176

Comprising Groceries, Jams, Tinned Fruit, Condiments, Sugar, Tobacco, Cigarettes, Ice Chest, small quantity Hardware, Produce, etc., etc."

Known descendants of Thomas Alexander Pryde and Margaret Dickson currently total 53.

As indicated at the beginning of this chapter, a sister to Alexander Pryde and Thomas Alexander Pryde also travelled on the same ship as them. **Janet Pryde (1855 – 1892)** travelled with her husband Adam Kerr, and their five children. Adam Kerr was a brother to Janet who had married Alexander Pryde so it was yet another example of close-knit and intermarried families who emigrated together.

Adam Kerr and Janet Pryde married at Stobhill, Midlothian, in 1872 and the children who arrived with them in Australia were **Jessie Kerr (circa 1875 – 1972)** aged eight years, **Isabella Pryde (circa 1877 – after 1884)** aged six years, **Alexander Pryde (circa 1879 – 1884)** aged five years, **Adam Kerr (circa 1880 – 1884)** aged three years and **Thomas Kerr (circa 1883 – 1884)** aged just one year, all of whom were 5 x great-grandchildren of James Pride and Helen Selkirk.

Tragedy struck immediately on their arrival in Sydney as Thomas was one of the ship's passengers who had contracted measles, and he died whilst still in quarantine. As the records are unclear there is some uncertainty regarding the fate of Adam Jnr. who also died in 1884. He may have died at the same time as his brother Thomas, or later that same year. A further tragedy was to strike the family as their third son

Alexander Kerr, aged only five years, passed away on 26th November 1884 in Lambton. On a happier note, a further child was born in August 1886, at Lambton, and named **John Alexander Kerr (1886 – 1958)**.

Apart from the above loss of their children Adam and Janet Kerr née Pryde seemed to have enjoyed a settled life in Lambton where by all accounts Adam Kerr worked as a bricklayer. However, just less than eight years after settling in Lambton Janet Kerr née Pryde died on 8th January 1892 aged only 36 years. Like her brother Alexander, Janet had been consumptive for years. Unusually, funeral notices were placed in the local newspaper not only by her husband, but by her brothers, Thomas, Alexander and Brodie, another by her half brother-in-law Walter Kerr and finally by her nephew Joseph Oldham.

Some three years later Adam Kerr married again, to Alice Young, and he carried on his trade as a bricklayer. However, he suffered a very bad accident on Monday 21st August 1898 when he fell off scaffolding whilst working on a chimney in Plattsburg. Amongst the injuries received were a badly fractured left arm, and an injury to a finger on his right hand which had to be amputated. Additionally he suffered a severe scalp wound halfway around his skull, but fortunately there was no fracture to the skull.

Later that same year there is evidence that the brothers-in-law Adam Kerr and Thomas Pryde had been in an argument as a notice placed in the local newspaper dated 18th November 1899 states:-

"PUBLIC NOTICES

I APOLOGISE to Mr. Adam Kerr for the language made use of by me, also his character, as I have no foundation for same, on November 9. (Signed) THOMAS PRYDE."

Adam Kerr died in 1920 in Lambton aged 71 years. Known descendants of Janet Pryde and Adam Kerr currently total 17. Their daughter Jessie, [as listed on page 177] who had been born in Scotland circa 1875, married Selby Walter Munsie in Queensland, Australia, in 1892. After starting work in the timber trade Selby Walter Munsie became a miner and was active in trade union affairs. In 1911 he was elected as a Labour member of the Australian Parliament and remained so until his death in 1938, the last position he held being the State Minister for Mines and Health.

Another brother to Alexander, Thomas, and Janet Pryde, namely **James Pryde (1847 – 1914)** also married another Kerr sibling, namely Isabella Kerr, at Stobhill, Midlothian, in 1874, but this family remained in Scotland.

However **Brodie Pryde (1860 – 1895)** brother to Alexander, Thomas, and Janet Pryde followed his siblings to Australia, arriving in Sydney in 1886. He joined them in Lambton and the following reports regarding his behaviour appeared in the local newspaper:-

5th July 1890:-

"*Lambton Police Court. FRIDAY, JULY 5TH.*

(Before Mr. R. I. Perrott, P.M.)

DRUNKENNESS.

Brodie Pryde pleaded guilty to drunkenness in Young-street, Lambton, on Sunday last, and was mulcted in the usual sum of £1 and costs."

15th June 1892:-

"*Lambton Police Court*

(Before Mr. R.I. Perrott, P.M.)

...Brodie Pryde pleaded guilty to the double charge of being drunk in Elder street and using obscene language on Friday last. Fined 10s. or 48 hours for drunkenness, and 10s. or seven days in the lockup for the language: concurrent sentences."

It is likely Brodie Pryde lived with his brother Thomas Pryde and family as he is listed as residing in Dickson Street, Lambton, and working as a Miner, in a Public Notice relating to the Electoral District of Waratah published in the local newspaper dated Tuesday 2nd October 1894. He does not appear to have married and he died aged 35 years in the Picton area of New South Wales, Australia.

As can be seen from the foregoing, the settlement of the above families in Australia, after emigration in 1884, was not easy. Although it is thought that Alexander and Jane Pryde, the parents of **John Kerr Pryde (1879 – 1950)**, pictured, had

 planned to send for him to join them at a later date, after he had been left behind in Scotland in 1884, the ill-health of his father brought on hard times for the family and then the deaths of both his parents meant the reunion never took place. Although he had surviving siblings, his elder sister Jessie was the only one who may have remembered her brother, and she had her own problems as has been evidenced; then it is likely she had taken on the care of her younger siblings after the death of her parents.

However, John Kerr Pryde was not without family as in 1891 he was living with his maternal grandparents, John and Isabella Kerr, at Cockpen, Midlothian, and by 1901 he was living with his maternal uncle, Peter Kerr and other family members, still in Cockpen. He emigrated from Scotland to America, arriving in May 1905 and in October of that year he married Mary Bremner in West Virginia. They settled in Marion, Illinois, because it was good coal-mining country. They had two children born there, **John Alexander Pryde (1907 – 1992)** and **Robina Pryde (1910 – 2006)**. The family of four returned to Scotland, arriving first at Liverpool, England, on 8th April 1914, but by October of that year they were in Hunterfield, Midlothian, for the birth of their third child, **George Bremner Pryde (1914 – 2004)**. John Kerr Pryde remained in Scotland and died in Stobhill, Midlothian, in 1950 aged 71 years. His wife Mary outlived him by some 29 years and died in Rhyl, Flintshire aged 100 years in 1979.

There is a happy footnote to the story of John Kerr Pryde who was left behind in Scotland. His son **John Alexander Pryde**

(1907 – 1992), pictured, who was obviously named after both his father and absent paternal grandfather, having been born in Illinois, America, but brought up in Scotland, took up employment as a Surveyor in the petroleum industry as can be seen from the following extract from The Dalkeith Advertiser Newspaper of 7th March 1929:-

"IMPORTANT APPOINTMENT FOR ARNISTON MAN - Mr John A Pryde, eldest son of Mr. & Mrs. John K Pryde, 4 Store Cottages, Arniston, left on Sunday for Puerto, Southern Mexico, where he is to take up the important duties of surveyor with the Mexican Eagle Petroleum Company. For nearly eight years he was attached to the surveying staff of the Arniston Coal Company, Ltd. Prior to his departure, he was made the recipient of a handsome set of surveying instruments by the colliery management, staff and friends. Mr James A Philips, the general manager, made the presentation. Mr Pryde suitably acknowledged the gift."

He returned to Scotland in 1932 to marry his childhood sweetheart, Rachael May Fortune Samuel, who was known as

May. After their marriage they went back to South America, for a while. They subsequently had one son **John Kerr Samuel Pryde (1937 – 2003)** who was born in Scotland in 1937. Sadly May died in 1943 in California, USA, aged 36 years.

John Alexander Pryde married his second wife, Mary Aileen Canny in New Jersey, USA, in 1957 and they had a daughter **Joan Aileen Pryde (Living)**, pictured, born in Connecticut, USA. Joan is a 7 x great-grandchild of James Pride and Helen Selkirk.

 As part of my early research I contacted Joan in late 1996. She was aware her grandfather had been left behind in Scotland when the rest of the family went to Australia, but did not know why he had not joined them later and I was able to explain about the circumstances surrounding this. I was also able to put Joan in touch with one of her close kin in Australia, so after just over 100 years both parts of this family were back in touch.

Fate was not to be so kind to another 7 x great-grandchild of James Selkirk and Helen Selkirk who descended through the same line as Joan. **Keith North Jnr. (1941 – 1965)**, was a son of Keith North and Elma Ott, and a great-grandson of Thomas Alexander Pryde and Margaret Dickson as featured in this chapter. Keith North had been working in America and was murdered just prior to his return to Australia, when he was just 24 years of age, as the following newspaper transcript shows:-

San Antonio Express dated 28th June 1965:-

"Party Crash Attempt Brings Death

NEW YORK (AP) – An Australian rugby player was slain Saturday night when five youths tried to crash a farewell party for him in his apartment, police said.

Other guests, most of them also rugby players, chased the fleeing youths and tackled four on the street. One was later charged with homicide. The others were released.

The victim, Keith North, 24, was stabbed when the youths tried to push their way into his basement apartment in Manhattan, police said.

North had been employed at the British Mission to the United Nations as a utility man. Unmarried, he had planned to return next Friday to Australia, where he had been a member of a rugby team. His parents live there in Lambton, Newcastle, New South Wales.

Nathaniel Alvarez, 16, was ordered held without bail at his arraignment in the slaying.

He and three companions were questioned by police after the four were apprehended during the pursuit on the street. The fifth party crasher was not caught."

To date details of the outcome of any criminal proceedings brought against the alleged perpetrator of the crime are not known.

CHAPTER 14

A HANGING AFFAIR

Robert Flockhart Vickers (1846 – 1884)
and
Esther Hare (circa 1849 – 1927)

Having outlined in the previous chapters something of the times of a few of those who left Scotland to make new lives for themselves, I would now like to illustrate the lives of some of those who remained in the land of their birth.

The story of the lives of Robert Flockhart Vickers and Esther Hare is one which has been extensively researched by others[23] as well as myself. It is also wide-reaching and includes many members of the extended Pryde family.

Esther Hare (circa 1849 – 1927), pictured, was born in
Newbattle, Midlothian, and was a 4 x great-granddaughter of James Pride and Helen Selkirk. She was a daughter of John Hare and **Janet Pryde (1820 – 1872)**.

---

[23] With grateful thanks to John Vickers for his permission to quote freely from his website at
http://homepages.ihug.co.nz/~johnvick/rfv.html and I also acknowledge the contributions to that website made by Bob Scott, David Gee, Colin Wilson and Lois Saleeba.

LINE OF DESCENT FOR ESTHER HARE
AS FEATURED IN CHAPTER 14

James Pride (circa 1678 – after 1748)
and Helen Selkirk
|
|
Robert Pride (1710 – after 1755)
and Christian Selkirk
|
|
Robert Pride (1741 – after 1792)
and Janet Wemyss
|
|
Brodie Pride (1767 – between 1837 and 1839)
and Catherine McQueen
|
|
David Pryde (1793 – 1856)
and Helen Richardson
|
|
Janet Pryde (1820 – 1872)
and John Hare
|
|
Esther Hare (circa 1849 – 1927)
and Robert Flockhart Vickers

Esther Hare married **Robert Flockhart Vickers (1846 – 1884)** at Newbattle, Midlothian, Scotland, in 1868. He is also generally accepted as a 4 x great-grandson of James Pride and Helen Selkirk. However, there is a slight uncertainty in one link of his ancestry regarding the parentage of William Selkirk who married Helen Hyslop. An in-depth review of material available, including the identification of witnesses at relevant baptisms and concurrent movement of fellow workers, would seem to confirm he was the son of the parents shown.[24] This means that Robert Flockhart Vickers and Esther Hare were fifth cousins as well as man and wife although it is highly unlikely they were aware of their kinship. After their marriage they had eight children born between 1868 and 1883, all in Midlothian, Scotland.

Robert Flockhart Vickers worked as a coal miner but he was also a convicted poacher. There was a history of poaching in the Vickers family as in 1848 **William Vickers (1812 – 1855)**, father of Robert Flockhart Vickers and 3 x great-grandson of James Pride and Helen Selkirk, pleaded guilty to an assault on gamekeeper Archibald White, and to assault by shooting of another gamekeeper, Robert Hume. Both assaults took place on the same night, 18th October 1847 near Dalhousie Castle, Cockpen.   At the time of the offence, his second son Robert

---

[24] Even if his ancestry is confirmed at any time in the future as being otherwise the story is still warrants inclusion because of the Pryde kinship of Esther Hare and others.

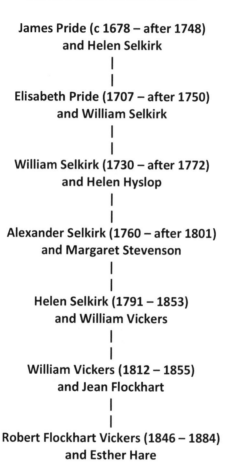

LINE OF DESCENT FOR ROBERT FLOCKHART VICKERS
AS FEATURED IN CHAPTER 14

James Pride (c 1678 – after 1748)
and Helen Selkirk
|
|
Elisabeth Pride (1707 – after 1750)
and William Selkirk
|
|
William Selkirk (1730 – after 1772)
and Helen Hyslop
|
|
Alexander Selkirk (1760 – after 1801)
and Margaret Stevenson
|
|
Helen Selkirk (1791 – 1853)
and William Vickers
|
|
William Vickers (1812 – 1855)
and Jean Flockhart
|
|
Robert Flockhart Vickers (1846 – 1884)
and Esther Hare

Flockhart Vickers was just one year old. As well as William Vickers the men who were involved included three of his brothers, **Alexander (1819 – 1893), George (1821 – Unknown)** and **Ramsay Vickers (1826 – 1889),** together with four other men. The sentence passed was that William Vickers and Alexander Vickers be transported for seven years, and that George and Ramsay Vickers be imprisoned for eight months in Perth if there be room for them and if not they were to be detained in prison at Edinburgh. It is likely the sentence in respect of William Vickers was commuted as by March 1851 he was back living with his wife and family including a four month old daughter at Cockpen. William Vickers died in Gorebridge some four years later, aged only 42 years.

We can be certain that the tradition of poaching continued within the family as on 5th January 1880 his son Robert Flockhart Vickers and another man, William Innes, were both found guilty of trespass with the intent of poaching on land called Lime Kiln Park, on the farm of D'Arcy [Newbattle]. They both pleaded guilty and were fined One Merk. [Old Scottish Pound].

On the 16th of December, 1883, Robert Flockhart Vickers and William Innes were again poaching, this time on land belonging to Lord Rosebery, at the Mansion House about five miles from Gorebridge. However, Lord Rosebery's head keeper, James Grossert, another keeper John Fortune, together with a local rabbit trapper and part-time gamekeeper, John MacDiarmid,[25] had decided to lay in wait for the suspected poachers. There was an encounter between the poachers and the gamekeepers; MacDiarmid was shot in the arm, Grossert was shot in the shoulder and another shot hit Fortune in the abdomen. Grossert managed to get away and made it to cover in woodland adjoining Edgelaw Farm, where he obtained the assistance of three workers and they went back to retrieve MacDiarmid and Fortune. A doctor and the police were summoned and Grossert told them he had recognised one of the poachers and identified him as William Innes, of Stobhill, the well-known poacher.

It was subsequently found that the second man was Robert Flockhart Vickers, who had earlier been in the company of Innes at a local public house. Vickers was arrested on Sunday morning after a search of his home revealed a double-barrelled shotgun. On the following Tuesday morning Fortune died of his injuries and both Vickers and Innes were charged with night poaching and murder. MacDiarmid had recovered enough to identify both men, stating Vickers was the man who shot him. MacDiarmid had received 38 pellet wounds in his right arm, and whilst the dressings were being changed he started bleeding and passed away, so Vickers and Innes were charged with the murder of both men. The trial took place on 10th March 1884 and they pleaded not guilty.   After the prosecution had put forward their case the defence for Vickers and Innes was that they were in their beds during the night of

---

[25] Also reported as McDermid and other variations

the offence. In support of this the following witnesses were called:-

1.   John Wallace, Miner, Stobhill, Gorebridge

2.   Elizabeth Young or Pryde, wife of James Pryde, Miner, Gorebridge. She was a neighbour of Robert Flockhart Vickers and stated that he had been in the house at ten in the evening; she had stayed up to three in the morning of the murder with a tooth ache, and had not heard Vickers leave the house till five the next morning. [Her husband **James Pryde (1848 – 1927)**, was a 4 x great-grandson of James Pride and Helen Selkirk, so was second cousin to Esther Hare, wife of Robert Flockhart Vickers, as well as being fifth cousin to Robert Flockhart Vickers].

3.   Helen Landles or Wilson, wife of James Wilson, Miner, Gorebridge.

4.   Isabella Moffat or Walkinshaw, wife of David Walkinshaw, Miner, Stobhill, Gorebridge.

5.   David Walkinshaw, aforesaid.

6.   **William Vickers (1868 – 1938)**, son of Robert Flockhart Vickers, Miner, Gorebridge. He would have been 15 years of age at this time and he stated that his father went to bed around ten at night. He woke his father at five in the morning to go to work. [See entry on page 246]

7.   **Jessie Vickers (1870 – after 1924)**, daughter of Robert Flockhart Vickers, Miner, Gorebridge [baptised as Janet]. She would have been 13 years of age at the time of the trial.

8.   Andrew Bernard, No. 19 of Crown List – who stated that he had the habit of tapping the door to wake up Innes, and on the morning of the murder he walked in to find Innes carelessly inspecting his gun at about 5 a.m. He also stated he had later gone down the mine in the same cage as Innes and his son.

9.   William Ramage, No. 21 of Crown List who stated that he had heard a shot that morning and entered the Innes house, to find him standing barefoot in the middle of the room holding the discharged gun. Ramage took the gun from him and discharged the remaining shot out of doors. Innes had told him the first shot had been caused by his inadvertently knocking the gun against the table.

10.   James Bernard, Miner, Stobhill, Gorebridge

11.   Neilson Flyn Fowler, No. 23 of Crown List of witnesses stated that he had seen two men hurrying along a public road towards Gorebridge Village at half past five in the morning but could not identify them as the accused although he was acquainted with them.

12.   George Thomson, Miner, Mossend, Gorebridge

When summing up the prosecution declared that as the prisoners had discharged their weapons at the unarmed gamekeepers, the only verdict could be a guilty one. They dismissed the evidence of the witnesses called for the defence as the shooting had occurred at two in the morning.

The men were found guilty by a majority verdict. The judge concurred with the verdict and issued the following sentence:-

"In respect of the verdict before recorded, Lord Young Decerns and Adjudges the Pannels Robert Flockhart Vickers and William Innes to be carried from the bar to the prison of Edinburgh, therein to be detained and fed on bread and water only till the thirty first day of March current, and upon that day between the hours of eight and ten o'clock forenoon, within the walls of the said prison, by the hands of the common executioner to be hanged by the neck upon a gibbet until they are dead, and their bodies thereafter to be buried within the walls of the said prison; and Ordains their whole moveable goods and gear to be escheat and inbrought to Her Majesty's use; which is pronounced for Doom :"

Both condemned men later admitted their crimes through confessions. A reprieve was hoped for and a petition, referred to at the time as a memorial, in support of a reprieve was completed by over 1,000 signatories. However, on 28th March 1884 it was refused. Both Robert Flockhart Vickers, aged 37 years, and William Innes, who was aged about 39 years, were hanged at Calton Prison, Edinburgh on 31st March

193

1884 and were buried within the grounds of the prison. The executioner was James Berry, and this was his first undertaking in the role. He later wrote about his experiences in a book entitled "My Experiences as an Executioner".

Known descendants of Robert Flockhart Vickers and Esther Hare currently total just under 60.

A memorial stone in memory of Fortune and MacDiarmid was installed on the shores of Edgelaw Reservoir, which reads:-

**HERE
ON DEC. 16TH. 1883
TWO BRAVE MEN
JOHN FORTUNE
AND
JOHN MACDIARMID
MET THEIR DEATH
IN THE
DISCHARGE OF DUTY**

The surviving Head Gamekeeper, James Porteous Watson Grossert, pictured, was 40 years of age at the time of

shootings. In a strange twist of fate there was a link between the family of Robert Flockhart Vickers and Esther Hare and James P. W. Grossert because he had a paternal first cousin, Mary Grossert (1823 – 1884) and she had married William

Terbit Pryde in 1851. **William Terbit Pryde (1822 – 1898)** was a great-great-grandson of James Pride and Helen Selkirk, and as such was related to both Robert Flockhart Vickers and Esther Hare. James P W Grossert died in 1897 at the age of 53 years and he had been a gamekeeper at Rosebery for 32 years.

In another quirk of fate, when I first researched the fore-going  in 2002, I discussed the case with another cousin, **Thomas Pryde (Living)**, pictured, 6 x great-grandson of James Pride and Helen Selkirk, and his response to me is as shown in the following letter, dated 2nd July 2002:-

"About 20 years ago while walking up the Camp I met a man about 80 years, fit and active who said his name was Jock Vickers. There was a dusting of snow and birds prints which he identified as being a hen partridge. How he knew the difference he did not explain. He then took me to see the site of Camp Meg's House which had been a Beacon House which was to give warning of the French Fleet coming up the Forth during the French Revolution. He poked his stick in the turf until it hit the flagstones. His brother Bob had years ago cleared the site and found various artefacts, clay pipes (smoking) etc. He then showed where the Long Lum Pit had been, ventilated by fire. The Cockhoolit pit upshaft where women had carried the coal up in creels. And where as a boy he had thrown stones down to break the rotting ladders. He then told of his time during the 26 strike when poaching and

digging for coal outcrops near Gowkshill and Mungo Mackay put up private property signs which the Vickers' threw in Masterton Quarry and that he was connected to the Bob Vickers that had been hung.

He told me that Vickers and friends had gone to a dance. A Barn Dance at Rosebery and had taken their guns to do a bit of poaching on the way home, the guns being hidden meantime. As there were a lot of serving girls there it may have leaked out. Anyway, they were accosted by the keepers and started an argument which became more and more heated with the result on your report. Bob Vickers was apprehended as he stepped off the bogies off the d/shift and went quietly. Jock said that when the Memorial was erected the Vickers' planned to set explosives and blow it to smithereens but decided not to as the police would know who had done it. If I had known I could have told Jock Vickers that we were connected many times removed.

When Vickers told me the story he said there was an exchange of fire which implied that the gamekeepers were armed which contradicts your report. And I find it odd that gamekeepers going to accost men they knew to have guns would challenge them with sticks and as Innes was wounded in the fracas would also indicate he had been fired upon. J Vickers told me it was not the guilty verdict but the sentence of death that made them want to blow up the memorial stone as they saw it as an argument that got out of hand and not deliberate or premeditated murder. Of course, at that time you could be

196

hung for stealing a sheep. P.S. The upshaft was a paler shade of green in a corn field."

In another letter dated 19th August 2002 he added:-

"Met an old workmate who knew the Vickers. He said there was BOB (ROBERT) WULL (WILLIAM) JOCK (JOHN) and DAVE (DAVID). He did not know their ages or their father's name, unaware of any sisters. He said I was mistaken about it being Jock that I had met as it was Bob who walked the Camp where I had met him and was still doing so when he was 90. The Camp was so called as it had been a Roman Encampment chosen for its all-round panoramic views. He also told me that one of the brothers whose name I now forget was a renowned poacher who one day caught a large salmon when he was happened upon by Lord Rosebery who said it was his. VICKERS: Not so, I caught it. ROSEBERY: In my river on my property. VICKERS: The water has flowed through many properties how can you claim what belongs to many - and offered to fight him for it. Now the veracity of these words I'm not sure about, but the encounter and Vickers belligerence I readily believe. What is a fact is that Vickers became one of Lord Rosebery's Game Keepers. I suppose Rosebery figured this was the easiest solution."

I was later able to confirm that the person who Thomas Pryde had met was **Robert Vickers (1902 - 1994)**, pictured, who was grandson to Robert Flockhart Vickers and

Esther Hare and 6 x great-grandson to James Pride and Helen Selkirk. He and Thomas Pryde were seventh cousins, although they were not aware of this during their discussion. Further research showed that although there was not a brother called William, there was a sister called Euphemia, and David Pryde was the brother who became a gamekeeper, although he later returned to the coal pits.

During my investigations I was also advised that the case is still talked about in the district to this day, with arguments both for and against the actions of all the men involved and their fate. I was able to verify this first hand myself whilst visiting Scotland in 2010 as I had a long and very interesting talk with a taxi driver, who was an ex-miner, aged about 50 years. During the course of our talk the subject of the Rosebery Murders came up and he was well aware of what had happened and felt very strongly the men should not have been hanged, that it was at worst a case of manslaughter.

Whatever the rights and wrongs of the case, there is no doubt it was a great tragedy for all concerned, the echoes of which still reverberate amongst the community today.

CHAPTER 15

QUOITING SUCCESS

Gideon Pryde (circa 1853 – 1890)
and
Elizabeth Blyth (circa 1854 – after 1892)

As an antidote to the sad events recounted in the previous chapters it would be good to remember there are instances of good fortune that also occurred within the family. One example of this involves another 4 x great-grandson of James Pride and Helen Selkirk, a contemporary and fifth cousin of Robert Flockhart Vickers and also of Esther Hare who was his second cousin. However, their lives and fortunes unfolded in very different ways.

Gideon Pryde (circa 1853 – 1890) was born in Newtongrange, Midlothian, son of **John Pryde (1825 – 1883)** and Gideon [otherwise known as Jane] Ann Gordon. He was brought up in Newtongrange and is shown there on the 1871 census, living with his parents and siblings and working as a Coal Miner, aged 18 years.

LINE OF DESCENT FOR GIDEON PRYDE
AS FEATURED IN CHAPTER 15

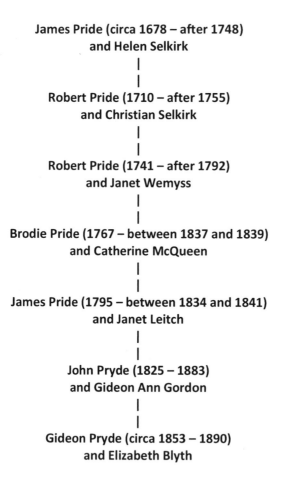

James Pride (circa 1678 – after 1748)
and Helen Selkirk
|
|
Robert Pride (1710 – after 1755)
and Christian Selkirk
|
|
Robert Pride (1741 – after 1792)
and Janet Wemyss
|
|
Brodie Pride (1767 – between 1837 and 1839)
and Catherine McQueen
|
|
James Pride (1795 – between 1834 and 1841)
and Janet Leitch
|
|
John Pryde (1825 – 1883)
and Gideon Ann Gordon
|
|
Gideon Pryde (circa 1853 – 1890)
and Elizabeth Blyth

The sport of quoiting [pronounced "koiting" or "kiting"] was popular in mining communities throughout Scotland at this time, and contemporary reports show Gideon was very successful at this sport.

Quoiting required a great deal of skill and strength as it involved throwing heavy iron or steel rings, weighing between six and twelve pounds (or between 2.7 and 5.5 kilograms), at a pin in the ground. The Scottish game used to be played by throwing the quoit a distance of 21 yards (about 19 metres) but the shorter distance of 18 yards (about 16.5 metres) was sometimes played. A game is played by the players each throwing two quoits at a three foot (almost one metre) square bed of clay or hob. The players then change ends and throw their quoits at the opposite hob. The player whose quoit is nearest the pin wins that end, scoring two points if both of their quoits are nearest the pin or, otherwise, just one point. The game is won by the first player to reach a score limit of 21, 51, 61, 71 or 81, the limit being agreed prior to the start of the match. Games could take a number of hours to reach their conclusion. As well as the often large prize money available, quoiting was commonly associated with gambling.

The following reports appear in The Scotsman newspaper on the dates shown:-

Monday 4th November 1872 –

"Quoiting for £20 prev. Sat. Gideon Pryde v James Armour[26].
Gideon lost 61 to 40.

Monday 30th June 1873 –

"Quoiting at Powderhall
Gideon Pryde, Newtongrange won against Armour, having
won several heats he got 1st Prize.
Also competing was J. Pryde of Newtongrange who was
beaten after several heats By Thom of Newliston, but came 5th
overall."

Report referring to Saturday 27th Jun 1874 -

"Quoiting,   Great Match for £50 at Powderhall
Gideon Pryde, Newtongrange v. James Armour, Rosewell,
Loanhead
G.P. won 61 to 47 after 5hrs play"

As can be seen from the above, Gideon Pryde, even whilst still
a teenager, was winning significant amounts of money.
Although wages earned fluctuated greatly at this time,
according to the price being obtained for coal, a coal miner
could expect to earn around 5s. per day so to win a cash prize

---

[26] **Helen Pryde (1737 – after 1775),** granddaughter of James Pride and
Helen Selkirk, married James Armour in 1757 at Liberton and it is through
this line there is a family link between these two quoiting adversaries,
Gideon Pryde and James Armour, although it is highly unlikely that they
were aware of this link.

of £50 would signify a great improvement in Gideon's finances and that is before any winnings from bets placed is taken into consideration.

In July 1874 Gideon Pryde, recorded as a Miner aged 21 years, married Elizabeth Blyth at Newbattle. His married state did not restrict his quoiting exploits to any great degree as another report in The Scotsman newspaper refers to a match which took place on 17th October 1874:-

"Quoiting, Great Match at Powderhall
Gideon Pryde, Newtongrange v, James Armour, Rosewell
G.P. won 61 to 42 after 8 hrs play"

A report about the above match also appears in the Dalkeith Advertiser dated 22nd October 1874:-

"Quoiting"

GREAT MATCH FOR £50

A very large number of quoiting enthusiasts assembled at Powderhall Grounds on Saturday to witness the match for the above sum between Gideon Pryde, of Newtongrange, and James Armour of Loanhead. The men are old opponents, having contended seven times previously, out of which number Armour has been successful four times, and Pryde three. As players, both are in the first rank, Armour having only a fortnight ago defeated Letham, the champion, in a tournament at Dumfries. This great performance caused him to be most fancied by those acquainted with the merits of the

203

competitors; but as Pryde had been doing wonders in practise, the Newtongrange division were extremely sanguine. At ten minutes to eleven Armour led off, but amidst loud cheering Pryde secured the first head. The next two fell to Armour for pairs, but he was shortly afterwards collared, and they "peeled" for the first time at 7 - Pryde then was most deadly, and reached 15 to 11, but Armour getting in soon made the score "19 all". This he further augmented and reached 24 without ever giving his opponent a chance. A run of eight successive shots by Pryde put a different aspect on the game, and when they stopped a few minutes for refreshment the score stood - Pryde, 31; Armour, 28. From this point the Newtongrange man played splendidly, while Armour seemed totally to have lost his form; there was a want of steadiness in his pitching and he failed to avail himself of the very few opportunities which Pryde afforded him. The latter increased his advantage, and after fully five hours' play won the game by 19 shots, the final score standing - Pryde, 61; Armour, 42. We append the scoring in the match:-

Pryde -
10020020201210102100
10110010000021111110
12001011202021111112
0101000111100212012- 61

Armour –
02201101020001010012
01002101111200000001
00210100010100000000
2020112000011000100- 42"

Gideon Pryde later became a Spirit Merchant in Blantyre, Lanarkshire, and it is probable his earnings from quoiting were significant enough to fund the change of occupation from coal miner. Sadly he died at the beginning of January 1890 aged only 38 years, having succumbed to Acute Meningitis. Gideon Pryde and Elizabeth Blyth had no issue.

In 1891, a year after the death of her husband, Elizabeth Pryde née Blyth was still carrying on the business of Spirit Merchant at Blantyre, supported by two of her siblings. In December 1891 she married William Naysmith, a coal miner, at Newbattle and her occupation is given as a Publican.

Finally, Gideon's name again appears in The Scotsman newspaper dated 27th August 1892, but this time it is for a less auspicious reason than previously:-

"Notice of Application for Bankruptcy 27 Aug 1892 -- Elizabeth Blyth or Pryde or Naismith [sic], sometime widow of Gideon Pryde, spirit merchant of Blantyre, now wife of William Naismith, spirit merchant, Black Bull Inn, Dalkeith."

There is no doubt when reading the above report many local readers would have remembered, hopefully with pleasure, the sporting exploits of Gideon Pryde.

CHAPTER 16

EXTRAORDINARY TIMES FOR ORDINARY PEOPLE

The family of George Thomas Pryde (1864 – 1922)
and
Margaret Hunter (circa 1864 – 1939)

As the later generations of the family move from the end of the 19th century to the beginning of the 20th century it becomes easier to obtain details of how they lived their day-to-day lives, and no-one of that era will have been unaffected by the Great War, which was later to become known as World War 1.

There are many more chapters I could write about this period describing the lives and times of a large number of the different families descended from James Pride and Helen Selkirk, especially those who have remained in Scotland but to do so would take this book in a different direction. Therefore I have chosen to include the following family details in this chapter to give examples of the outside influences which affected many during this time, especially those residing in the east of Scotland.

George Thomas Pryde Snr. (1864 – 1922), pictured, was born  in Newcraighall, Midlothian. He was a 4 x great-grandson of James Pride and Helen Selkirk and the fifth child of **John Pryde (1835 – 1905)** and his first wife Margaret Ratcliffe. As mentioned in Chapter 5 John Pryde had 19 children from his two marriages.

Shortly after the birth of George Snr. the family moved from the Newcraighall area to live at West Calder, West Lothian. Just a month before George Thomas was four years old his mother, Margaret Pryde née Ratcliffe, died of Puerperal Fever, ten days after the birth of her seventh child, **Mary Pryde (1867 – 1868)**, in November 1867. The birth of Mary and the death of her mother were both registered by John Pryde (husband and father) on the same day, 10th December, 1867. Mary died the following year aged eight months.

The family were still in West Calder in 1871 and on the census George Snr. aged seven years, is shown to be living there with his widowed father, sisters Margaret and Catherine, and elder brother William. Both John Pryde his father and William Pryde his brother, at this time aged 15 years, are working as Shale Miners. **William Pryde (1855 – 1872)** died one year later, aged only 16 years, from Tuberculosis Mesenterion, leaving George Snr. as the eldest surviving son. By 1881 George Snr. is shown on the census aged 17 years and he is also working as a Shale Miner. He is still living at West Calder with his father and stepmother.

LINE OF DESCENT FOR GEORGE THOMAS PRYDE
AND SOME OF HIS FAMILY AS FEATURED IN CHAPTER 16

James Pride (circa 1678 – after 1748)
and Helen Selkirk

|

George Pride (1716 – 1759)
and Margaret Fraser

|

Thomas Pride (1753 – after 1796)
and Henrietta Maria Pride (1755 – after 1796)
(Granddaughter of James Pride and Helen Selkirk
and daughter of James Pride and Agnes Smith)

|

George Pride (1779 – 1832)
and Elizabeth Pettigrew

|

William Pryde (1815 – 1871)
and Agnes Marshall

|

John Pryde (1835 – 1905)
and Margaret Ratcliffe

|

George Thomas Pryde (1864 – 1922)
and Margaret Hunter and three of their sons:-

William Hunter (1893 – 1970)
Charles Ratcliffe (1904 – 1996)
George Thomas Jnr. (1901 – 1984)

George Thomas Snr. married Margaret Hunter at Edinburgh in 1891 when he was 27 years age – he was still a shale miner at West Calder. They had two children born in West Lothian and then a further six children born in different parts of Lanarkshire. By 1901 George Snr. and his wife and family had settled in Shotts, Lanarkshire, and he was employed as a coal miner.

The family moved after 1906 and by 1911 were living at Ballingry in Fife. On the night of the 1911 census Margaret is shown as living at 21 Waverley Street, Ballingry, with her children but George Snr. is a listed as one of four prisoners being held at the Police Station in Ballingry with his usual occupation being shown as a Coal Miner. There is no report in the local newspapers indicating his misdemeanour so it is likely it was only a minor offence.

These were volatile times for coal miners, with wages varying a great deal in accordance with the price being obtained for the coal, and there were a number of disputes between the coal miners, represented by the Scottish Miners' Federation, which was formed in 1894, and the coal mine owners.

The first national strike by coal miners in Britain took place in 1912, in an effort to secure a minimum wage. Nearly one million miners took part and after 37 days the strike was ended, the coal miners having gained what they wanted, and the Coal Mines (Minimum Wage) Act 1912 was passed.

In addition to the workplace turmoil at this time the onset of the Great War in 1914 meant that a great many coal miners rushed to join the Armed Forces, reported as being a quarter of the workforce in the first year alone. This had such an impact on coal output, fuel which was desperately needed, that in 1916 mining became a reserved occupation, taking preference over military service. Some miners were even recalled from the front line.

William Hunter Pryde (1893 – 1970), pictured, eldest son of  George Thomas Pryde Snr. and Margaret Hunter and 5 x great-grandson of James Pryde and Helen Selkirk, enlisted in the Black Watch on 4th January 1912 when he was aged 18 years and 6 months, with his occupation being listed as a coal miner. However, after a short but somewhat chequered military career, he was discharged at his own request on payment of £18. He married Robina Wood in Newbattle in 1915 and they had five children together between 1915 and 1926 but they subsequently divorced. William then had six children with his second wife Mary Shearer Aitchison. According to oral family history William was regarded as the black sheep of the family, prone to getting into fights, but he was also a good dancer and very musical, being a member of the Kelty Band. He taught his younger brother George Thomas Pryde Jnr. these same skills.

By 1921 George Snr., with sons Charles and George Thomas Jnr., had returned to their Midlothian roots and were living at Newtongrange, Midlothian, which was the site of the Lady Victoria Colliery.

The Lady Victoria Colliery at Newtongrange was opened in 1895 by the Lothian Coal Company who at the same time had built dwellings, capable of housing over 6,500 people. These dwellings were regarded at the time as the best-built housing for miners in Scotland. The standards of the houses and village were maintained by the Mine Manager, Mungo Mackay, who had been appointed in 1894 at the age of 27 years. By a number of accounts it is known that he ruled the village with a very firm hand and dealt with any transgressions, both major and minor, in what many would refer to as a harsh manner. Any individual thought guilty of an offence was called to his office which was "up the stairs" to be faced by Mungo Mackay sitting behind his green table which was legendary within the village.

The extent of the control wielded by Mungo Mackay was felt by many, including the family of George Thomas Snr. In April

 1921 George Snr. and his wife Margaret, their son **Charles Ratcliffe Pryde (1904 – 1996)**, pictured, who was single, and also their son **George Thomas Jnr. (1901 – 1984)** and his wife Agnes and their one month old son, **George Thomas III (1921 – 2014)**, all lived together at Newtongrange.

All the men of the house, that is George Thomas Pryde Snr. the father, and his two sons, George Thomas Jnr. and Charles not only lived together, they were also all employed underground at Lady Victoria Pit. At the end of April 1921 Charlie had an altercation with the shift boss at the end of the

shift. No blows were struck; by all accounts it was more or less a shouting match only. Charlie, who was aged 17 years at the time, was summoned to the "office" upstairs and Mungo Mackay sacked him from his job. Charlie was also told to tell his father and brother there was no more work for them and ordered to have his father's house keys turned in. The family travelled almost a whole day to Fife in very bad weather where they were successful in finding work. Amongst those who made the journey was seven weeks old **George Thomas Pryde III (1921 – 2004)**, the first born child of George Thomas Pryde Jnr. and Agnes Dalzeil.

In addition to the personal problems being experienced within the family in 1921 there was also another national strike. The Miner's Federation had refused to accept a reduction in wages brought in by the coal owners after they had regained control of the mines following the end of the Coal Emergency Act brought in during the Great War. The strike lasted three months.

George Thomas Pryde Snr. died in 1922 aged 58 years and his wife Margaret died in 1939 at Bowhill, Fife, aged 75 years. Known descendants currently total just over 100. The majority of the children of George Thomas Pryde Snr. remained in Fife and brought up their families there.

However, in the late 1920s the two brothers, Charles and George Thomas Jnr. with his family, were able to return to Midlothian where they gained employment at Easthouses Mine, one mile from Newtongrange.

George Thomas Pryde Jnr. (1901 – 1984), pictured, was a 5 x
 great-grandson of James Pride and Helen Selkirk. By the time of their return to Midlothian he and his wife Agnes Dalzeil had four children and they were to have another child born after their move. In the 1930s he was involved in an underground gas explosion whilst working as a coal stripper in a team of twelve men. Six were found dead and three died on arrival at hospital. He suffered facial burns and his hair was 'burned to a crisp'. He spent two years recovering whilst living on dwindling compensation and was one of the first persons to receive what was then called "Miracle Treatment for Burns" - Tannic Acid[27]. His hair turned different colours until finally returning to its natural chestnut colour and when his burnt skin finally peeled off the new skin had no scars. George Thomas Jnr., who was a gifted accordion player, emigrated from Scotland to California in 1954 and he died there in 1984 aged 82 years, predeceasing his wife by some 8 years.

---

[27] The introduction of Tannic Acid treatment for severe burns in the 1920s significantly reduced mortality rates.

The eldest son born to George Thomas Jnr. and Agnes Dalzeil was **George Thomas Pryde III (1921 – 2014)** [28] , pictured, who was known as Geordie. He was a 6 x great-grandson of James Pride and Helen Selkirk and was the seven-week old child who made the journey from Newtongrange to Fife with his parents, grandparents and Uncle Charlie after their sacking by Mungo Mackay. Upon their return to Midlothian he lived in what was known locally as the "Bogwood", in Gorebridge. As the eldest child of five he recalled stealing potatoes to keep food on the table after his father was injured down the pit in the 1930s as recounted on the previous page.

When he was 14 years of age his father got him a job as an Apprentice Slater and Roofer, because he did not want his son to go down the pit. However, after a month or so, Geordie left his apprenticeship and went down the pit, doubling his wages, so he was able to "keep up" with his mates. His father said "You have made your ain bed and you'll hae ti lie on it!"

He worked as a miner until joining the Army in 1941 but after one year he was returned to the mines, transferring to the Territorial Army Reserve in 1942. He married Margaret Docherty in 1945 and soon after this he joined Edinburgh City Police and became a Pipe Drummer in their Pipe Band, only

---

[28] I am indebted to the late George Thomas Pryde for our many years of shared correspondence during which he recounted the lives of his family in detail.

after they agreed to waive their minimum height requirement to permit his entry as a constable.

He emigrated from Scotland to Canada in the second half of the 1950s after seeing an advert placed by the Powell River Co. who were seeking pipers and drummers to boost their band. He became a member of the Powell River Pipe Band which won all the major awards for Senior Pipe Bands on the Pacific Coast. He worked in security for the Powell River Co. at their paper and pulp mill and named his home "Bogwood", never forgetting his roots. George Thomas Pryde III passed away in 2014, having been predeceased by his wife 10 years previously.

As the story of our family has now reached living memory and living members I hope I have recounted enough of our connected but diverse family history to enable us all to get a flavour of the times in which our ancestors lived.

CHAPTER 17

LIVES ENDED TOO SOON

As shown in the foregoing chapters some lives were brought to an untimely end, either by accident or conflict. The following list shows some of those within the family who were so affected.

Mining Fatalities

Catherine Pryde (1801 – 1839) – daughter of **Brodie Pride (1767 – between 1837 and 1839)** and Catherine McQueen, and 2 x great-granddaughter of James Pride and Helen Selkirk. She was a niece of Walter Pride who some three years after her death was to give evidence to the Franks Report as referred to in Chapter 3. Her burial record shows she was aged 38 years, with cause of death given as Accidental Death. A report of her death appears in the Caledonian Mercury newspaper dated 7th March 1839 as follows:-

"22 February 1839

On Friday the 22d ultimo as one of the workmen in Newbattle Colliery were setting off one of their waggons, on an inclined lane, underground, it was not observed that it was unconnected with the crane which regulates the descent of the vehicle, when it came with its accumulated violence against Catherine Pryde, and produced such severe injury on her body that she died on her way home to the village of Easthouses. An aged and blind widowed mother has, by this event, been derived of her principal means of support."

David Pryde (1793 – 1856) – son of **Brodie Pride (1767 – between 1837 and 1839)** and Catherine McQueen, and 2 x great-grandson of James Pride and Helen Selkirk. He was a brother of Catherine Pryde who lost her life as shown in the previous paragraph. David Pryde was married to Helen Richardson and they had six children, born between 1814 and 1833, four of whom it seems had successfully reached adulthood when David Pryde lost his life. His death record shows that he was Coal Weigher, aged 64 years and that cause of death was from a fall down a coal pit. Instantaneous death, Not Certified. The informant was Thomas Stewart, Overseer. Thomas Stewart's daughter Marion was married to John McIntosh, who was a 3 x great -grandson of James Pride and Helen Selkirk, and therefore first cousin once removed to the deceased.

The entry in the Mines Inspectors' Report shows that David Pryde died on 10th May 1856. He was a Weigher of Dalkeith, working at a pit owned by the Duke of Buccleuch, Dalkeith,

Midlothian, and he sustained his injuries by falling down a pit whilst assisting a pitheadman.

William Pryde (1855 – 1879) – son of **David Pryde (1822 – 1897)** and Marion Meek and 4 x great-grandson of James Pride and Helen Selkirk. He was a grandson of David Pryde (1793 – 1856) who also lost his life in a pit accident, as outlined in the previous entry. The death record shows that William was an Ironstone Miner, single and aged 23 years when he died from Internal Injuries from an accident, duration three hours.

An entry in the Register of Corrected Entries Vol. 1 P60 for Penicuik states that the following Report of a Result of Precognition has been received touching the death of William Pryde, registered under No. 16 in the Register Book of Deaths for 1879:-

William PRYDE, 23 years, a male - died Shottstown 21st March 1879 - Injuries received while engaged in mining operations. Survived accident about three hours.

An entry in list of deaths taken from the Mines Inspectors' Report shows that William Pryde, aged 24 [sic] years, an Ironstone Miner of Penicuik, who was employed in a mine owned by the Shotts Iron Co., Edinburgh, was killed by a fall of ironstone at face.

Charles Pryde (1875 – 1893) – son of William Pryde (1841 – 1924) and Beatrice Cossar and 5 x great-grandson of James Pride and Helen Selkirk. His death record shows that he died on 7th February 1893 and that he was a Pony Driver, aged 17 years, with the cause of death being an accident in pit. The death was reported by John Richardson, Uncle, present.

An article in the Dalkeith Advertiser Newspaper dated 9th February 1893 states:-

"FATAL ACCIDENT AT NEWBATTLE COLLIERY

On Tuesday evening an accident which was attended with fatal consequences occurred at Newbattle Colliery. The unfortunate party was Charles Pryde, a young man of eighteen [sic] *years of age. From inquiry it appears that the unfortunate person was employed as a dook-fitter, and whilst at work a bogey which had become loose came in contact with him, injuring him much about the side. He was taken to his home in Newtongrange and lingered on in a very precarious condition, but in an hour after his removal he succumbed to his injuries. The sad affair has cast quite a gloom over the village."*

Mungo Pryde (1870 – 1894) – son of William Pryde (1841 – 1924) and Beatrice Cossar and 5 x great-grandson of James Pride and Helen Selkirk. He was brother to Charles Pryde listed above and he lost his life just over a year after the death of his brother. His death record shows he was a Coal Miner, single, aged 23 years. The cause of death is given as Accident in Pit, not certified, at Engine Pit, Lingerwood. Death was reported by David Cossar, Brother-in-law.

An entry in the Mines Inspectors' Report states that Mungo Pryde, aged 23 years, a Dookheadman, of Newbattle, working for Lothian Coal Co. Ltd., Edinburgh, was killed on 10th July 1894 by being crushed by a tub.

From Main body of report: *Deceased was acting temporarily as a hanger-on at the head of an engine dook, which has a dip of 1 in 2, and on which the tubs are drawn by two endless ropes, to which they are attached singly at intervals of about 20 yards. One rope passes along each side of the tubs, and each tub is attached to the ropes by four horns, one at each of its corners. A tub loaded with bricks was being sent down the dook, and owing probably to the horn on one side catching the rope slightly in advance of that on the other, the tub went over on the dook with the left front horn twisted too far back. Deceased signalled to stop the engine, and going down after the tub for a distance of about 8 yards, he knocked the outer side of the horn forward with a brick. Observing that the right front horn had also become twisted, he crossed in front of the tub to put it right, and while doing so the ropes slipped through the horns and the tub ran away, driving him down the dook before it, and crushing him against the next tub. His back, left thigh, and several ribs were fractured, and he died in a few moments without having regained consciousness. The accident was evidently due to want of caution on the part of deceased. It was exceedingly rash to attempt to shift the grip*

*of the horn which apparently was carrying most of the load,
more especially while standing directly below the tub.*

An article in the Dalkeith Advertiser dated 12th July 1894
states:-

"NEWTONGRANGE - FATAL ACCIDENT

*Very general regret was expressed in Newtongrange on
Tuesday when it became known that a young man named
Mungo Pryde, residing at St. Davids Row, Newtongrange, had
met with his death by accident in the pit that morning. He was
employed as an oncost man, and was engaged in connecting
a loaded batch of bricks with the haulage chain at the top of
the incline, when, the hutch, breaking away from its fastening,
he was carried with it down the incline. From the injuries he
received death must have been instantaneous. Pryde was a
native of Newtongrange, and was greatly esteemed for his
high personal character, and the great interest he took in
several village societies."*

George Pryde (1865 – 1923) – son of **Mary Pryde (circa 1834
– 1911)** and 4 x great-grandson of James Pride and Helen
Selkirk. He was a Pitheadman aged 57 years when he was
involved in an accident at New Chum No. 4 Colliery, Ipswich,
Australia, and he died in Ipswich Hospital. He left a wife and
one adult daughter. Full details and photo as reported in
Chapter 12.

Alexander McIntosh Millar (1888 – 1932), pictured - son of

William Jamieson Millar and **Beatrice McIntosh (1863 – 1935)** and 5 x great-grandson of James Pride and Helen Selkirk. His death record shows that when he died on 12th December 1932 he was aged 45 years and single, with cause of death given as Rupture of Diaphragm, General Bruising, and Chronic Bright's Disease.

The record in the Register of Corrected Entries for Dunfermline 1933, Entry No. 58 states Alexander McIntosh Millar died from Injuries received on 8th December 1932 in the underground workings of Bowhill Colliery in the course of his industrial occupation as a Miner there, caused by a fall from the roof of his working place - per Verdict of Jury.

John Wesley Cooper (1895 – 1934), pictured - son of Joseph

Cooper and **Janet McIntosh (1854 – 1939)** and 5 x great-grandson of James Pride and Helen Selkirk. He died in Krings, Pennsylvania, aged 39 years. John Wesley Cooper and Alexander McIntosh Millar as reported above were second cousins who would have been contemporaries but would have never met. It is sadly ironic that they both lost their lives in a similar manner but on different continents.

The Johnstown Tribune newspaper, date 10th October 1934 reported [abridged]:-

223

"JOHN W. COOPER FATALLY INJURED AT LORAIN MINE Kring's Station Man Crushed Between Roof of Mine and Mine Motor

INQUEST UNDECIDED

John W. Cooper, 40, [sic] of Kring's Station was fatally injured late yesterday in an accident at the Ingleside No. 5 mine of the Lorain Steel Company. He was dead on admission to Memorial Hospital a short time after the accident. Mr. Cooper, a veteran of 19 years' experience in the mines, was crushed between the roof of the mine and a mine motor while "spragging" on the tripless motor. He suffered fractures on the skull and neck. Coroner Cyrus W. Davis viewed the body at the hospital and announced that an inquest will be governed by the report of Mine Inspector M. W. Thomas, who is handling the State investigation. Known to a large number of friends as "Cappy," John W. Cooper was a leader in sports and played third base on the miners' mushball team. He was popular in Kring's Station, where he lived. Mr. Cooper was born March 11, 1895, and was a son of Joseph and Janet (McIntosh) Cooper."

He was married to Trella Viola Mishler and left behind two young children.

 John Pryde (1895 – 1941), pictured in photo taken in WW1 – son of **John Pryde (1871 – 1945)** and Isabella Chalmers Stenhouse and 5 x great-grandson of James Pride and Helen Selkirk. John Pryde, coal miner, aged 45 years died on 14th

June 1941 in West Fife Hospital, Dunfermline, from injuries sustained by a roof fall at Lindsay Colliery, Kelty, Beath Parish, Fife, nine days earlier, on 5th June 1941. An article in the Scotsman newspaper dated 6th June 1941 reported:-

"Fife pit accident - Three men dead; two injured - Extensive roof fall - Three pit workers lost their lives and two were injured when they were buried under an extensive fall yesterday morning in the underground workings of the Lindsay Colliery, Kelty, belonging to the Fife Coal Company Ltd. The three men killed were: -Bernard Lynch 65, conveyor engine attendant, Woodend Park, Kelty; Peter Wilson 29, stripper, Main Street, Lumphinnans; and Robert Nicol 29, stripper, Naysmith Place, Kelty

The injured are: - Edward Drummond, 23, stripper, Naysmith Place, and John Pryde 45, shot firer, Lower Oakfield, Kelty. The men had just begun work in the Lochgelly splint section of the colliery, when there was an extensive fall of material from the roof, and they were trapped. Rescue parties under the direction of Dr J N Williamson, the company's Safety Engineer; Mr W E S Peach, colliery agent; Mr T Thyne, manager; and Mr A Thomson, under manager, made heroic efforts to extricate the men. The body of Lynch was recovered shortly before midday. Drummond and Pryde were extricated at about the same time, and it was found that, although injured, their condition was not serious. Several hours elapsed before the bodies of Wilson and Nicol were brought to the surface. Drummond and Pryde, who were removed to Dunfermline and

West Fife Hospital suffering from shock and general bruising."

A report for the same date in the Evening Telegraph newspaper also reported the following:-

"TRAPPED IN FIFE PIT - THREE DEAD, TWO INJURED - Three miners were killed and two injured in a Fife accident to-day. The men had commenced work in the Lochgelly Seam of the Lindsay Colliery belonging to the Fife Coal company, when there was a very heavy fall of coal and they were trapped. Under Mr W E S. Peach, colliery agent, and Mr Thomas Thyne, colliery manager, a rescue party was quickly at work. Before noon the body of Bernard Lynch (65), 11 Woodend Park, Kelty was recovered. Edward Drummond (23), 44 Naismyth Place, Kelty and John Pryde, Lily bank, Lower Oakfield Kelty, were taken out injured, but not seriously. The rescue party continued their efforts and this afternoon the bodies of Robert Nicoll (29), Naismyth Place, Kelty, and Peter Wilson (29), 45 Main Street, Lumphinnans, were brought to the surface. Lynch leaves a wife and a large grown-up family.

Nicoll was a well-known junior footballer. He played for Kirkford Juniors and was well-known locally as "Tippy" Nicoll because of his neat passing."

John Pryde was married to Catherine Hunter Forsyth and left behind two children who were in their teens.

Alexander Pryde (1913 – 1958) – son of **James Smith Pryde** **(1886 – 1956)** and Jane Forbes Sneddon Black and 5 x great-grandson of James Pride and Helen Selkirk. His death record shows he was a Coal Miner (Brusher), married aged 45 years. Cause of death was Asphyxia (Pit Accident) at Lady Victoria Colliery, Newtongrange. He was married to Georgina Richardson Anderson and left behind three young children as an article in the Edinburgh Evening News dated 5th April 1958 reported:-

"NEWTONGRANGE MINER KILLED

A 43 [sic] year old Newtongrange miner, Alexander Pryde, was killed by a roof fall at the Lady Victoria Pit, Newtongrange, yesterday.

It is believed that one of the roof support beams collapsed trapping him under tons of rubble. Pryde, whose home was at The Square, Newtongrange, leaves a widow and 3 children.

He was a former Arniston Rangers and Leith Athletic footballer, and his brother W Pryde played for Newtongrange Star and Airdrieonians."

MAY THEY ALL REST IN PEACE

American Civil War Fatalities

William Henry Harrison Brown (circa 1836 – 1863) – 3 x great-grandson of James Pride and Helen Selkirk and son of George Brown and **Alison Pride (1803 – after 1880),** who feature in Chapter 8. William was aged 27 years when he died after contracting Typhoid Fever caught whilst in the line of duty, as he was serving as a Sergeant, Co. H, in the 17th Pennsylvania Cavalry. He was married to Harriet Anne Brazier and left two very young children. He had five brothers, at least three of whom served in the Civil War and survived.

James Simpson Pryde (1845 – 1864), pictured – son of **John Pryde (1811 - 1894)** and Mary Ann Knowles and 3 x great-grandson of James Pride and Helen Selkirk. He was single, aged 19 years, when he lost his life whilst fighting on the Confederate side. See Chapter 7 for full details.

Robert B Pryde (1848 – 1864) – son of **John Pryde (1811 - 1894)** and Mary Ann Knowles and 3 x great-grandson of James Pride and Helen Selkirk. Brother to James Simpson Pryde above, he was killed aged just 16 years, one month after the death of his brother, whilst fighting on the Union side. See Chapter 7 for full details.

The Great War or World War 1 Fatalities[29]

Alexander George Howden (1888 – 1915), pictured – son of William Thomson Howden and **Janet Buchanan Polson (1866 – 1941)** and 5 x great-grandson of James Pride and Helen Selkirk. He was single and serving as a Private in the 1st. Bn. of the Argyll and Sutherland Highlanders when he was killed at Ypres, Belgium, on 24th February 1915. His name is commemorated on the Ypres (Menin Gate) Memorial.

The Menin Gate is one of four memorials to the missing in Belgian Flanders which cover the area known as the Ypres Salient. The site of the Menin Gate was chosen because of the hundreds of thousands of men who passed through it on their way to the battlefields. It commemorates casualties from the forces of Australia, Canada, India, South Africa and the United Kingdom who died in the Salient. The Ypres (Menin Gate) Memorial now bears the names of more than 54,000 officers and men whose graves are not known. The memorial, designed by Sir Reginald Blomfield with sculpture by Sir William Reid-Dick, was unveiled by Lord Plumer on 24th July

---

[29] Some of the information contained in this chapter about individuals and in particular the burial sites has been obtained from the Commonwealth War Graves Commission website under whose terms of copyright this material is used.

1927. Each night at 8.00 p.m. the traffic is stopped at the Menin Gate while members of the local Fire Brigade sound the Last Post in the roadway under the Memorial's arches.

Joseph Pryde (1889 – 1915) – son of **Alexander Pryde (circa 1865 – 1933)** and Hannah Shotton and 5 x great-grandson of James Pride and Helen Selkirk. He was a Sapper in the 174th Field Coy., Royal Engineers when he was killed in action on the Somme Battlefield, France, on 2nd August 1915, aged 26 years. He is buried at Perrone Road Cemetery, near Maricourt Village, Somme, France.

Maricourt was, at the beginning of the Battles of the Somme 1916, the point of junction of the British and French forces, and within a very short distance of the front line; it was lost in the German advance of March 1918, and recaptured at the end of the following August. The Cemetery, originally known as Maricourt Military Cemetery No.3, was begun by fighting units and Field Ambulances in the Battles of the Somme 1916, and used until August 1917; a few graves were added later in the War, and at the Armistice it consisted of 175 graves which now form almost the whole of Plot I. It was completed after the Armistice by the concentration of graves from the battlefields in the immediate neighbourhood and from certain smaller burial grounds including Authuile Communal Cemetery Extension which contained the graves of 108 French soldiers and those of 23 from the United Kingdom who fell in 1915 and early 1916.

George Hannah Pryde (1896 – 1915) – son of **James Darling Pryde (circa 1586 – 1932)** and Elizabeth White and 5 x great-grandson of James Pride and Helen Selkirk. He was single and serving as a Private in the 1ˢᵗ Bn. Argyle & Sutherland Highlanders when he was killed in action on 13ᵗʰ September 1915, aged 19 years.

He is buried at the Brewery Orchard Cemetery, Nord, France. The cellar of the brewery was used as a dressing station and the cemetery was started in the orchard nearby in November 1914. It was sheltered from enemy observation by ruined houses and continued in use until January 1918. Brewery Orchard Cemetery contains 339 Commonwealth burials of the First World War. There are also four Second World War burials and five German war graves. The cemetery was designed by Sir Herbert Baker.

Peter Lowe Currie (1883 – 1916) – son of John Archibald Currie and **Margaret Lowe (circa 1854 – 1915)** and 5 x great-grandson of James Pride and Helen Selkirk. He was serving as a Lance Corporal in the 124ᵗʰ Field Coy., Royal Engineers, when he was killed in action on the 11ᵗʰ July 1916 aged 33 years. He was married to Margaret Little and left behind four sons aged between ten years and two years of age.

He is buried at Flatiron Copse Cemetery, Mametz, Somme, France. Flatiron Copse was the name given by the army to a small plantation a little to the east of Mametz Wood. The ground was taken by the 3rd and 7th Divisions on 14th July 1916 and an advanced dressing station was established at the copse. The cemetery was begun later that month and it remained in use until April 1917. After the Armistice, more than 1,100 graves were brought in from the neighbouring battlefields and from smaller cemeteries. There are now 1,572 Commonwealth servicemen of the First World War buried or commemorated in this cemetery. The cemetery was designed by Sir Herbert Baker.

James Sheriff Robertson (1894 – 1916), pictured – son of James Sheriff Robertson and **Isabella Robertson (1868 – 1948)** and 6 x great-grandson of James Pride and Helen Selkirk. He was single and a Private in the 9th Bn. of the Seaforth Highlanders when he was killed in action on the Somme Battlefield, France, on 16th July 1916 aged 22 years. He is buried at Abbeville Communal Cemetery, Somme.

For much of the First World War, Abbeville was headquarters of the Commonwealth lines of communication and No.3 BRCS, No.5 and No.2 Stationary Hospitals were stationed there variously from October 1914 to January 1920. The communal cemetery was used for burials from November 1914 to September 1916, the earliest being made among the French military graves. Abbeville Communal Cemetery contains 774

Commonwealth burials of First World War. It was designed by Sir Reginald Blomfield.

Irvine Lawson Pryde (1895 – 1916) – son of **John McKay Pryde (1867 – 1903)** and Mary Jane Lawson and 4 x great-grandson of James Pride and Helen Selkirk. Irvine had attended Leith Walk Public School in Edinburgh after which he had travelled to Australia when aged 19 years. He was a Private in the 51st Bn., Australian Infantry, A.I.F., when he was killed in action on 3rd September 1916 in France aged 21 years.

His name is commemorated on the Villers-Brettoneux Memorial. The memorial is the Australian National Memorial erected to commemorate all Australian soldiers who fought in France and Belgium during the First World War, to their dead, and especially to name those of the dead whose graves are not known.

The Australian servicemen named on this memorial died on the battlefields of the Somme, Arras, and in the German advance of 1918 and the Advance to Victory. The memorial stands within Villers-Bretonneux Military Cemetery, which was made after the Armistice when graves were brought in from other burial grounds in the area and from the battlefields. Both the cemetery and memorial were designed by Sir Edwin Lutyens. The memorial was unveiled by King George VI on 22nd July 1938.

Robert Pryde (1892 – 1917) – son of **William Pryde (circa 1853 – 1926)** and Isabella Wallace and 4 x great-grandson of James Pride and Helen Selkirk. He was single and serving as a Lance Corporal in the 9th Bn. Royal Scots when he was killed in action on 23rd April 1917 in France, aged 24 years. He is buried at the Level Crossing Cemetery, Fampoux, France.

Fampoux village was taken by the 4th Division (passing through the 9th (Scottish) Division in which Robert Pryde was serving) on 9th April 1917. It remained close behind the Allied front line, but part of it was lost on 28th March 1918 during the German advance. The village was cleared by the 51st (Highland) Division on 26th August 1918.

The cemetery was begun in June 1917 when a number of graves of April and May were brought in from the battlefield. It was used until March 1918 and two further burials were made in October 1918. In addition to the 9th and 51st Division, the 15th (Scottish) Division fought in the area, and over half the graves are those of soldiers of Scottish regiments.

Level Crossing Cemetery contains 405 burials and commemorations of the First World War. The cemetery was designed by Sir Reginald Blomfield.

George Robertson (1877 – 1917), pictured – son of **Robert**  **William Robertson (1850 – 1908)** and Christina Cairns and 5 x great-grandson of James Pride and Helen Selkirk. George was working as a miner and aged 38 years when he enlisted in December 1915. He was serving as a Private in the 35th Bn. of the Australian Infantry, A.I.F., when he was killed in action in Belgium on the 7th June 1917. He was aged 39 years, married to Elizabeth Williams and he left five children.

His name is commemorated on the Ypres (Menin Gate) Memorial, details as provided previously.

George Pryde (1884 – 1917) – son of **George Pryde (1846 - 1916)** and Janet Brunton and 4 x great-grandson of James Pride and Helen Selkirk. George was a serving soldier aged 18 years according to the 1901 census. He was single and a Lance Corporal in 6th Bn. Kings Own Yorkshire Light Infantry, formerly of 2nd Dragoon Guards (Royal Scots Greys), when he was reported missing in action at Ypres, Belgium, on 23rd August 1917, aged 32 years.

His name is commemorated on the Tyne Cot Memorial Panel, Zonnebeke, West Vlaanderen, Belgium. The Tyne Cot Memorial is another of the four memorials to the missing in Belgian Flanders, as mentioned previously. The memorial now bears the names of almost 35,000 officers and men whose graves are not known. Designed by Sir Herbert Baker with sculpture by Joseph Armitage and F.V. Blundstone, it was unveiled by Sir Gilbert Dyett on 20th June 1927.

Robert Newlands Glen (1898 – 1917) – son of Peter Glen and **Barbara Herkes Wilson (1863 – 1954)** and 6 x great-grandson of James Pride and Helen Selkirk. He was single and a Private in the 9th Bn. of the Royal Scots (Lothian Regiment) when he was killed in action in France on 8th September 1917, aged 19 years. His name is commemorated on the Tyne Cot Memorial Panel, Zonnebeke, West Vlaanderen, Belgium, details as referred to previously.

Malcolm McGregor (1898 – 1917) – son of **Malcolm McGregor (1872 – 1957)** and Isabella Paterson and 5 x great-grandson of James Pride and Helen Selkirk. He was single and a Private in the 1st/4th Bn. of the Gordon Highlanders when he was killed in action near Cambrai, France, on the 21st November 1917, when he was 19 years of age. He is buried at the Orival Wood Cemetery, Flesquieres, which is a village situated some five kilometres from Cambrai.

Flesquieres was attacked by the 51st (Highland) Division, with tanks, on the 20th November 1917, in the battle of Cambrai, but held for a time by a German officer with a few men; it was captured on the 21st which is the day Malcolm McGregor lost his life. The Bois d'Orival is a small wood on the road from Flesquieres to Fontaine-Notre Dame, cleared by the 2nd

236

Grenadier Guards on the 27th September 1918. The Cemetery was begun in November 1917, during the Battle of Cambrai and used again in September-October 1918. There are now nearly 300 casualties of the 1914-18 war commemorated in this site.

William Henry Bond (1898 – 1918) – son of Joseph John Bond and **Janet Pride Gray (1863 – 1934)** and 6 x great-grandson of James Pride and Helen Selkirk. He was single and a Lance Corporal in the Australian Infantry, A.I.F., and already a holder of a Military Medal awarded in March 1917, when he was killed in action on the 6th April 1918 on the Somme Battlefield, France, aged 20 years. He is commemorated at the Villers-Bretonneux Memorial at the Somme, France, details as referred to previously. See also Chapter 18.

Robert Goldie (1895 – 1918) – son of **William Goldie (1867 – 1907)** and Helen Robertson and 5 x great-grandson of James Pride and Helen Selkirk. He was single and a Gunner in "D" Bty. 58th Bde. of the Royal Field Artillery when he was killed in action in France on 23rd August 1918. He is buried at the Hersin Communal Cemetery Extension which is situated about five kilometres south of the village of Bethune, Pas de Calais, France.

The extension to Hersin Communal Cemetery was begun by French troops, who made over 100 burials, and was taken over by Commonwealth troops and field ambulances in March 1916. It was used until October 1918. The extension contains 224 Commonwealth burials of the First World War and was designed by Sir Edwin Lutyens.

Thomas Denholm Pryde (1882 – 1918) – son of **William Pryde (1841 – 1984)** and Jane Fairholm and 4 x great-grandson of James Pride and Helen Selkirk. He was a 2nd Corporal in the 175th Tunnelling Company of the Royal Engineers when he was killed during the Battle of Le Cateau, France, on 14th October 1918 aged 36 years. He was married to Elizabeth Smith and it seems he left three surviving young children. He is buried at Honnechy British Cemetery.

Honnechy is a village in the Department of the Nord, eight kilometres south-west of Le Cateau. Honnechy British Cemetery is north-east of the village, on the north-west side of the road to Reumont. Honnechy was part of the battlefield of Le Cateau in August 1914, and from that time it remained in German hands until the 9th October 1918, when the 25th Division and the 6th Cavalry Brigade captured it. It had been a German Hospital centre, and from its capture until the end of October it was a British Field Ambulance centre. The village was inhabited by civilians during the whole of the War.

The cemetery stands on the site of a German Cemetery begun in the Battle of Cambrai 1917 and used by German troops and then by the British until the 24th October 1918. The 300 German graves were removed to another burial ground,

238

leaving 44 British graves. The cemetery was re-made in 1922 and 1923 by the concentration of British graves almost entirely from German Cemeteries. There are now over 450 war casualties commemorated in this site.

World War 2 Fatalities

Tragically, the first three entries in this section are brothers, being 5 x great-grandsons of James Pride and Helen Selkirk. They were three of the four sons of the Revd. **John Marshall Pryde, B.D. (1872 – 1954)** and Jane Janet Symington. The Revd. John M. Pryde had served in the Great War, being Chaplain to the 4th Royal Scots in Ireland and he also served as Chaplain to the Forces at Salonika, Greece.

William Symington Pryde (1917 – 1939), pictured – he was

single and a Flying Officer (Pilot) in the Royal Air Force when he lost his life aged 22 years on 24th September 1939. It is believed his aircraft crashed near Newton, Sleaford, Lincolnshire. He is commemorated on the Memorial at Anstruther New Cemetery, Fife, as are his two brothers shown as follows.

George Archibald Marshall Pryde, D.F.C., (1910 - 1940), pictured. He was a Squadron Leader in the Royal Air Force,

aged 30 years, when he lost his life over the sea off Bizerta, Tunisia, on 18th June 1940. He was married to Honor Brown. His name is additionally commemorated on the Runnymede Memorial, near Windsor, England. See also Chapter 18.

The Air Forces Memorial at Runnymede commemorates by name over 20,000 airmen who were lost in the Second World War during operations from bases in the United Kingdom and North and Western Europe, and who have no known graves.

The memorial was designed by Sir Edward Maufe with sculpture by Vernon Hill. The engraved glass and painted ceilings were designed by John Hutton and the poem engraved on the gallery window was written by Paul H Scott. The Memorial was unveiled by The Queen on 17th October 1953.

David Douglas Pryde, D.F.C., (1918 – 1942), pictured. He was

single and a Squadron Leader with the Royal Air Force when he was reported missing on operations on 9th June 1942, aged 24 years. Poignantly the following report appears in The Scotsman newspaper on 20th June 1942:-

"R.A.F. OFFICER CASUALTIES

OFFICIAL intimation has been received that Squadron-Leader David Pryde, D.F.C., son of the Rev. J. Marshall Pryde and Mrs Pryde of Kilrenny, Fife, is reported missing on operations. He was reported missing on a previous occasion, but made a safe return, and hopes are entertained of the same good fortune. He received the D.F.C. for bravery in action in June 1940. Mr and Mrs Pryde have lost two sons in the war, Flying-Officer William Pryde and Squadron-Leader George Pryde, D.F.C. A fourth Son, Flying-Officer Jack Pryde, is at present serving in Central Africa."

Like his brother George he is also commemorated on the Runnymede Memorial in Windsor. See also Chapter 18.

In addition, the brothers are remembered on the following panel, see Fig. 12, in Kilrenny Church, Fife, where their father served as Minister.

Fig. No. 12 - Memorial Panel at Kilrenny Church, Fife.

Peter Glen (1914 – 1941) – son of **William McIntosh Glen (1890 – 1951)** and Christine Liddle Tullis and 7 x great-grandson of James Pride and Helen Selkirk. He was an Aircraftman 2nd Class in the Royal Air Force Volunteer Reserve when he was killed in Fylde, Lancashire on 18th January 1941, aged 26 years. He was married to Marian Hamilton Cranston and is buried at Portobello Cemetery, Edinburgh.

William Mitchell (1906 – 1941), pictured – son of Alexander  McGregor Mitchell and **Isabella Storey Laurie (1883 – 1965)** and 5 x great-grandson of James Pride and Helen Selkirk. He was a Lieutenant in the Royal Naval Reserve and served aboard the Armed Merchant Cruiser H.M.S Rajputana. He died on 13th April 1941, aged 34 years when this ship was attacked by the German U-boat U-108 in the North Atlantic Ocean.

His name is commemorated on the Liverpool Naval Memorial which is situated on the Pier Head at Liverpool, Lancashire. The Liverpool Naval Memorial commemorates 1,400 officers and men of the Merchant Navy, who died on active service aboard more than 120 ships, and who have no grave but the sea. The memorial was designed by C. Blythin and S.H. Smith and was unveiled by the Admiral of the Fleet, The Viscount Cunningham of Hyndhope, K.T., G.C.B., O.M., D.S.O., on the 12th November 1952.

Donald Joseph Gedye (1917 – 1942) – son of Charles Gedye and **Anne Pryde (1891 – 1981**) and 6 x great-grandson of James Pride and Helen Selkirk. He enlisted on the 24th April 1941 as a Private in the 132nd Illinois Volunteer Infantry Regiment which was inducted into federal service on 5th March 1941. The regiment arrived in the Guadalcanal area in the South Western Pacific on 8th December 1942 where it engaged in fierce fighting to capture Japanese positions. Donald Gedye was killed in action here on 3rd January 1943 aged 24 years. His body was recovered and he is buried in Peru City Cemetery, Peru, Illinois. He was single and in June 1948 his mother Mrs. Ann Gedye née Pryde applied for a Headstone for a Military Veteran[30] and this was granted.

Thomas Hamill (circa 1914 – 1942), pictured – son of Thomas

Hamill and **Mary Jane Pryde (1877 – 1953)** and 5 x great-grandson of James Pride and Helen Selkirk. He was single and a Private in the 2nd Bn. of the Royals Scots and by 1942 he was a prisoner of war of the Japanese, held aboard the *Lisbon Maru* ship in Hong Kong harbour which was also being used as a troop transport. The ship was not marked as a prisoner of war ship and was sunk

---

[30] On 3rd March, 1873, U.S. Congress granted burial rights in national military cemeteries to all honourably discharged veterans of the Civil War (17 Stat. 605). An act of Congress on 3rd February, 1879 (20 Stat. 281), extended the privilege of government-provided gravestones to soldiers buried in private cemeteries. Over time, the government expanded burial honours and benefits available to all honourably discharged U.S. soldiers.

by the American submarine *Grouper* on 1ˢᵗ October 1942. Some 700 Japanese soldiers were able to leave the ship before it sank but the prisoners, who had been captured and incarcerated some nine months earlier, were trapped in the holds as the hatches had been battened down by the Japanese soldiers as they left. Thomas Hamill lost his life aged 28 years. He is commemorated on the Sai Wan Memorial, Hong Kong, China.

The Sai Wan Memorial forms the entrance to Sai Wan War Cemetery and bears the names of more than 2,000 Commonwealth servicemen who died in the Battle of Hong Kong, or subsequently in captivity, who have no known grave. Both the cemetery and memorial were designed by Colin St Clair Oakes. The memorial was unveiled by Sir Alexander Grantham, the Governor of Hong Kong, on the 20ᵗʰ February 1955.

Ronald Pryde Hordon (1920 – 1943) – son of John William Hordon and **Zillah Pryde (1900 – 1932)** and 6 x great-grandson of James Pride and Helen Selkirk. He was a Sergeant (Pilot) in 44 Sqdn. of the Royal Air Force Volunteer Reserve when he was killed in action on 2ⁿᵈ February 1943 aged 23 years. He is buried at Eindhoven (Woensel) General Cemetery, Noord-Brabant, Netherlands. There are nearly 700 war casualties commemorated on this site, with almost four-fifths of the men buried here belonging to the air forces, who lost theirlives in raids over this part of Holland or when returning from Germany, between 1941 and 1944.

Richard Wallace Reid (1924 – 1945) – son of James Richard Reid and **Jane Stonestreet Pryde (1898 – 1988)** and 7 x great-grandson of James Pride and Helen Selkirk. He was a Sergeant (Flight Engineer) in 622 Sqdn. of the Royal Air Force Volunteer Reserve and died on 20th April 1945 when he was 21 years of age. He is buried at Durnbach War Cemetery, which is located in the south west of Germany, some 45 kilometres south of Munich.

The great majority of those buried there are airmen shot down over Bavaria, Wurtemberg, Austria, Hessen and Thuringia, brought from their scattered graves by the Army Graves Service. The remainder are men who were killed while escaping from prisoner-of-war camps in the same areas, or who died towards the end of the War on forced marches from the camps to more remote areas. Durnbach War Cemetery contains 2,934 Commonwealth burials of the Second World War, 93 of which are unidentified.

ADDENDUM FEBRUARY 2018

Robert Flockhart Vickers (c 1892 – 1917) – son of **William Vickers (1868 – 1938)** and Marion Moffat Black and 6 x great grandson of James Pride and Helen Selkirk. He was a Private in the 7th Bn. Royal Scots Fusiliers and died aged 25 years of wounds received on 6th May 1917 whilst serving in France. He is buried at St. Sever Cemetery Extension, Rouen. [See page 191, Robert's father William lost his own father who was executed in 1884 and then his eldest son was killed in action].

VIETNAM WAR

 **William Elwood Hannings (1948 – 1968)**, pictured – son of Ellwood Hannings and **Helen Davie Rankine Pryde (1922 – 1990)** and 7 x great-grandson of James Pride and Helen Selkirk. He was single and serving as a Lance Corporal in the 1st Bn. of the United States 4th Marine Corps when he was killed in action in Quang Tri, South Vietnam, on 6th June 1968, aged 19 years. A report in the Philadelphia Inquirer newspaper dated 15th June 1968 states:-

"Marine Lance Cpl. William E. Hannings, 19, son of Mr. and Mrs. Elwood Hannings Jr., of 608 Derstine ave., Lansdale.

Cpl. Hannings, who was due to come home next month, was killed June 6 when the helicopter he was in was shot down. He enlisted in December, 1966, and had been in Vietnam since

June 12, 1967. He led a Marine mortar team. His last letter stated he was going on a 10-day mission beginning June 2 in the Khe Sanh area. "Say a prayer for me, Mom," he wrote."

His body was recovered and he is buried at Greenlawn Cemetery, Lansdale, Montgomery County, Pennsylvania, USA. His name is commemorated on the Vietnam Veterans Memorial which is a national memorial in Washington, D.C. It honours U.S. service members of the armed forces who fought in the Vietnam War, service members who died in service in Vietnam/South East Asia, and those service members who were unaccounted for (Missing In Action) during the War.

WE WILL REMEMBER THEM

CHAPTER 18

ACHIEVEMENTS AND AWARDS

As can be seen from the previous chapters just surviving and bringing up a family without even adding in the rigours of emigration, accidents and conflict was a significant achievement on its own for many of our family. However some of the family left behind more of a footprint than is usual and below is a celebration of just a few of those achievements and awards.

David Pryde (1835 – 1910) – son of **John Pryde (1811 – 1864)** and Helen Lawson and 3 x great-grandson of James Pride and Helen Selkirk. His father was a coal miner then colliery contractor as outlined in Chapter 6. When David Pryde married Margaret Rutherford in Dalkeith, Midlothian, in 1861 his occupation was shown as a Colliery Clerk. He obviously progressed in his career as from 1875 to 1888 he was employed by the Broughton Coal Co., in the Brymbo and Wrexham area of North Wales and he directed the sinking of Gatewen Pit, see Fig. 13. After it opened in 1877 he stayed on as the manager there under the auspices of the Broughton and Plas Power Coal Co. There are numerous newspaper reports showing his involvement in the many aspects of the mine and these demonstrate he was well-regarded as being a fair and knowledgeable manager.

Fig. 13 – Gatewen Colliery, date unknown[31]

The high esteem in which he was held is evidenced in the following extract from the Wrexham Advertiser newspaper dated 20th October 1888 which states:-

"PRESENTATION TO MR. D PRYDE, MANAGER OF GATEWEN COLLIERY

On Friday evening, a deputation of workmen, representing the testimonial committee at Gatewen Colliery, waited upon Mr. D. Pryde, at Broughton Hall, for the purpose of presenting him with a testimonial from the officials and workmen at the colliery, and other friends, on resigning his appointment as colliery manager.

This position Mr. Pryde had held for upwards of 12 years, during which period he had gained the good will and respect

---

[31] Reproduced by kind permission of Graham Lloyd of northwalesminers.com

of the workmen under him, who were most anxious that the presentation should in every way be commensurate with the sterling qualities he displayed in the successful management of this important colliery. Subscriptions were readily given by the workmen, who took the matter up most spontaneously, and a considerable amount was realised. The testimonial took the form of a purse of gold, and an illuminated address, executed by Mr. H Boothey, Wrexham, expressing the regret the workmen felt at his (Mr. Pryde's) departure from the colliery. The presentation was made in suitable terms by Mr. T. Jones, one of the workmen, and Mr. Pryde thanked the men for their good wishes, and trusted that the same good feeling which had existed at the colliery between himself and the workmen would continue for a long time, and the deputation then withdrew."

After leaving the management of Gatewen Colliery David Pryde and his family moved to the Manchester area where he became a leather merchant and he died there in 1910, aged 74 years, some six years after the death of his wife. Gatewen Colliery closed in 1932.

John Pryde (1862 – 1932) eldest son of the above **David Pryde (1835 – 1910)** and Margaret Rutherford and 4 x great-grandson of James Pride and Helen Selkirk. He is shown on the 1881 census living with his parents at Broughton Hall, near Wrexham, and his occupation is given as Mining Engineer and Surveyor, even though he was aged only 19 years of age at the time. John Pryde married Janet Rutherford Liddle in 1886 at Cambuslang, Lanarkshire, Scotland. He worked on various engineering projects including being engaged in making surveys of Brymbo Ironworks and Collieries and the Parliamentary Plans and Sections for the Wrexham, Mold and Connah's Quay Railway Extensions and Dock Bill 1881-1882. From 1883 to 1887 he worked on the same railway, engaging in the doubling of the line and construction of a branch therefrom. However, one of his more notable achievements was that from November 1887 to November 1891 he was the Engineer on the No. 8 section of the Manchester Ship Canal which included the Barton Lock, Barton Aqueduct and Barton Swing Bridge.

The Barton Swing Aqueduct, see Fig. 14, is a moveable navigable aqueduct in Barton-upon-Irwell in Greater Manchester, Lancashire, England. It carries the Bridgewater Canal across the Manchester Ship Canal. The swinging action allows large vessels using the ship canal to pass underneath and for smaller narrowboats to cross over the top. The aqueduct, the first and only swing aqueduct in the world is now a Grade II* (Grade 2 starred) Listed Building.

After working on many other similar feats of engineering, including bridges, tunnels, and viaducts, mostly to do with the expansion of the railways, John Pryde became a Full Member of the Institution of Civil Engineers in 1902. At that time he was living in Barnet, London. He died in 1932 aged 70 years, some 17 years after his wife.

Fig. 14 – The Barton Swing Aqueduct in the closed position, showing the Bridgewater Canal crossing over the ship canal. The Barton Road Swing Bridge is on the right.[32]

In an interesting twist **David Barnes Pryde (1889 – 1923)** – son of the above **John Pryde (1862 – 1932)** and Janet Rutherford Liddle and 5 x great-grandson of James Pride and Helen Selkirk also became an Associate Member of the Institution of Civil Engineers albeit under unusual circumstances.

Like his father he worked on railway projects, including working for the Great Western Railway installing new railway lines in South Wales. However, his application to become a member of the Institution was made whilst he was prisoner-of-war in Güstrow, Germany. He had joined the 14th County of London Regiment (the London Scottish) on 15th September 1914 and was captured in November 1914. From January 1915

---

[32] Author of the photo is RuthAS via Wikipedia Commons

he was placed in charge of the English Post in Güstrow, Germany. He was accepted as an Associate Member of the Institute of Civil Engineers on 3rd December 1918.

William Henry Bond (1898 – 1918), son of Joseph John Bond and **Janet Pride Gray (1863 – 1934)** and 6 x great-grandson of James Pride and Helen Selkirk. William Bond enlisted in the 45th Bn. of the Australian Imperial Force at Holdsworthy, New South Wales, Australia, on the 19th August 1915. He was awarded the Military Medal (M.M.), see Fig. 15, whilst on active service in France. He was recommended for this award by Lt-Col. S.C.E. Herring, D.S.O., in a citation which read:-

"For courage and determination shown by him in an attack upon enemy strong point and trench at Gueudecourt on the morning of 21st February 1917. He acted with skill and coolness as a bomb thrower in the progress along the trench and owing to this tenacity of purpose was one of the first to reach the objective where he showed great bravery in the face of a German counter bombing attack."

The award was cited in the London Gazette dated 24th April 1917 and also in the Commonwealth of Australia Gazette dated 21st August 1917.

Lance Corporal Bond was injured twice during his war service and just four months after rejoining his regiment for the second time he was killed in France on 6th April 1918. See also Chapter 17.

Fig. 15 – Military Medal[33]

His parents chose to have his Military Medal awarded to them privately, saying that as *"...as he was a boy that was very reserved in life and would never allow himself to be praised or made much of we would prefer to have his medal presented privately..."*. In accordance with these wishes the Military medal was forwarded to his father on 12th August 1918 and the accompanying letter stated the following [partial transcription]:-

---

[33] Author of the photo is PalawanOz via Wikipedia.

"Dear Sir

It is with feelings of admiration at the gallantry of a brave Australian soldier who nobly laid down his life in the service of our King and Country, that I am directed by the Honourable The Minister to forward to you, as next of kin of the late No. 3689 W.H. Bond, M.M., 45th Battalion, Australian Imperial Force, the Military Medal which His Majesty the King has been graciously pleased to award to that gallant soldier for conspicuous bravery and devotion to duty while serving with the Australian Imperial Expeditionary Force.

I also ask you to accept his deep personal sympathy in the loss which, not only you, but the Australian Army has sustained by the death of Lance Corporal Bond, whose magnificent conduct on the field of battle has helped to earn for our Australian soldiers a fame which will endure as long as memory lasts."[34]

 Robert Pryde (1849 – 1930), pictured - son of **John Pryde (1811 – 1864)** and Helen Lawson and 3 x great-grandson of James Pride and Helen Selkirk. Robert Pryde is shown on the 1881 census as a 24 year old soldier in the Royal Horse Artillery stationed at Aldershot. He had joined the Army in 1870 as his parents wanted him to become a Church Minister. After a varied early military career in June 1886 he was appointed Battery Sergeant Major. Robert served with his

---

[34] NAA: B2455 Bond WH

regiment in India where he was to remain for the rest of his life, although he did make trips back to Britain to see his family.

After his service with the army he joined the Bombay Police Force. He was awarded the King's Police Medal and the citation in the London Gazette dated 8th January 1915 cites the award made to *"Robert Pryde, Inspector of the mounted branch of the Kathiawar Agency Police, Bombay Police"*.

The King's Police Medal, see Fig. 16, was introduced in 1909 by His Majesty King Edward VII to reward "courage and devotion to duty in the Police & Fire Services of the UK and Overseas Dominions". Robert died in 1930 and was buried in Bangalore, India. See also Chapter 6.

Fig. 16 – King's Police Medal

Arthur Walter Pryde (1896 – 1986), pictured – son of **Robert**

Pryde (1849 – 1930), as reported in the preceding entry, and Margaret Mabel Milner Prager and 4 x great-grandson of James Pride and Helen Selkirk. He became an Officer of the Most Excellent Order of the British Empire (Civil) (O.B.E.), see Fig. 17, on 2ⁿᵈ January 1939 when he was cited in the Edinburgh Gazette dated 6ᵗʰ January 1939 as "Arthur Walter Pryde Esq., Indian Police, Labour Officer for the City of Bombay and Bombay Suburban District, Bombay".

Fig. 17 – O.B.E.

On 12ᵗʰ June 1947 Arthur Walter Pryde, O.B.E., Deputy Inspector-General of Police, Special Duty, Karachi, Sind was awarded the King's Police and Fire Service Medal for

Distinguished Service, the same award his father had received some 30 or so years before.

On 1st January 1948 it was reported in the London Gazette that the O.B.E. held by Arthur Walter Pryde had been promoted to a Commander of the Most Excellent Order of the British Empire, (C.B.E.) with the citation listing "Arthur Walter Pryde, O.B.E., Indian Police, Inspector-General of Police, Sind". See also Fig. 18.

Arthur Walter Pryde retired from the above role in 1951 and left India in 1954. On his return to Britain he worked at the Ministry of Supply and then the Treasury where he was Head of Security for staff working at No. 10 Downing Street, the official residence of the British Prime Minister. In later life he went to Australia to join his daughters and he died in the Templestowe area of Melbourne in 1986 aged 89 years. See also Chapter 6.

Fig. 18 – Arthur Walter Pryde (far left) being presented with an award in India (specific date and award unknown but likely pre-1947)

George Archibald Marshall Pryde (1910 - 1940) – family details and photo as shown in the previous chapter. He was awarded a Distinguished Flying Cross (D.F.C.), see Fig. 19, posthumously. A D.F.C. was awarded for "an act or acts of valour, courage or devotion to duty whilst flying in active operations against the enemy". Reports recount that on 18th June 1940 Squadron Leader Pryde was in control of a Blenheim aircraft making for North Africa accompanied by five Hurricane aircraft. A number of the Hurricanes turned back due to various reasons. As they neared the African coast a very red light was seen to come from Squadron Leader Pryde's Blenheim aeroplane. Shortly afterwards it crashed into the sea. The announcement of his award appeared in the London Gazette dated 9th July 1940.

Fig. 19 – D.F.C.

His brother **David Douglas Pryde (1918 – 1942)** – family details and photo as shown in the previous chapter, was also awarded a Distinguished Flying Cross on the 12th June 1940. This was announced in the London Gazette and the citation stated:-

"On 20th May 1940, this officer was detailed for a collaboration operation involving an attack on the communication centre at Hannapes. Despite difficult conditions, he succeeded in identifying the target from a very low altitude. Although his aircraft was hit heavily, Flying Officer Pryde climbed to 3,000 feet and executed a successful bombing attack. His aircraft subsequently caught fire, but he continued flying and when height could no longer be maintained, the entire crew landed by parachute. Flying Officer Pryde has completed sixteen operational flights during six months of war flying and has displayed considerable courage and determination."

On 9th June 1942 Sqdn. Leader David Douglas Pryde, D.F.C., was on a night flight in order to carry out an anti-submarine patrol. At 1230hrs the aeroplane was intercepted by enemy fighters about 30 miles southwest of Brest and shot down. Sqdn. Leader Pryde and at least two others were killed in action.

Duncan McLean Pryde (1937 – 1997), pictured - son of

 **William Darnley Pryde (1909 – 1980)** and Georgina McLean and 7 x great-grandson of James Pride and Helen Selkirk. Duncan McLean Pryde had a troubled upbringing and he and his siblings were brought up in various institutions in Scotland. He joined the Merchant Navy aged 15 years. When he was 18 years old he saw an advertisement placed in the Glasgow Sunday Post in 1955 which read *"Single, ambitious, self-reliant young man required, must be prepared to live in isolation."* He was successful in his application for the post and this led Duncan to travel to Canada and try his hand at fur trading.

He spent three years in Cree country in Northern Manitoba and Ontario, during which time he learned the Cree language. The Indians taught the young Scot how to trap and after three years he asked for a transfer to the Arctic.

Whilst there he learned more and more of the Eskimo way of life and formed life-long friendships, eventually being treated by the Eskimo as one of their own. He fathered several children with Eskimo women due to the very tolerant sexual customs prevailing at that time within their community.

He wrote a book entitled 'Nunaga – Ten Years of Eskimo Life', about his life with the Eskimo, and this was published in 1971. This led to his appearance on various television programmes. After becoming the first Inuit Member of Parliament in the late 1960s he resigned in 1975 when he moved to Alaska to take up the chair of Eskimo studies in Inupiat University of the Arctic, where he was commissioned to compile an Eskimo dictionary.

He later moved back to Britain and after the death of his first wife, he remarried and set up home on the Isle of Wight where he bought a newsagent's shop. He was still working on the compilation of the Inuit dictionary when he died in 1997 aged 60 years. An appreciation of his life stated: - *"Duncan Pryde was a trapper, explorer, linguistic scholar, and politician. He is one of the most extraordinary Scots to have ventured to remote Canada. "*

Herbert Marshall Pryde (1906 – 1983), pictured – son of **John Marshall Pryde (1877 – 1925)** and Florence Louise Sargent

and 5 x great-grandson of James Pride and Helen Selkirk. Master-at-Arms Herbert Marshall Pryde was awarded the Distinguished Service Medal, (D.S.M.), see Fig. 20. The D.S.M. was a military decoration awarded to personnel of the Royal Navy and members of other services for bravery and resourcefulness on active service at sea. Herbert Marshall Pryde was given his award for services on H.M. Aircraft Carrier *Indomitable* during the Malta Relief Operation in 1942. This was cited in a supplement to the London Gazette dated 10th November 1942 for *"bravery and dauntless resolution .... when an important Convoy was fought through to Malta in the face of relentless attacks by day and night from enemy submarines, aircraft and service forces."*

Fig. 20 – Distinguished Service Medal

Herbert Marshall Pryde died in 1983 aged 77 years, having never married.

James Pryde (1916 – 1982) – son of **James Smith Pryde (1886 – 1956)** and Jane Forbes Sneddon Black and 5 x great-grandson of James Pride and Helen Selkirk. He was awarded the Oak Leaf Award, see Fig. 21, after being mentioned in despatches. This was cited as follows in the London Gazette dated 31st January 1947 which stated:-

"The King has been graciously pleased to give orders for the publication of the name of the following personnel who have been mentioned in despatches: - 990458 W/O Pryde, James, R.A.F.V.R."

Fig. 21 – Bronze Oak Leaf Award

An abridged extract from Dalkeith Advertiser dated 27th February 1947 states:-

"NEWTONGRANGE MAN'S OAK LEAF AWARD

Shot down over France in a blazing aircraft which broke in half: the rear-gunner seriously injured, and himself badly burned, was what happened to Warrant Officer Jas. Pryde during the second year of the war.

But that wasn't all. James, whose father and mother live at 49 Rear [sic] Park, Newtongrange, was captured by the enemy and taken to the notorious Luft. III prison for British "terror fliegers" where 50 airmen were shot whilst attempting to escape in 1944.

There he joined the camp escape committee and by forging passports assisted the successful escape of an English wing-commander, whom he was to meet afterwards in London.

Educated at Newtongrange, and a painter and sign writer before the war, James was employed with the Lothian Coal Company. In 1941 he joined the RAF as a wireless operator,

265

and completed 27 raids over enemy and enemy-held territory
before being shot down. He was a prisoner of war for 4 years."

The escape attempt referred to above was later immortalised in the films The Wooden Horse (1953) and the better known The Great Escape (1963).

After the war James Pryde married Margaret Elizabeth Mack and he died in 1982 aged 65 years.

James Pryde (1929 – 2009), pictured – 7 x great-grandson of James Pryde and Helen Selkirk. Pipe Major James (Jimmy)  Pryde served with the Royal Scots Greys and was the senior Pipe Major of the Scottish Regiments. He became a Member of the Most Excellent Order of the British Empire (M.B.E.), see Fig. 22, in the New Year Honours List 1972 as listed in the London Gazette. He performed in the Edinburgh Military Tattoo every year from 1948 until he retired from the Army in 1971. That year, he arranged and recorded a version of Amazing Grace with the Royal Scots Dragoon Guards. This became a surprise hit, reaching the top five in the pop charts. He passed away in Melrose, Scotland, in 2009 aged 79 years.

Fig. 22 – M.B.E.

James McQueen (Living) – son of James McQueen and **Janet Brown Pryde (1908 – 1978)** and 5 x great-grandson of James Pride and Helen Selkirk. He was awarded the British Empire Medal (Civil Division) (B.E.M.), see Fig. 23, at the start of 1990. The B.E.M. is awarded for meritorious civil or military service worthy of recognition by the Crown. This award was reported in the London Gazette in December 1989 when he is cited as "James McQueen, Sgt, Royal Parks Constabulary, Scottish Office".

Fig. 23 – B.E.M.

Robert Pryde (Living) – son of **William Hunter Pryde (1893 –
1970)** and Mary Shearer Aitchison and 6 x great-grandson of
James Pride and Helen Selkirk. He became a Member of the
Most Excellent Order of the British Empire (Civil) (M.B.E.) in
the New Year Honours List of 2005. This award was reported
in the London Gazette dated 31st December 2004 when he is
cited as "Robert Pryde. For services to the Scottish Ambulance
Service, Kinross, Perthshire".

Sir Christopher Andrew Hoy (Living), pictured – son of **David** **Austen Hoy (Living)** and Carol Jane Morrison Reid (Living) and 7 x great-grandson of James Pride and Helen Selkirk. He is a British former track cyclist who has represented Great Britain at the Olympics and World Championships and Scotland at the Commonwealth Games.

Amongst his many achievements he is an eleven-time world champion, six-time Olympic champion and a winner of a total of seven Olympic Games medals comprising of six gold medals and one silver medal. When he won two gold medals at the London 2012 Olympics he became the most successful British Olympian of all time in terms of gold medals.

He became a Member of the Most Excellent Order of the British Empire (Civil) (M.B.E) in the New Year Honours List of 2005. This award was reported in the London Gazette dated 31st December 2004 when he is cited as "Christopher Hoy. For services to cycling".

He was awarded a Knight Bachelor, see Fig. 24, in the New Year Honours List in 2009 for services to sport. This was reported in the London Gazette dated 30th December 2008 when he is cited as "Christopher Andrew HOY, M.B.E., Cyclist. For Services to Sport."

Concurrently his mother Carol Hoy also received an M.B.E. for her work on sleep-related illness. Carol Hoy and Chris Hoy became the first mother and son to be recognised for separate achievements on the same list.

Fig. 24 – Insignia of a Knight Bachelor

In September 2012 Sir Chris Hoy was awarded the Freedom of the city of Edinburgh.

It is suitably fitting this chapter ends here; as it is pleasing that a 7 x great-grandson of a man who was in bondage during all his lifetime, not only becomes titled but obtained what his 7 x great-grandfather James Pride never did – freedom, something which we now mostly take for granted.

CHAPTER 19

RESEARCH AND DNA

When I speak about my research to someone who does not research their own family history I am often asked "How do you do that?" Usually that question is qualified by adding that they would love to do "that" themselves.

When I started my research over 20 years ago one had to visit local Record Offices and trawl through the records they had available there, mostly using microfiche readers – often the records were not indexed so searches could be time-consuming. If the records that you wanted to search were not held in the local Record Office then you had to travel to the area which held those records or pay a professional researcher to do it for you.

Similar to many other amateur genealogists I am grateful for the like-minded people who were prepared to look at out-of-area records on my behalf and I have often reciprocated in kind, making good friends along the way. In addition, the Church of Jesus Christ of Latter-day Saints holds many records which they freely shared as long as you were able to visit one of their local history centres. Again, I have always been given much assistance and a warm welcome whenever I have availed myself of their facilities.

As time has progressed the availability of computers, especially in our own homes, has changed the manner of carrying out family history research in many respects, with numerous indexed records being available to search on-line. One example of this is the Familysearch.org website which gives access to the records compiled by the Church of Jesus Christ of Latter-day Saints, which were previously only accessible to those in the UK as described in the previous page. These new indexed records, online access to which is increasing all the time, together with newspapers extracts, information about different localities and not least the ease with which the researcher can store and produce different formats of results achieved has totally transformed genealogical research in recent years.

In addition to the above it is now possible to make contact with other researchers around the world, by the use of e-mail. In 1996 and 1997 I sent out hundreds of letters to recipients in the UK and abroad who were listed as having the Pryde surname but that all seems very antiquated now.

Many researchers now make their tree outlines and research freely available on-line for other researchers to use. Whilst this can be invaluable I have always found it wise to use these as a guide only, and to confirm the accuracy of the information presented using official records.

Another big step forward in genealogical research has come about with the opportunity of using DNA tests and this has proved to be the case with my own Pryde research.

Male DNA is passed through the paternal line from father to son and son to grandson, etc. On its most basic level female DNA is passed from mother to daughter, and daughter to granddaughter etc. Even though a son inherits his mother's DNA he cannot pass it on to his own children. As the maternal surname is usually changed in each generation, this can make it more complicated to use maternal DNA testing in our genealogical research.

Put simply, a DNA test allows determination of a person's genetic profile by observing scientifically established DNA "locations" in the test. Haplotype is the scientific name for this type of profile and each person will belong to a certain haplogroup. This will indicate which area of the world our ancient ancestors came from.

In some cases, as will be illustrated, because of the unavailability of records, it is only by comparison of one person's DNA results with those of another person, that we can find if there is a common ancestor, be they in recent or distant ancestry. The measurement of kinship in these instances is referred to as MRCA, or the Most Recent Common Ancestor. It should be borne in mind that, especially when using DNA to investigate paternal ancestry, there is always the possibility of a "cuckoo in the nest" i.e. a claimed father not being the biological father of child somewhere along the line. Therefore a control of at least one other DNA result for comparison is always advisable.

By the time DNA testing for genealogical purposes became
 generally affordable and available my father
had passed away but my paternal uncle
Vincent Harold Pryde (1922 – 2013),
pictured, was delighted to provide a DNA
sample and to know his DNA was being used
in this way, as he had a great interest in and
had shown much support for my research. The results showed
this line of Prydes belongs to Paternal Haplogroup R1b, known
as The Artisans, as can be seen in Fig. 25.

About 70% of individuals currently residing in southern
England are members of the Artisans and they can also be
found in high rates in the modern day populations of Spain,
Portugal, France, Wales, Ireland – and Scotland.

As interesting as it was to find out the above origins of our
ancient ancestors it was more exciting to be able to utilise the
results in other ways. To date it has not been possible to
identify the likely parents of our earliest known Pride
ancestor, James Pride who married Helen Selkirk, nor even to
find out where in Scotland this line of Prydes originated before
him. The county of Fife holds the highest demographic profile
of Prydes in Scotland so I always considered it a possibility that
"our" line of East and then Mid Lothian Prydes may have come
from Fife, in that at some time an ancestor crossed the Firth
of Forth from Fife to Midlothian for work, or indeed that they
had been moved from one area to another by the masters
who owned them.

PATERNAL LINEAGE TEST RESULTS FOR PRYDE

Your DNA test results show that you belong to haplogroup *R1b*, The Artisans.

PATERNAL
HAPLOGROUP

R1b
THE ARTISANS

This map shows the likely migration pathways of your ancient ancestors, The Artisans (haplogroup *R1b*). Your ancestors may have been responsible for the first cave paintings, and probably lived in present day England, France, Spain or Portugal. To use your test results to build your family tree, visit dna.ancestry.com and learn about other participants with genetic profiles similar to your own.

ancestry.com | DNA

YOUR HAPLOTYPE

Location	19a	19b	385a	385b	388	389i	389ii	390	391	392	393	426	438	439	447	448
Value	14	-	11	14	12	13	29	24	10	13	13	12	12	11	14	25	19
Location	449	454	455	458	460	461	463	464a	464b	464c	464d	Y-GATA-H4	YCAIIa	YCAIIb	Y-GGAAT-1B07
Value	30	11	11	18	11	12	24	14	15	17	-	19	23	22

Fig. 25 - Pryde DNA

I have been in contact with another long-time Pryde researcher, **Ronald Andrew Pryde (Living)**,  pictured, of Fife, Scotland, for a good number of years, and we often work together on our research. Despite our best efforts we have been unable to find out if his line of Prydes, which goes back to Andrew Pride born circa 1642, at Leuchars, Fife, and his wife Margaret Henderson, had any kinship connection to my line of Prydes i.e. to James Pride and Helen Selkirk. As soon as the DNA result for my line of Prydes was available Ron also took a DNA test. When the two results were compared it showed we had matching haplogroups with a MRCA of 22 – so we were cousins – and it was more likely that the line of Prydes originated in Fife than the other way around. With the link being around 22 generations back it would be practically impossible to find out our common ancestor using normal research methods, but thanks to DNA testing we now know we are kin.

The DNA results have also proved to be of great help with other more recent queries within the family as will be shown by the following examples.

 A DNA test was taken by **David Allen Pryde (Living)**, pictured, of Illinois, USA. David is the son of **Robert John Pryde (1933 – 2004)** and Nancy Darlene McIlvenna and a 7 x great-grandson of James Pride and Helen Selkirk. David is a fourth-generation

American and his great-great-grandfather **John Pryde (1849 – 1903)** was born in Newbattle, Midlothian, Scotland, where he had married Jane Taylor at Dalkeith in 1879. This was his second marriage as his first wife, Elspeth Jack, had died 10 days after giving birth to their first child, **Elspeth Johnston Pryde (1875 – 1875)**, who also died some 15 days after the death of her mother. John Pryde emigrated from Scotland to America in late 1879 and his second wife and their young son followed about a year later. He worked in the coal fields mainly around Decatur, Illinois.

I was confident the line of descent I had entered for David Allen Pryde was correct, but it was reassuring when his DNA test results confirmed the same haplogroup with a MRCA of 3 – this was the control test that was needed to confirm there had been no substitutions in the father-to-son descent on my line, and indeed that of David's line.

Another query which was solved with the use of DNA was that

concerning **Stephen Ross Pryde (Living)**, pictured, of Colorado, USA.

His Pryde ancestry was fairly straightforward back to his 3 x great-grandfather **John Pryde (circa 1782 – 1848)** who had married Helen Weddel circa 1805. This couple had eight children born between 1806 and 1822 in Newbattle, Midlothian.

Despite a great deal of in-depth research it has not yet been possible to positively identify the parents of this John Pryde but a DNA test taken by Stephen shows a haplogroup match with a MRCA of 3. This confirms that whoever are the parents of John Pryde who married Helen Weddel, they are closely related to James Pride who married Helen Selkirk, and Stephen can be confident that James Pride who was married to Helen Selkirk is a direct-line ancestor of his.

As a final example of how useful DNA can be when trying to match families, I was contacted in 2013 by a gentleman who was acting on behalf of another man who I shall call WW. WW is over 80 years of age and was born in Detroit, Michigan, USA, and he was adopted soon after birth. WW had taken a DNA test and this again came up with the same Pryde haplogroup and the MRCA was 9. This gave a strong indication that whoever was the father of WW he was likely to be a direct descendant or very closely related to James Pride and Helen Selkirk. Even though it was not possible for me to give WW exact details of his direct line he was very pleased to know the details of his Pryde line in general terms and to know his paternal ancestry originated in Scotland.

The above are only a few examples of how DNA testing has managed to solve a few queries within the orbit of family-history research, some of which, such as that for WW, would have been impossible to solve in any other way.

The accuracy and scope of the tests is improving year on year, added to which even as I have been writing this book, the format of the tests has moved from paternal Y-DNA and maternal Mt-DNA tests to autosomal tests. With autosomal tests the results are gender neutral, with results being shown

278

for both the paternal and maternal lines. It also targets more recent family history, so any matches should be more relevant.

Time will tell how useful or successful autosomal testing will be, but I have no doubt that in time to come using DNA testing for family history research will become more the norm rather than the recent innovation it is still considered to be today.

Update – as at October 2017 both myself and my brother have taken an autosomal DNA test. Results have confirmed matches for both of us on our paternal and maternal lines, and the Pryde results go back to the MRCA of James Pride who was married to Helen Selkirk. Happily this confirms the overall accuracy of the research undertaken so far, going back to James Pride and Helen Selkirk.

CHAPTER 20

PRYDE GATHERINGS / REUNIONS

In the penultimate chapter of this book it would be remiss of me not to detail events which have taken place which can be described as Pryde family gatherings or reunions.

Just as there are many persons before me who have carried out research into their Pryde ancestry and no doubt there will be many after me, I am sure that there are many others who have arranged such gatherings or reunions. Nevertheless, the first Pryde reunion of which I am aware took place at Byron, Wyoming, USA, in the mid 1960s. This mainly involved the descendants of both the Pryde and the Young families, some of whom are featured in Chapter 9.

As indicated earlier, between them the two families of John Pryde and Janet Young, and Robert Pryde and Christina Young, have over 170 known living descendants. They had settled in Byron, Wyoming in the early 1900s.

See Fig. 26 and details which follow for those who attended the reunion[35].

---

[35] I am grateful to Roselin Pryde-Kylander of Wyoming, USA, for providing the photograph and information regarding this reunion and for her long-standing and ongoing support.

**Fig. 26 – Pryde and Young reunion at
Byron, Wyoming in the 1960s**

All names listed left to right:-

Front Row:-

1. Janet Kay (1903 – 1973) later Cauble and then Hoge,
   daughter of James Kay and Margaret Young
2. **Janet Lucille Pryde (1900 – 1982)** later Bland,
   daughter of Robert Pryde and Christina Young and 4
   x great-granddaughter of James Pride and Helen
   Selkirk
3. **Margaret Louise Pryde (1903 – 1998)** later Crowder
   then Smith, daughter of Robert Pryde and Christina
   Young and 4 x great-granddaughter of James Pride
   and Helen Selkirk
4. Unknown

5. Maria Mae Abraham (1903 – 1988) later Ames, daughter of John Morgan Abraham and Catherine Young.
6. Unknown
7. Unknown

Middle Row:-

1. **Margaret Laird (1919 – 1966)** later Harkens then Cima, daughter of Edward Laird and Ruby Isabelle Pryde and 5 x great-granddaughter of James Pride and Helen Selkirk
2. **Mary Pryde (1897 – 1997)** later Henderson, daughter of Robert Pryde and Christina Young and 4 x great-granddaughter of James Pride and Helen Selkirk.
3. **Ruby Isabelle Pryde (1895 – 1971)** later Laird, then Gifford, daughter of Robert Pryde and Christina Young and 4 x great-granddaughter of James Pride and Helen Selkirk.
4. **Gladys Catherine Pryde (1893 – 1982)** later Borders, daughter of Robert Pryde and Christina Young and 4 x great-granddaughter of James Pride and Helen Selkirk.
5. Jennette (Jessie) Young Fletcher (1910 – 1993) later Johnson, daughter of Robert Shaw Fletcher and Elizabeth Young.
6. **Janet Pryde (1897 – 1974)** later Heasler then Davis, daughter of John Pryde and Janet Young and 4 x great-granddaughter of James Pride and Helen Selkirk.

7. Unknown
8. **Catherine Pryde (1891 – 1974)** later Dowlen then Neville, daughter of John Pryde and Janet Young and 4 x great-granddaughter of James Pride and Helen Selkirk.

Back Row:-

1. James John Johnson (1908 – 1999), husband of Jennette Young Fletcher
2. Fred Carrington Henderson (1895 – 1971), husband of Mary Pryde (1897 – 1997)
3. **Adam Pryde (1889 – 1964)**, son of John Pryde and Janet Young and 4 x great-grandson of James Pride and Helen Selkirk.
4. Samuel Fletcher (1903 – 1976), son of Robert Shaw Fletcher and Elizabeth Young.
5. George Morgan Abraham (1898 – 1983), son of John Morgan Abraham and Catherine Young.
6. Cordelia Marguerite Watson (1900 – 1995) later Abraham, wife of George Morgan Abraham.
7. Ernest Hoge (1905 – 1972), husband of Janet Kay.
8. Walter Gillins Stevens (1898 – 1978), widower of Catherine Grace Abraham.
9. Unknown

PRYDE AND FRIENDS REUNION 2005
NEWTONGRANGE, SCOTLAND

This took place on 15th June 2005 and was reported in the Dalkeith Advertiser on 28th July, 2005 as follows:-

"Gathering with Pryde

The Dean Tavern in Newtongrange was the venue for a gathering of Prydes recently. More than 100 people attended the event organised by Eve Pryde-Roberts from North Wales and Yvonne Taylor of Newtongrange and they also provided a buffet for all guests.

All those who attended were descended from James Pride and Helen Selkirk who were born circa 1678 and are recorded as colliers under the Laird of Prestongrange in 1748.

Later generations moved to Liberton and the extended family spread locally to Newbattle, Lasswade, Gilmerton and Newtongrange as well as other local villages and abroad.

The Dean Tavern was chosen as the venue because of its links to the mining community of Newtongrange.

Earlier in the evening many people attended an open evening at Lothian Family History Society at Lasswade High School where all were made welcome.

The Function Room of the Dean Tavern had more than 20 large family trees on display and guests were able to find their own family on these and link up with other guests.

The event was the culmination of 10 years of research undertaken by many lines of the family, and currently Eve has 13,000 entries in the tree over 16 generations.

The patriarch in attendance was 83 year old Vincent Harold Pryde who had travelled from Cleethorpes with his sons Paul from Norwich and Richard from Leicester.

A local attendee who only just missed out on the patriarch title was Thomas (Tam) Pryde of Dalkeith, formerly of Newbattle. Youngest attendees were Leona Pryde from Galashiels and Danny Stuart from Newtongrange, both aged 10 years.

Many participants brought items of interest and the star attraction was a walking stick owned by Colin Marshall Pryde of Galashiels, which had 'James Pride 1722' inscribed upon it.

Others attending came from Canada and the USA as well as from Scotland, England and Wales." [Out of date contact information has been omitted.]

No formal group photograph was taken on this occasion but Fig. 27 gives a general impression of the evening and a few of the tree displays referred to in the Dalkeith Advertiser newspaper report can be seen along the left hand wall.

Fig. 27 – Pryde Reunion at Dean Tavern, Newtongrange
15th June 2005

Some of those who attended were:-

5 x great-grandchildren of James Pride and Helen Selkirk:-

Elizabeth Blythe Pryde Jackson née Halliday and Charles Jackson, Midlothian, Scotland
James McQueen with Marie Louise McQueen, Midlothian, Scotland
Peter Brown Pryde McQueen with Margaret McQueen, Midlothian, Scotland
Vincent Harold Pryde (1922 – 2013), Lincolnshire, England

Arthur Baxter Reid with Dorothy Helen Reid, Edinburgh, Scotland
Kenneth Graem Reid (1936 – 2006) with Lillian Norma Reid, Edinburgh, Scotland
Janet Brown Stuart née Halliday, Midlothian, Scotland
Thelma Joan Tweedie née Reid, North Lanarkshire, Scotland

6 x great-grandchildren of James Pride and Helen Selkirk:-

Morven Andrews née Reid, Edinburgh, Scotland
Harriet (Hetty) Wright Bennie née Cowan and Archie Bennie, West Lothian, Scotland
Rebecca Dickson Bowerman née Pryde, Maryland, USA
Thomas Ian Bradshaw and June Edith Bradshaw (1933 – 2007), Washington, USA
Janet (Etta) Chapman Adams Campbell née Pryde and John Campbell, Fife, Scotland
Agnes Keenan Deighan née Stuart, Midlothian, Scotland
Fiona Forster née Tweedie, Stirling, Scotland
Valerie Jean Fox née Ripley and David John Storrs Fox, Lancashire, England
Fraser Harris, Edinburgh, Scotland
Jill Rodanthe Harrup née Homewood, Cornwall, England
Elinor Laing Hickey née Rennie, Ontario, Canada
Scott Daniel McFarlane, Midlothian, Scotland
Rosemary Douglas McLeod née Hoy, Edinburgh, Scotland
Matilda Pryde Halliday Mitchell née McFarlane with Richard Adam Mitchell, Midlothian, Scotland
Joan Margaret Poole née Hoy and John Poole, West Sussex, England

Colin Marshall Pryde with Vivien Evelyn Pryde, Selkirkshire, Scotland

James Pryde, Midlothian, Scotland

James Bendall Fair Pryde and Pamela Joyce Pryde (1938 – 2012), Mid Glamorgan, Wales

Jeannie Pryde (1928 – 2013), widow of **William Hunter Pryde (1926 – 2002)**, Midlothian, Scotland

Paul Christopher Pryde, Norfolk, England

Richard Kevin Pryde, Leicestershire, England

Thomas Pryde, Midlothian, Scotland

Eve Pryde-Roberts née Pryde, Wrexham C.B., Wales

Barbara Jane Rodger née Reid and Graham Walker Rodger, Edinburgh, Scotland

Elizabeth Penman Taylor née Pryde (1929 – 2009), Fife, Scotland

Yvonne Janet Halliday Taylor née Stuart, Midlothian, Scotland

Kathleen Josephine Tully, representing husband **Charles Thomas Tully**, Texas, USA

Martin Stuart and Tracey Stuart, Midlothian, Scotland

Walter Stuart, Midlothian, Scotland

Helen Elizabeth West née Bradshaw and Basil West, Norfolk, England

7 x great-grandchildren of James Pride and Helen Selkirk:-

George Irvin Akin and Natalie Akin, California, USA
Ronald Stanley Akin and Laurie Susan Akin, California, USA
Lynda Baillie née Pryde, Cambridgeshire, England
Anthony Douglas Barr, Perth and Kinross, Scotland
Maureen Bell née Pryde, Midlothian, Scotland
Irene Brown née Lister, Falkirk, Scotland
Warren Deighan, Midlothian, Scotland
Deborah Forster, Stirling, Scotland
William David Henderson and Rita Henderson, Midlothian, Scotland
Gordon Lister with Kathy Ludbrook, London, England
Ronald Lister, Fife, Scotland
Lee Richard Mitchell and Gillian Mitchell, Midlothian, Scotland
Geoff Thomas Pryde, Selkirkshire, Scotland
Leona Sarah Pryde, Selkirkshire, Scotland
Margaret Janet Russell née Lawrence (1930 – 2008), North Carolina, USA
William Glover Scott and Ann Margaret Scott, East Renfrewshire, Scotland
Danny Stuart, Midlothian, Scotland
Melanie Stuart, Midlothian, Scotland
Joseph Taylor, Midlothian, Scotland
Sophie Taylor, Midlothian, Scotland
Mary Kathleen Tully, Illinois, USA
Brenda Ure née Pryde, Midlothian, Scotland
Susan Wilson née Reid, Midlothian, Scotland

8 x great-grandchildren of James Pride and Helen Selkirk:-

Dawn Akin, California, USA
Garret Irvin Akin, California, USA
Jennifer Susanne Akin, California, USA
Kelsey Noelle Akin, California, USA
Kristie Lynn Akin, California, USA
Morag Elizabeth Hulse née Scott, Suffolk, England
Linda Joyce Wilson née Russell, North Carolina, USA

Other kin and friends who also attended were:-

Peter, Susan, Kirsty and Jonny Bath, Midlothian, Scotland
Mel Jade Chisholm, Midlothian, Scotland.
Craig Ellery, Edinburgh, Scotland
Sarah Flockhart, Midlothian, Scotland
Barbara Harper, Ontario, Canada
Ronald Andrew Pryde, Fife, Scotland

AUSTRALIAN PRYDE GATHERING 2008
LAKE SOMERSET, QUEENSLAND, AUSTRALIA

Inspired by the 2005 Pryde Gathering, the next such gathering took place on 9th February 2008 at Lake Somerset, Queensland, Australia. This sought to celebrate the lives of James Pryde and Jane Drysdale Russell and George Pryde and Margaret Drysdale Russell and their descendants, as featured in Chapter 12.

The event was organised by **Marilyn Fay Pryde now Deuter** **(Living)**, pictured, 7 x great-granddaughter of James Pride and Helen Selkirk. The following handout prepared by her was given to all guests:-

Pryde Gathering 2008

With pride (Pryde) we are gathering today to renew friendships, meet more of the Pryde family, celebrate and give thanks for the lives of our great-grand parents :-

James Pryde & Jane (Drysdale Russell) and their children Jane Drysdale Pryde, Mary Pryde, Marion Pryde, William Russell Pryde, Alison Pryde, George Pryde & Margaret Russell Pryde.

George Pryde & Maggie (Russell) and their child, Margaret Drysdale Pryde.

We honour them and are thankful for our lives and our lifestyle here in this lovely part of the world.

We thank too, Eve Pryde-Roberts, living in Wales, UK, as she continues to encourage and motivate a number of us to explore our roots and remember those who came before.

Eve has given us so much of herself with her extensive research of the Pryde Family. She willingly shares this knowledge she has gathered with all who are remotely interested." [Out-of-date contact information has been omitted]

Much of the information and handouts today have been sourced from Eve for which I am very grateful.

As most of you know, our branch of the Pryde family has been involved in coal mining since before 1670. In the handout today I have put together a brief history in a few leaflets on our coal mining past. There are possibly errors in these leaflets, so please excuse these, and inform me of any corrections.

You may know of really personal stories regarding our coal mining ancestry. I would love to collect these stories to collate and print. [Out-of-date contact and other information has been omitted]

Do have a look at the "All Descendants of Mary Pryde" family tree displayed today [see Fig. 28].

Enjoy the gathering, and the memories that follow. Marilyn"

Fig. 28 – Family Tree Chart on display in Australia 2008

Some 60 or so persons attended the Gathering and most are shown in Fig. 29. Guests included the following who were from the Brisbane, Ipswich, Toowoomba, Gatton and Sunshine Coast areas of south east Queensland, Australia

6 x great-grandchildren of James Pride and Helen Selkirk:-

Clifford Norris Pryde (1920 – 2014)
Frances Pryde, widow of **Robert Ezra Pryde (1917 – 1992)**
Edna Sollitt née Grove

7 x great-grandchildren of James Pride and Helen Selkirk:-

Gary John Bachman
Meryl Blair née Feldhahn and Douglas Blair
Joyce Frances Boon née Pryde
Jill Brigginshaw née Pryde and George Brigginshaw
Susan Collins née Heath, former widow of **Lloyd Robert Pryde (1950 – 1998)** and Robert Collins
Marilyn Fay Deuter née Pryde and Peter Deuter
Delma Joy Drew née Pryde
Neil Feldhahn and Dianne Feldhahn
Desley Joyce Peach née Pryde
Desmond Pryde and Avril Pryde
Donald Pryde and Beverley Pryde
Edwin James Pryde and Cecily Pryde
George Pryde and Janice Elizabeth Pryde
Graham Clifford Pryde
Ronald John Pryde and Bronwyn Jean Pryde
Linda Rosenthal née Harris
Alison Margaret Trim née Bailey
Michelle Leah Waghorn née Morris and Graham Douglas Waghorn
Miriam Joan Worsnop née Pryde and Phillip William H Worsnop

8 x great-grandchildren of James Pride and Helen Selkirk:-

Chloe Bachman
Ethan Bachman
Danielle Doman née Pryde and Neal Doman
Karen Narelle Fraser née Pryde
Michelle Anne Gascoyne née Peach
Sharon Wendy Kruger née Pryde

Darren Keith Peach
Ross James Pryde and Emma-Jean Clare Pryde
Daniel Graham Pryde and Kerren Pryde
Cassandra Joy Wriede née Drew

9 x great-grandchildren of James Pride and Helen Selkirk:-

Angela Maree Blazer née Kruger
James Preston Doman
Danielle Sheree Fraser
Matthew Colin Fraser
Nicholas Lawrence Fraser
Riley Keith Gascoyne
Brandon Mitchell Kruger
Randall Matthew Kruger
Corey James Pryde
Jake Cameron Pryde
Kady Clare Pryde
Luke Adam Pryde
Amber Joy Wriede

Fig. 29 – Australian Pryde Gathering

9th February 2008

297

PRYDE REUNION AT THE
SCOTTISH MINING MUSEUM,
NEWTONGRANGE, MIDLOTHIAN – 2010

Just at the end of the evening of the gathering held at the Dean Tavern, Newtongrange, in June 2005 I was asked by a guest to arrange another one "next year", to which my off-the-cuff response was "we'll have another one in five years' time". Inevitably that soon became next year and it was decided to go ahead with plans for another event. The joint organisers this time were myself, Bill Scott and Linda Wilson.

As the previous venue was no longer available it was eventually decided that the Scottish Mining Museum, Newtongrange, would be a suitable site for the event which was held on 16th June 2010. The event was reported in the Dalkeith Advertiser as follows:-

"PRYDE IN THEIR FAMILY

More than 200[36] members of the Pryde family from around the world gathered in Newtongrange recently for a reunion event.

---

[36] This figure was incorrectly reported, the correct figure was approximately 130, which was the capacity of the venue. Additionally, later in the article the date of the event was incorrectly shown as June 12th.

People came to event at the Scottish Mining museum – apt as the Prydes descended from coal miners in the area – from as far afield as Canada, USA and New Zealand, as well as locals from Newtongrange and Scotland.

Among the many items on display were 683 photographs of Pryde family members taken throughout the years, the oldest image being taken circa 1849.

Also on display was an Olympic skinsuit donated by gold medal winning cyclist Sir Chris Hoy, who is also a member of the Pryde family, and tickets were on sale for this to raise funds for the British Heart Foundation. The winner is due to be announced at the end of the month.

Pride of Dunbar performed on the evening including a song especially written for the event called Gathered with Pryde. Songwriter Paul Pryde's grandfather was a miner himself and the tough, dirty and hard working environment of the underground is captured with gritty realism in a special song cycle and poem "The Blue and the Black".

The event on June 12 followed on from a successful gathering in the Dean Tavern, Newtongrange in 2005." [Out of date contact details omitted.]

The article was also accompanied by a group photo as shown in Fig. 30[37].

---

[37] Photo published by kind permission of Chris Radley Photography at chrisradleyphotography.com

Fig. 30 – Guests at the 2010 Pryde Gathering 16th June 2010

Amongst those who attended on the evening were the following:-

5 x great-grandchildren of James Pride and Helen Selkirk

Elizabeth Blythe Pryde Jackson née Halliday and Charles Jackson, Midlothian, Scotland
Jean Marshall-Pryde, Arizona, USA, widow of **John Marshall Pryde (1915 – 2006)**
Arthur Baxter Reid and Dorothy Reid, Edinburgh, Scotland
Thelma Joan Tweedie née Reid, North Lanarkshire, Scotland

6 x great-grandchildren of James Pride and Helen Selkirk

Mary Ann Anderson née Pryde, (1940 – 2014), Illinois, USA
Joseph Colin Bain and Grace Annabella Bain, Fife, Scotland
Aileen Jenedith Barr née Grant, Perth and Kinross, Scotland
Valerie Barton née Lloyd, Midlothian, Scotland
Rebecca Dickson Bowerman née Pryde, Maryland, USA
Janet Chapman Adams Campbell née Pryde and John Campbell, Fife, Scotland
Margaret Theresa Davies née Pryde, Wrexham C.B., Wales
David Buchan Douglas and Millie Douglas, Perth and Kinross, Scotland
Fiona Forster née Tweedie, Stirlingshire, Scotland
Valerie Jean Fox née Ripley and David John Storrs Fox, Lancashire, England
Sandra Foxon née Cleaver and Steve Davison, Clackmannanshire, Scotland
Agnes Sylvia Gibbs née Pryde and Dudley Gibbs, Merseyside, England
Fraser Harris, Edinburgh, Scotland
Jill Rodanthe Harrup née Homewood, Cornwall, England

6 x great-grandchildren of James Pride and Helen Selkirk continued:-

David Austen Hoy and Carol Jane Morrison Hoy, Edinburgh, Scotland
John Derek Hoy (1954 – 2012), Edinburgh, Scotland
Lynne Jennifer Isaacs née Ripley, Cornwall, England
Alun Vincent Jones, Norfolk, England
Shaun Douglas Marshall-Pryde, Montana, USA
Cynthia Margaret Milne née Pryde, Midlothian, Scotland
Matilda Halliday Pryde Mitchell née McFarlane, Midlothian, Scotland
Joan Margaret Poole née Hoy and John Poole, West Sussex, England
Brian Keith Pryde and Janice Ann Pryde, Leicestershire, England
Colin Marshall Pryde, Selkirkshire, Scotland
David John Pryde and Falmai Pryde, Conwy C.B., Wales
Dennis Pryde, Wrexham C.B., Wales
James Pryde, Midlothian, Scotland
James Bendall Fair Pryde and Pamela Joyce Pryde (1938 – 2012), Mid Glamorgan, Wales
Lynda Mary Pryde and Duncan Alexander Joiner, Khandallah, New Zealand
Paul Christopher Pryde and Susan Pryde, Norfolk, England
Thomas Pryde and Mary Madeleine Pryde, Midlothian, Scotland
Eve Pryde-Roberts née Pryde, Wrexham C.B., Wales
Barbara Jane Rodger née Reid and Graham Walker Rodger, Edinburgh, Scotland
Melvyn Turner and Barbara Turner, Cambridgeshire, England
Helen Elizabeth West née Bradshaw and Basil West, Norfolk, England
April Williams née Pryde, Wrexham C.B., Wales

7 x great-grandchildren of James Pride and Helen Selkirk

Lynda Baillie née Pryde, Cambridgeshire, England
Anthony Douglas Barr, Perth and Kinross, Scotland
Maureen Bell née Pryde, Midlothian, Scotland
Yvonne Bisset née Pryde, Edinburgh, Scotland
William David Henderson and Rita Henderson, Midlothian, Scotland
Lilian Mary Joiner, Khandallah, New Zealand
Stirling Douglas Marshall-Pryde, Montana, USA
Mavis Pace née Stephenson and Archie Dickie, Hampshire, England
Geoff Thomas Pryde, Selkirkshire, Scotland
Martin James Pryde, Flintshire, Wales
William Pryde and Jeanette Pryde, Edinburgh, Scotland
Mary Reid, Midlothian, Scotland, widow of **John Pryde Reid (1934 – 1997)**
Eunice Richardson née Naylor and Robert Max Richardson, Waikato Region, New Zealand
Jessie Margaret Ormiston Robertson née Scott, Edinburgh, Scotland
William Glover Scott and Ann Margaret Scott, East Renfrewshire, Scotland
Agnes Pryde Smith née Stewart (1932 – 2012), Midlothian, Scotland
Madeleine Stevenson née Pryde, Midlothian, Scotland
William John Stewart, County Durham, England
Isabel Robertson Taylor née Duncan, Midlothian, Scotland
David William Pryde Turowski, South Carolina, USA
Brenda Ure née Pryde, Edinburgh, Scotland
Hannah McAlister Young née Henderson and Andrew Cumming Young, Selkirkshire, Scotland

8 x great-grandchildren of James Pride and Helen Selkirk

Sean Bell, Midlothian, Scotland
Grahame Foggo and Fiona Napier, East Lothian, Scotland
David Henderson and Jaqueline Henderson, Midlothian, Scotland
Morag Elizabeth Hulse née Scott, Essex, England
John William James Reid, Midlothian, Scotland
Lindsay Elizabeth Robb née Robertson, Perth and Kinross, Scotland
Irene Lewis Turpie née McKinlay and Craig Thomson Turpie, South Lanarkshire, Scotland
Catriona Jane Welsh née Scott, British Columbia, Canada
Linda Joyce Wilson née Russell, North Carolina, USA

9 x great-grandchildren of James Pride and Helen Selkirk

Holly Reid, Midlothian, Scotland
William Euan John Robb, Perth and Kinross, Scotland
Gary Turpie, South Lanarkshire, Scotland
Christopher Lawrence Wilson, North Carolina, USA
Stephen Michael Wilson, North Carolina, USA

Other extended kin and friends who also attended included:-

Joanne Allan and Ian Allan, Midlothian, Scotland
Gary and Clare Dungar, with Oliver, Gordon and Conna Dungar, Norfolk, England (Pride of Dunbar)
Diane Maxwell, Edinburgh, Scotland
Roddie Meredith and Sheila Meredith, Devon, England
Rochelle Mooth, Illinois, USA
Ronald Andrew Pryde, Fife, Scotland
Jason and Gay Tyrrell, Norfolk, England (Pride of Dunbar)

Ann McGill Watson Valentine, East Lothian, Scotland
Gordon Watson, Midlothian, Scotland
Susan Windsor, Midlothian, Scotland
Roger and Jane Woodrow, Norfolk, England (Pride of Dunbar)

N.B.   My apologies to any of those who attended the events referred to in this chapter who may have been inadvertently excluded.

CHAPTER 21

IN CONCLUSION
- A MINING VILLAGE CHILDHOOD

Until I married I lived in the same house in which I was born, situated in the mining village of Llay, North Wales. I have mentioned in Chapter 6 how my great-grandfather **Alexander Pryde (1847 – 1927)** came to the local area to visit his brother David Pryde who was involved in the management of a local colliery. Alexander and his wife Harriet Powell had 11 children, one being my grandfather **Richard Pryde (1885 – 1966)**,

 pictured, 4 x great-grandson of James Pride and Helen Selkirk. He married Agnes Theresa McHale in 1908 in Wigan, Lancashire. Coincidentally they had fled to Wigan to get married in the face of family opposition, as his parents had done before him. This time it was not opposition because of perceived class, but because of religious differences.

Richard served in the Royal Engineers (Transportation Branch) from 1915 to 1918. After he was demobbed my grandparents returned to their home area around Wrexham, North Wales, in 1918 and they were reconciled to his wife's parents at this time. Apart from his war service Richard had always worked as a coal miner and my father, who was the eldest child, also began work as a coal miner when he was aged just 14 years in 1923. He had passed a scholarship but

LINE OF DESCENT FOR RICHARD PRYDE AND FAMILY AS
FEATURED IN CHAPTER 21

James Pride (circa 1678 – after 1748)
and Helen Selkirk
|
|
George Pride (1716 – 1759)
and Margaret Fraser
|
|
John Pride (1755 – after 1807)
and Mary Sharp
|
|
George Pride (1790 – 1855)
and Catherine Miller
|
|
John Pryde (1811 – 1864)
and Helen Lawson
|
|
Alexander Pryde (1847 – 1927)
and Harriet Powell
|
|
Richard Pryde (1885 – 1966) and Agnes Theresa McHale
and their children:-
Joseph Anthony (1909 – 1985) *[+ Eva Hewitson=parents of Eve]*
Alexander (1912 – 1967)
Winifred Mary (1914 – 1988)
James (1919 – 1998)
Vincent Harold (1922 – 2013)
Sheila Catherine (1924 – 1987)

was unable to take this up because as the eldest child of six his earnings were needed to help keep the family. He started work alongside his father at Gatewen colliery but was never aware his great-uncle David had been responsible for the founding of that colliery.

In 1927 my grandparents Richard and Agnes, together with their six children moved from a nearby village to the village of Llay. There had been small mining operations in the general area previously but in 1908 coal was discovered at a depth of just under 2,500 feet and this was developed over the next 14 years until it was the largest colliery in Wales and the deepest pit in Europe. Men were needed to work in the colliery and housing was required for these men so house- building began in earnest in 1920. It was always the intention of the owners that good living conditions be provided for their workers and on some of the earlier plans it was even called Llay Model Village.

As with many mining villages the streets were unimaginatively named First Avenue, Second Avenue, Third Avenue and so on, but the streets and pavements were wide, the houses were quite large by standards of the day, and still thought to be spacious to this day. Unusually for workers' houses for the time they each had an inside toilet and bathroom.

As the village developed churches, chapels, public houses and primary, junior and senior schools all appeared. By the time I was born in the early 1950s, Llay was a thriving village that provided everything a child could want, including a youth club, tennis courts, a recreation ground, library, picture-house and the ever-present Miners' Welfare Institute.

Many facilities provided to improve the social well-being in the village came about because of the Miners' Welfare Fund set up in 1920. The fund was raised from a penny levied on every ton of coal, and with contributions from the mine workers themselves, with local committees where the funds had been raised deciding on how the money should be spent to improve the lot of the workers.

The development of the village and facilities for the miners in this way followed the same pattern in many other mining villages throughout the country, including Scotland, as I soon found out in the course of my research.

My father **Joseph Anthony Pryde (1909 – 1985)**, pictured, 5 x great-grandson of James Pride and Helen Selkirk, married my

mother Eva Hewitson in 1935 and they too lived all their married lives in Llay. Just before I was born they moved to a newly built local-authority property within the village, again in an echo of what my paternal grandparents had done some 25 years or so earlier.

There must have been hard times for them but as the youngest child of four after Margaret, June and Michael, I was not aware of these, even though I can remember my Dad being on strike at one time, and also him being injured down the pit and being brought home from hospital in an ambulance with his leg in plaster. We were all well-loved and well-fed, with a lot of produce coming from our own garden which my Dad enjoying working in as did many of his fellow workers. There was always a fire in our hearth and we were safe amongst our own.

The background music of my childhood was the daily sounding of the pit-hooter, at 6.00 a.m., 2.00 p.m. and 10.00 p.m., the echoes of which reverberated around the village and signalled the start and end of each shift. As a young child I thought nothing of the blue-black scars that I saw on my Dad or on the other men in the village, they were normal in my world. Everyone knew everyone else, and you knew if you needed help you would get it, and if you were naughty you would "get it" too!

We were all the same which meant that an incident which happened when I was about five or six years old stayed in my memory, only to be recalled many years later. I was outside our home with my Mum and I remember her speaking to a very well-dressed older woman, who turned to me, as I half hid alongside my Mum, holding her hand, and she said "So, your father is a miner, is he child?" I must have nodded my head in acquiescence although my memory on any other detail is vague. What has remained crystal clear in my memory – even though I could not have articulated it in these terms as a child – was the total disdain in her voice as she asked the question. It was perfectly clear to me she thought that being a miner was something to be looked down upon – and that was confusing to me although quickly put to the back of my mind with the ease of youth, to remain there until I started on my family-history research many years later.

By the mid 1960s, after a good few years of declining output, Llay Main Colliery closed, and after some 40 years of employment there my Dad, again like many of his fellow workers, was transferred to nearby Gresford colliery. The only tangible evidence of his years of labour in Llay Main Colliery, apart from his injuries and scars, was his lamp tally, pictured, which he brought home with him after his final shift. Although the majority of the workers from Llay went to work at other pits most remained living in the village as we did. Some years later my Dad transferred to a local steelworks where he remained until the end of his working life, a path once again also followed by many of his co-workers.

Llay village went into a slight decline in the 1980s, especially during the 1984 Miners Strike – thankfully at that time my Dad was retired but he held very strong opinions about what was right and what was wrong about the strike – but better minds than mine can debate that. Happily in the last decade or so there has been resurgence in the village; there is a local history society which has published some very good books about the village and the coal mining industry there. The Miners' Welfare building is home to a small mining museum and outside of it there is a display of pithead gear as there is in other local villages. Mining heritage is now being appreciated throughout the country with the opening of the National Coal Mining Museum for England, at Wakefield, Yorkshire; the Big Pit National Coal Museum at Blaenavon, South Wales, and the Scottish Mining Museum at Newtongrange, Scotland.

My Dad always said if he had the chance he would go back into the pit because of the comradeship; they relied on each other to keep safe and to save each other's lives and this sentiment has been repeated to me by other mine workers time and time again. I have not set out in this book to glorify coal miners, they toiled at their jobs from day-to-day as did many other workers in different industries, but they certainly played their part in the development of the country through the ages, working very hard in terrible conditions for much of the time as my research has confirmed.

Whilst it is sad in many ways to see the demise of the coal-mining industry in this country it is also pleasing to know that so many men do not have to spend their lives in such working conditions, although we can be gratified with what has been achieved by their hard work over the centuries.

So if I had the opportunity today to be that young child again, when being asked if my father was a miner, I would answer loud and clear "Yes, my Dad is a coal miner, as were his forefathers for at least eight generations before him, and I am proud he is a coal miner, and proud to be a **PRYDE**."

INDEX

Battle of Prestonpans – see Prestonpans, Battle of

Baxter, Andrew 54

Baxter, Lawrence Ferrier 54; Marshall Pryde 54-5; Mary, née Pride 38,54,55; Thomas 54

Bayless-Telford, Sally – see Pryde, Sallie

Beaufort, Australia 148

Bennett, Jamieson 62,63,65,68,69,70,72

Bernard, Andrew 192; James 192

Berry, James 194

Big Horn, Wyoming 124,125,127

Big Pit National Coal Museum, Blaenavon, South Wales 313

Billings, Montana 125,127

Birel, John 10

Black, Catherine – see Young. Catherine; Jane Forbes Sneddon – see Pryde, Jane Forbes Sneddon

Blackside 22

Blair, Robert, senior and junior 40; William 40

Blantyre 205

Blyth, Elizabeth – see Pryde, Elizabeth

Bombay, India 91,257,258

Bo'ness 10,13

Bond, Janet Pride, née Gray 237,254; Joseph John 237,254; William Henry, M.M. 237,254-6

Bonnie Prince Charlie – see Stuart, Charles Edward

Booval, Australia 155

Borrowstounness - see Bo'ness

Borthwick 22

Bowie, Hunter 40

Braidwood, Illinois 123

Brazier, Harriet Anne – see Brown, Harriet Anne

Bremner, Mary – see Pryde, Mary

Bridgewater Canal 252

Brisbane, Australia 155,156

British Empire Medal 268

Broughton Hall 250,251; Broughton Coal Company 249-51; Broughton Coal and Plas Power Company 249-51;

Brown, Alexander 39,43; Alison, née Pryde 113,228; Andrew 80; Elizabeth (born 1823) 113-4; Elizabeth (born 1832) 80; George 113,228; Harriet Anne, née Brazier 228; Helen, née Pride 79-80; Honor – see Pryde, Honor; James 39,43,45-6; Marion 121; Mary – see Pryde, Mary; William Henry Harrison 228

Brunton, Janet – see Pryde, Janet

Brymbo, Wales 249,252

Buccleuch, Duke of 81,218

Buffalo Gap, Virginia 95

Burnett, Mr 42

Burnetts, Hamblen County, Tennessee 95

Burnley, Jessie, née Pryde 165,168-9,171,181; John 169,171

Burnside, David 40

Burg, Alderman 170,171

Byron, Wyoming 124,126,127; reunion at, 281-4

Cadel, William 8

Cairns, Christina – see Robertson, Christina

California 214

Campbell, Betsey 62,65,72; George 62,72; John 39,45-6

Candelaria, Esmeralda, Nevada 89,90

Canny, Mary Aileen – see Pryde, Mary Aileen

Canterbury, New South Wales 89

Carngham, Australia 148

Carstairs, Christian – see Pryde, Christian

Carter, Samuel Ellis 157,159

Carter County, Tennessee 109

Carthall 45

Chambers, Helen, née Tait 138,142; John 142

Chesterhill 30

Children's Employment Commission (1842) 27

Chisholm, H.J. 174

Cholera 79-80,139

Church of Jesus Christ of Latter-day Saints – see Mormon Church

Clayfield Limeworks 54

Fairholm, Jane – see Pryde, Jane

Falkirk 88

Farm, Alexander 40

Fife Coal Company Ltd 225-6

Fleming, James 131

Fletcher, Mr 174

Flockhart, Matilda – see Pride, Matilda

Flockhart, Violet – see Pryde, Violet

Floyd County, Virginia 106

Forsyth, Catherine Hunter – see Pryde, Catherine Hunter

Fortune, John 189-94

Fowler, Neilson Flyn 192

Franks Report (1846) 13,28-9,33,217

Franks, Robert Hugh 28

Fraser, Rev. Donald 168; Margaret – see Pride, Margaret

Frizzell, Margaret – see Pride, Margaret

Frow, Robert 39

Fryar, T. 173

Gatewen Colliery 88,249-51,309

Gatherings, Pryde – see Reunions

Gedye, Anne, née Pryde 244; Charles 244; Donald Joseph 244

Gee, David 185fn

Geelong, Australia 142,149,150

George, Isabella, née Pryde 112,116; Mary 116; Robert Pryde 116; William 116; William junior 116; William III 116; George II 4

Genealogical research 271-9

Gibb, Alexander 39

Gilmerton 7,19,39,41,44,47,49,51,52,80,285

Glasgow 262

Glass, Rev. John R. 76; Louisa 76

Glen, Barbara Herkes, née Wilson 236; Christian Liddle, née Tullis 243; Marian Hamilton, née Cranston 243; Peter (1), 236; Peter (2) 243; Robert Newlands 236; William McIntosh 243

Gold Hill, Storey, Nevada 115

Goldie, Helen, née Robertson; Robert 237-8; William 237

Goodlet, Jane – see Pryde, Jane

Goodson, Tennessee 95

Gordon, Alexander 39; David 39; Gideon 'Jane' Ann – see Pryde, Gideon 'Jane' Ann

Gorebridge 189, 215

Granger County, Tennessee 93

Grant, Mr 8

Graves, Dr Thomas B. 119

Gray, Janet Pride – see Janet Pride Bond; Mr 156

Great Escape 266

Great Western Railway 253

Greenrigg 52

Grieve, Mr John 24,27

Griffith, A., M.P. 168

Grossert, James Porteous Watson 189-95; Mary – see Pryde, Mary

Güstrow, Germany 253-4

Hall, Talton 104-7; Mr 171; Thomas 129

Hamilton, Australia 148

Hamilton, Duke of 10,13

Hamill, Mary Jane, née Pryde 244; Thomas senior and junior 244-5

Hannings, Ellwood 247; Helen Davie Rankine, née Pryde 247; William Elwood 247-8

Hardy, Mr E 168; Mr G. 170

Hare, Esther – see Vickers, Esther; Janet, née Pryde 185,186; John 185,186

Hartwick, Mrs W.I. 76

Hassler, Mrs J.E. 76

Hay, Peter 59-72

Hedrick, Detective 106
Henry, W.E. 173
Henderson, Margaret 276
Henty family, Australia 147,148
Herring, Lt. Col. S.C.E., D.S.O., 254
Hetherington, Robert 169
Holdsworthy, Australia 254
Hong Kong 244-5
Hoods, David 39; George 39; Thomas 39
Hope, Sir John 27,51,81
Horden, John William 245; Ronald Pryde 245-6; Zillah, née
    Pryde 245
Howden, Alexander George 229; William Thompson 229;
    Janet Buchanan, née Polson 229
Hoy, Carol Jane Morrison, née Reid, M.B.E. 269-70; Sir
    Christopher Andrew, M.B.E. 269-70,299; David Austen
    269
Hubbard, Anne – see Cleveland, Anne
Huerfano, Colorado 124
Hume, Robert 187
Hunter, James, senior and junior 39; Margaret – see Pryde,
    Margaret; William 39
Hutchie 2
Hutchie, James 8; William 8
Hutchison 2
Hyslop, Helen – see Selkirk, Helen

Illinois, U.S.A. 276-7,277
Ingles 2
Ingles, William 8,10
Innes surname 2; William 189-94
Innis, R., 8; William 8
Inveresk 18
Ipswich, Australia 155,156,162,222
Irvine, James 39; William 39
Isle of Wight 263

Jack, Andrew 39; Elspeth – see Pryde, Elspeth; James 39; John 39

Jeffrey, Alexander Bell 157,158,159,162; Mary – see Pride, Mary; Robert 157,158

Johnson City, Tennessee 108

Jones, June Dorothy, née Pryde 310

Jonesboro, Arkansas 108

Journal of Management (Prestongrange) 6-9

Karachi, India (now Pakistan) 258

Keddie, George 39

Kelty 225

Kemp, Janet – see Paterson, Janet

Kentucky 105

Kentucky Flat, California 74

Kerr, Adam 177-9; Adam junior 177; Alexander 178; Alexander Pryde 177,178; Alice, née Young 178; George 39.44-6; Isabella 181; Isabella junior 177; Isabella – see Pryde, Isabella; Jane – see Pryde, Jane; Janet, née Pryde 163,164,177-8; Jessie – see Munsie, Jessie; John 181; John Thomas 177; Peter 181; Walter 178

Kilpatrick, Mr 159,161

King, John 8; King, Katherine, née Pride 8

King's Police Medal 257

Kinloch, Mr David 19

Knowles, Mary Ann – see Pryde, Mary Ann

Knox County, Tennessee 105,109

Lake Bolac, Australia 148

Lake Goldsmith, Australia 148

Lambton, Australia 165,166,167-76,178,170,180,184; Marquis of Lorne Hotel 172-6

Landles, Helen – see Wilson, Helen

Lang, Wood & Company Ltd 176

Lansdale, U.S.A. 247

Laramie, Wyoming 113

Lasswade 285

Latta, Thomas 40
Laurie, Isabel Storey – see Mitchell, Isabella Storey
Lawless, Elizabeth – see Pryde, Elizabeth; John 99; Walter 99
Lawson, Helen – see Pryde, Helen; Mary Jane – see Pryde,
   Mary Jane
Letham (male) 203
Leitch, Janet – see Pryde, Janet
Leith Athletic (football team) 227
Liberton 19,44,285
Liddle, Janet Rutherford – see Pryde, Janet Rutherford
Lindsay, Agnes – see Pride, Agnes
Little, Margaret – see Currie, Margaret
Little Rock, Arkansas 103
Llay, North Wales 307,309-13; Miners' Welfare Fund 310
Loanhead 53,202
Longside 18
Lorain Steel Company (USA) 224
Lothian Coal Company Ltd 221,265
Lothian Family History Society 285
Lowe, Margaret – see Currie, Margaret
Lumphinnans 225
Lumsdale, Elizabeth, née Pride 2,8; John 8; Robert 2,8
Lumsden – see Lumsdale
Lynch, Bernard 225-6

Mack, Margaret Elizabeth – see Pryde, Margaret Elizabeth
Mackay, Mungo 195-6,212-3,215
Madden, David Andrew 150; James 146,147-50; James
   junior 150; Margaret, née Tait 138,146,151; her diary
   146-50; Margaret junior 150; William Baldy 150
Manchester 251; Manchester Ship Canal 252-3
Manitoba, Canada 262
Marion, Illinois 181
Marshall, Agnes – see Pride, Agnes; John 37,39,44,45,50,52;
   use of as Christian names 52,55; Margaret – see Pride,
   Margaret
Mason, David, senior and junior 39 and 40

Mathieson, George 157,158,159,161

McCune, Detective 100

McDermid/Macdiarmid, John 190-4

McGregor, Isabella, née Paterson 236; Malcolm senior and junior 236-7

McHale, Agnes Theresa – see Pryde, Agnes Theresa

McIntosh, Beatrice – see Millar, Beatrice; Janet – see Cooper, Janet; John 218; Marion, née Stewart 218

McKechnie, Isabella, née Pryde 25,31; William 31

McLean, Georgina – see Pryde, Georgina;

McIlvenna, Nancy Darlene – see Pryde, Nancy Darlene

McNeal, Gen 103-4

McQueen, Catherine – see Pryde, Catherine; James senior 267; James, B.E.M. 267

Measles 165

Meek, Marion – see Pryde, Marion

Melanosis 81-2,87

Melbourne, Australia 142,143,151,259

Memphis, Tennessee 95-107

Menin Gate, Ypres 229-230,235

Merino Downs, Australia 147,148

Mexican Eagle Petroleum Company 182

Midway, Green County, Tennessee 107

Military Medal 255

Millar, Alexander McIntosh 223; Beatrice, née McIntosh 223; William Jamieson 223

Miller, Catherine – see Pride, Catherine; Colonel 108; James 40

Minersville, Schuylkill County, Pennsylvania 114,116; Miners' Memorial Statue 116-9

Mining fatalities 217-27

Mishler, Trella Viola – see Cooper, Trella Viola

Mitchell, Alexander McGregor 243; Isabel Storey, née Laurie 243; William 243

Moffat, Abram 27; Isabella – see Walkinshaw, Isabella; William 27

Montana 124

Mormon Church 123,126

Mozingo, Rachel Elizabeth – see Robertson, Rachel Elizabeth

Muir, Archibald 39,45-6; Helen – see Pride, Helen

Munsie, Jessie, née Kerr 177,179; Selby Walter 179

Musselburgh 60

Mutter, John 129; Mary, née Pryde 129

Naismyth, Margaret 42

Naysmith, Elizabeth, née Blyth, formerly Pryde
199,200,202,205; Mary – see Pride, Mary; William 205

National Coal Mining Museum, Wakefield 313

Nationalisation of Mines 86

New Orleans 101

New Statistical Account for Scotland - Newton 80-4

Newbattle 54,80,285; colliery 220

Newbyth 8

Newcastle, Australia 168

Newliston 202

Newton Village 32,80,82

Newtongrange 202,203,204,212,222,264,285,298; East
Houses Mine 214; Lady Victoria Colliery 212,227; Star
(football team) 227

Nic[h]olson, Jean, née Pride 60

Nic[h]olson, John 60,62,63,64,65,72

Nicol, Robert 225-6

Noble, Mrs C. 168; Alderman G. 167; Mr H.J. 168

North, Elma, née Ott 183; Keith junior 183-4; Keith senior
183;

Norton, Virginia 105

Norwegian, Schuylkill, Pennsylvania 113

Oak Leaf award 264-5

Oakland Township, Alameda, California 115

Oamaru, New Zealand 132

Order of the British Empire: C.B.E. 259; O.B.E. 258; M.B.E.
267

Ogden, M.L. 109

O'Haver, Capt. (police) 107
Old Pretender – see Stuart, James Francis Edward
Oldham, Joseph 178
Otago Antimony Mining Company 129-131
Ott, Elma – see North, Elma
Oxfurdhall 22

Paterson, Adam 89; David Pryde 89; Isabella – see
  McGregor, Isabella; Janet, née Kemp 89; Margaret – see
  Pride, Margaret; Mary née Pryde 85,87,89
Patterson, Robert 39; William 39
Peach, Mr W.E.S. 225-6
Peacock, Mr, surgeon 42
Penicuik 219
Penman, David 39; Elizabeth – see Pride, Elizabeth;
  Katherine – see Pride, Katherine; Thomas, 40
Pentland, David 40,47-9; Isobel, née Sharp 49; Robert 40
Perrott, R.I. 180
Perth 189
Peru, Illinois 244
Petition (1746?) 9-13,28; (1823) 37-47; (1824) 47; (1824 (2))
  49
Pettigrew, Elizabeth – see Pride, Elizabeth
Philips, James A. 182
Picton, New South Wales 180
Pinkey 7,8,18
Pitfield, Australia 142,148
Placerville, California 73
Plaquemine, Louisiana 102-3
Plattsburg, Australia 178
Poaching 185-98
Polson, Janet Buchanan – see Howden, Janet Buchanan
Port Philip, Australia 142,143,145
Port Seton 4
Portland, Australia 147,150
Powderhall 202,203
Powell, Harriet – see Pryde, Harriet

James (1823, unidentified) 39

Pryde, Alexander (born 1823) 163,164; Alexander (born 1847) 85,87,90-1,307,308; Alexander (born 1849) 163,164,165-71,178; Alexander (born c1865) 230; Alexander (born 1912); Alexander (born 1913) 227

Pryde, Alison Tait Isabella 156; Alison – see Brown, Alison

Pryde, Ann – see Gedye, Ann

Pryde, Arthur Walter, C.B.E., K.P.M., 91-2,258-0

Pryde, Beatrice, née Cossar 220

Pryde, Brodie 163,164,178-80,186,200,217,218; Brodie John Adamson 25,32,154,164

Pryde, Catherine (born 1801) 217-8; Catherine (born c1850-64) 209; Catherine, née McQueen 154,164,186,200, 217,218; Catherine, née Wilson 153,154; Catherine Hunter, née Forsyth 227

Pryde, Charles 220; Charles Albert 99; Charles Ratcliffe 209,211,212-3,215

Pryde, Christian, née Richardson 30

Pryde, Christina, née Sutherland 135; Christina, née Young 121,122,124,127

Pryde, Colin Marshall 14; David (born 1793) 186,218-9,219; David (born 1835) 85,87,88,249-51,251,307,309; David (born 1855) 219; David Allen 276; David Barnes 253-4; David Douglas, D.F.C. 241-2,261

Pryde, Duncan McLean 262-3

Pryde, Elizabeth, née Blyth – see Naysmith, Elizabeth; Elizabeth 'Lizzie', née Lawless 99; Elizabeth, née Rodger 88; Elizabeth, née Smith 238; Elizabeth, née White 231; Elizabeth, née Young 191

Pryde, Elspeth, née Jack 277; Elspeth Johnston 277

Pryde, Eva, née Hewitson 308,310

Pryde, Eve – see Pryde-Roberts, Eve

Pryde, Florence Louise, née Sargent 263

Pryde, Frederick Faithful Begg 130,132,135

Pryde, George (born 1811) 25,31; George (born 1821) 37,52,121,122; George (born 1824) 25,31,32,33; George (born 1833) 85,88; George (born 1846) 235; George (born 1865) 153,154,155-62,222-3; George (born 1884)

235-6; George Archibald, D.F.C. 240-1,242,260; George Bremner 181; George Hannah 231; George Thomas (born 1864) 207-12,213; George Thomas (born 1901) 209,211,212,213,214,215; George Thomas 'Geordie'(born 1921) 212,213,215-6

Pryde, Georgina, née McLean 262; Georgina Richardson, née Anderson 227

Pryde, Gideon (male) 199-205; Gideon 'Jane' Ann, née Gordon 199,200

Pryde, Hannah, née Shotton 230

Pryde, Harriet, née Powell 91,307,308

Pryde, Helen (born 1737) – see Armour, Helen; Helen Davie Rankine – see Hannings, Helen David Rankine; Helen, née Lawson 79,85,86,88,249,256,308; Helen, née Richardson 186,218; Helen, née Weddel 277-8; Helen May, née Curline 135

Pryde, Herbert Marshall, D.S.M. 263-4

Pryde, Honor, née Brown 240

Pryde, Irvine Lawson 233-4

Pryde, Isabella 165; Isabella Merton 165; Isabella, née Kerr 179; Isabella, née Wallace 234; Isabella, née Young 121,122; Isabella – see George, Isabella; Isabella – see McKechnie, Isabella; Isabella Chalmers, née Stenhouse 225

Pryde, J. (1873 unidentified quoit player) 202

Pryde, Jack 242

Pryde, Jacka Adamson 25,32

Pryde, James 'Jimmy', M.B.E. 266; James (born 1795) 164,200; James (born 1840) 85,87,88-9; James (born 1847) 163,164,179;James (born 1848) 191; James (born 1858) 153-5,156; James (born 1916) 264-6; James (born 1919) 308; James Darling 231; James Simpson 94,107,109,228; James Smith 227,264

née Ratcliffe 73,74,208,209; Margaret, née Rutherford 88,249,251; Margaret Drysdale, née Russell 153,154, 156; Margaret Drysdale 156; Margaret Elizabeth, née Mack 266; Margaret Louise – see Crowder, Margaret Louise; Margaret Theresa – see Davies, Margaret Theresa

Pryde, Marilyn Fay – see Deuter, Marilyn Fay

Pryde, Marion, née Darling 32; Marion, née Meek 219; Marion, née Young 121,122,125-7

Pryde, Mary (born c1830) 25,33; Mary (born c1834); 153,154,155,222; Mary (born 1867) 208; Mary (born 1897) 127; Mary Jane – see Hamill, Mary Jane; Mary, née Bremner 181; Mary, née Brown 111,112,113,115; Mary, née Grossert 194; Mary – see Mutter, Mary; Mary – see Paterson, Mary; Mary Aileen, née Canny 183; Mary Ann, née Knowles 93,94,110,228; Mary Henrietta 95; Mary Jane, née Lawson 233; Mary Shearer, née Aitchison 211

Pryde, Mattie F., née Smith 95,97-8; Mattie J., née Roddy 99,110

Pryde, Michael 310

Pryde, Mungo 220-2

Pryde, Nancy Darlene, née McIlvenna 276

Pryde, Nicol 25,32

Pryde, Paul 286,299

Pryde, Peter 153,154

Pryde, Rachel May Fortune, née Samuel 181

Pryde, Richard (born 1885) 307-10; Richard 286

Pryde, Robert, M.B.E. 268; Robert, K.P.M., 85,87,91,256-7; Robert (born 1710) 25,32,33; Robert (born 1795) 111-115; Robert (born 1837) 112,114,115; Robert (born 1867) 121,122,124-7; Robert (born 1868) 88; Robert (born 1892) 234; Robert B. 94,107-9,228; Robert John 276-7; Robert William 91

Pryde, Robina 181; Robina, née Wood 211

Pryde, Ronald Andrew x,276

Pryde, Sallie, née Bayless-Telford 95

Pryde, Sheila Catherine 308

Pryde, Stephen Ross 277-8

Pryde surname ix,1,19

Pryde, Thomas 'Tam' 195-7,286; Thomas Alexander (born 1857) 163,164,172-7,178,179; Thomas Alexander (born 1902) 172; Thomas Denholm 238-9

Pryde, Vincent Harold 274,286,308

Pryde, Violet, née Flockhart 88

Pryde, Walter (born 1808) 25,30,92.217

Pryde, William (born c1810) 85-6; William (born 1832) 112,115; William (born 1841) 220,238; William (born 1845) 85,87.89; William (born c1845) 73-5; William (born c1853) 234; William(born 1855) 208,219-20; Pryde, W[illiam] (born 1926) 227; William Alexander 172; William Darnley 262; William George 94,95-107,110; William H. (born 1877) 95; William Hunter(born 1893) 209; William Symington 240,242; William Terbit 194

Pryde, Winifred Mary 308

Pryde, Zillah – see Horden, Zillah

Pryde-Kylander, Roselin 281

Pryde-Roberts, Eve, née Pryde 285,293,298,310

Puerto, Mexico 182

Punishments (Miners) 9,29

Purcell, Mrs B., née Pride 76

Purnel, Dr H.W. 100-2

Queensland Colliery Employees' Miners' Union 155,159,162

Quoits 201-5

Ramage, William 192

Ratcliffe, Margaret – see Pryde, Margaret

Reid, Carol Jane Morrison – see Hoy, Carol Jane Morrison; Ellen 62,72; James (1) & (2) 62,63,68,72; James Richard 246; Jane Stonehouse, née Pryde 246; John 62,63,64, 69,70,72; Richard Wallace 246; Thomas 62,72; William 40

Reunions, Pryde – 281-305 *The names of person attending reunions are to be found listed in Chapter 20 – they are not included in this index.* Byron, Wyoming 1960s 282-4;

Newtongrange 2005 285-91; Queensland 292-7;
Newtongrange 2010 298-305

Richardson, Christian – see Pryde, Christian; Helen – see
Pryde, Helen; John 220

Richmond, Virginia 59,93,105

Richmond, John 39

Rio de Janeiro 141

Roberts, Eve – see Pryde-Roberts, Eve

Robertson, Charles 40,44,45-6; Christina, née Cairns 235;
Elizabeth, née Williams 235; George 235; Isabella 232;
Helen – see Goldie, Helen; James Sheriff senior and junior
232; John A. 99; Mr 10; Rachel Elizabeth, née Mozingo
98-9; Robert William 235

Robinson, William Robert 157,158,159-60

Rocksprings, Wyoming 124,126

Roddy, Mattie J. – see Pryde, Mattie J.

Rodger, Elizabeth – see Pryde, Elizabeth

Rolland, Adam, Crown Agent 42,51

Rosebery, Lord 189,197

Rosewell 202,203

Rushton, Mr 174

Russell, Jane Drysdale – see Pryde, Jane Drysdale; Linda
Joyce – see Wilson, Linda Joyce; Margaret Drysdale – see
Pryde, Margaret Drysdale

Rutherford, Margaret – see Pryde, Margaret

Saleeba, Lois 185fn

Salter, Sergeant 174

Samuel, Rachel May Fortune – see Pryde, Rachel May
Fortune

San Antonio, U.S.A. 184

Sargent, Florence Louise – see Pryde, Florence Louise

Schuylkill Township, Pennsylvania 114

Scott, Arch[ibald] 42,44,46,48,51; Bob 185fn; G.F. 175; G.P.
176;Capt. S.M. 108-9; Mr 156; William Gilbert ix; William
Glover 'Bill' 298

Scottish Miners' Federation 210,213

Scottish Mining Museum, Newtongrange 299,313
Selkirk 2
Selkrig - see Selkirk
Selkirk, Christian – see Pride, Christian; Elizabeth, née Pride
7,18; Helen, née Hyslop 187; Helen – née Pride, Helen;
William (born c1698) 7,18; William (born ?) 187
Serfs (slaves) 2-3,21,23,26,28,40,
Sessions, Byron 126
Shaw, Janet 62,72
Sharp, Burrell 40; Charlotte – see Armour, Charlotte; Helen –
see Armour, Helen; Isabel – see Pentland, Isabel; James 1
and 2 39; John 40; Mary – see Pride, Mary; Thomas 39;
William 39
Shelby, Tennessee 99
Shelton, Mr 156
Sheriffhall 80-81
Shotton, Hannah – see Pryde, Hannah
Shotts Iron Company7 219
Shottstown 219
Silver State, Humboldt, Nevada 89
Simon, Mr 171
Sind, India (now Pakistan) 91,259
Skipton, Victoria, Australia 143,146,149,150
Smith, Agnes – see Pride, Agnes; Isobel 111; Elizabeth – see
Pryde, Elizabeth; Nancy – see Pride, Nancy; Mattie – see
Pryde, Mattie; John 39
Smythe's Creek 150
Sneddon, John 40
Society of Writers to Her Majesties Signet 42fn
Somme 230-231,232-3,233,237
Sparke, Mr 173
Stafford, Mr 159
St Enochs, Australia 149
Steel, Mr George 24,27
Stenhouse, Isabella Chalmers – see Pryde, Isabella Chalmers;
Messrs, mine owners 61
Stephens, ?, Australia 150

Stewart, Marion – see McIntosh, Marion; Thomas 218

Stuart, Charles Edward, 'The Young Pretender' and 'Bonnie Prince Charlie' 4; Danny 286

Stuart, James Francis Edward, ['The Old Pretender'] 4
Streatham, Australia 148

Sutherland, Christina – see Pryde, Christina
Sydney, Australia 163

Symington, Jane Janet – see Pryde, Jane Janet
Symons, Tom D. 117fn

Tacoma, Washington State 115

Tait, Alison 138,145; Andrew 137,138,139-42; Catherine 137,138,139-42; Charlotte – see Baldy, Charlotte; Helen, née Armour 137,138,139,151; Helen (born 1819) – see Chambers, Helen; John 137,138,139,151; John junior 138,146,150; Margaret – see Madden, Margaret; Margaret née Coyne 146

Tannic Acid – treatment for burns 214

Taylor, ?, US Marshall 105; Alfred M. 109; Jane – see Pryde, Jane; Yvonne 285

Thomas, M.W. 224

Thomson, George 192; Isabel[la] – see Pride, Isabel[la]; Robert 10

Thompson, Mr A, 225; Mr L.E. 176

Thorn (male) 202

Thyne, Mr T. 225-6

Tranent 4,8; colliery waggonway 4-5

Triplett brothers 106

Tullis, Christine Liddle – see Glen, Christine Liddle

Turnbull, Mr J. 170

Unions 39,40,41,44-5,47-8,50,51; strikes (1912) 210, (1921) 213; (1984) 312

Vaughn, General 108
Vance, Dick 106

336

Vickers, Alexander 190; Bob 195; David 'Dave' 197,198; Esther, née Hare 185,186,187,188,191,195,197,199; Euphemia 198; George 189; Jack 195-6; Janet 'Jessie' 192; John 'Jock' 197; John 185fn; Ramsay 189; Robert 197; Robert 'Bob' Flockhart 85,186-94,195,196,197,199; William 'Wull' (born 1812) 187; William (born 1868) 191,246

Victoria 146

Vietnam war 247

Vogrie 22

Waddel, Thomas 40

Waldie, Helen 47-8

Walking stick 14-15,286

Walkinshaw, David 191; Isabella, née Moffat 191

Wallace, Isabella – see Pryde, Isabella; John 191

Waratah, Australia 180

Watauga, River, Tennessee 108

Wauchope, John 81

Wear, John – see Weir, John

Weddel, David (born 1808) 34-5; David (born 1829) 34-5; David (born pre 1848) 35; Elizabeth, née Young 34-5; Helen – see Pryde, Helen

Weir, John 47

Wemyss, Janet – see Pride, Janet

West Calder 208

White, Archibald 187; Elizabeth – see Pryde, Elizabeth

White Rock, California 74,76

Whitehill, Dalkeith 52; fall of rock at Whitehill Mains Grounds/High Pressure Pit 59-72,93

Whitelaw, James 153

Wickliffe, Australia 148

Wilcox, C.C. 109

Willaura, Australia 148

Williams, Elizabeth – see Robertson, Elizabeth; General 108; Henry 171; Jack 96

Williamson, Dr J.N. 225

Wilson, Barbara Herkes – see Glen, Barbara Herkes;
  Catherine – see Pryde, Catherine; Colin 185fn; George
  103; George (2) 129-131; Helen, née Landles 191; James
  191; Linda Joyce, née Russell 298; Peter 225-6; William
  39

Wood, Robina – see Pryde, Robina

World War I 229-39.253

World War II 240-6

Wrexham 249,250-1,.251

Wrexham, Mold and Connah's Quay Railway 252

Wright, John 105-6

Wyoming 124

Yedom, Margaret 62,72

Young, Alice – see Kerr, Alice; Benjamin, 40; Catherine, née
  Black 123; Christina – see Pryde, Christina; Elizabeth – see
  Pryde, Elizabeth; Elizabeth – see Weddel, Elizabeth;
  George 123; Isabella 121; Janet 121; Marion – see
  Pryde, Marion

Young Pretender – see Stuart, Charles Edward

Ypres 229,235